Contemporary Human Rights Challenges

The Universal Declaration of Human Rights was drafted by the United Nations (UN) Commission on Human Rights in the aftermath of World War II in an attempt to address the wrongs of the past and plan for a better future for all. The process was led by Eleanor Roosevelt, René Cassin and John Humphreys amongst others, and the Declaration continues to be a powerful and profound template for our age.

This new collection of essays by academics, practitioners and activists brings a contemporary perspective to the original principles proclaimed in the Declaration's 30 Articles. Examined through these universal principles which have enduring relevance, the authors grapple with some of today's most pressing challenges, some of which would not have been foreseen by the original drafters of the Declaration. The essays cover a wide range of topics, such as an individual's right to privacy in a digital age, freedom to practice one's religion and the right to redress.

Contemporary Human Rights Challenges is of interest to researchers, academics, practitioners and students in the fields of human rights, international relations, political science and international law, and social justice.

Dr Carla Ferstman, Senior Lecturer at the Faculty of Law, University of Essex, UK.

Rev Alexander Goldberg, barrister and human rights activist, Jewish Chaplain to the University of Surrey, UK.

Dr Tony Gray, Director of Words by Design, Oxford, UK.

Dr Liz Ison (daughter of the late Clemens Nathan), London, UK.

Richard Nathan (son of the late Clemens Nathan), Director, Bosquet Capital, London, UK.

Michael Newman, Chief Executive, The Association of Jewish Refugees (AJR), London, UK.

Routledge Research in Human Rights Law

Available titles in this series include:

The Right to Religious Freedom in International Law
Between group rights and individual rights
Anat Scolnicov

The Right to Development in International Law
The Case of Pakistan
Khurshid Iqbal

Global Health and Human Rights
Legal and Philosophical Perspectives
John Harrington and Maria Stuttaford

Human Rights, Constitutional law and Belonging
The Right to Equal Belonging in Democratic Society
Elena Drymiotou

Dignity, Degrading Treatment and Torture in Human Rights Law
The Ends of Article 3 of the European Convention on Human Rights
Elaine Webster

The Right to Housing in Law and Society
Nico Moons

Human Rights and America's War on Terror
Edited by Satvinder Juss

Beyond Human Rights and the War on Terror
Edited by Satvinder Juss

For more information about this series, please visit: www.routledge.com/Routledge-Research-in-Human-Rights-Law/book-series/HUMRIGHTSLAW

Contemporary Human Rights Challenges

The Universal Declaration of Human Rights and its Continuing Relevance

Edited by
Carla Ferstman, Alexander Goldberg, Tony Gray, Liz Ison, Richard Nathan and Michael Newman

Routledge
Taylor & Francis Group
LONDON AND NEW YORK

First published 2019 by Routledge

2 Park Square, Milton Park, Abingdon, Oxfordshire OX14 4RN
52 Vanderbilt Avenue, New York, NY 10017

Routledge is an imprint of the Taylor & Francis Group, an informa business

First issued in paperback 2019

Library of Congress Cataloging-in-Publication Data
Names: Ferstman, Carla, 1968–, editor.
Title: Contemporary human rights challenges : the Universal Declaration of Human Rights and its Continuing Relevance / Edited by Carla Ferstman, Alexander Goldberg, Tony Gray, Liz Ison, Richard Nathan and Michael Newman.
Description: New York : Routledge, 2018. | Series: Routledge research in human rights law | Includes bibliographical references and index.
Identifiers: LCCN 2018021161 | ISBN 9780815364634 (hbk) | ISBN 9781351107129 (web pdf) | ISBN 9781351107112 (epub) | ISBN 9781351107105 (mobipocket)
Subjects: LCSH: United Nations. General Assembly. Universal Declaration of Human Rights. | Human rights—International unification.
Classification: LCC K3238.31948 .C66 2018 | DDC 341.4/8—dc23
LC record available at https://lccn.loc.gov/2018021161

ISBN: 978-0-8153-6463-4 (hbk)
ISBN: 978-0-367-48150-6 (pbk)

Typeset in Galliard
by Apex CoVantage, LLC

Dedication

For a time during my judicial career I thought that those who live in the United Kingdom could take for granted that their human rights would be adequately protected by English Law. But I am now worried as to whether this will remain the position. Certainly, in the future, I am now confident human rights, as they did in the past, will need the support of champions. That is, individuals who are totally committed to furthering and protecting our human rights. In referring to champions, I have in mind individuals like the late Clemens Nathan, in honour of whom this book is dedicated, who stoically fought to further human rights for the reasons clearly explained in the section of the book contributed by his daughter, Liz Ison, and son, Richard Nathan.

My current concerns were alerted by the campaign by the UK Government initially to repeal the Human Rights Act 1989. That Act made the European Convention of Human Rights part of our domestic law, enforceable in our courts. For a time it was the policy of our current government to repeal the 1989 Act and replace the European Convention with a *British* Bill of Rights. The terms of that Bill have never been published and fortunately that campaign has petered out.

However we would be unwise to set too much store by this apparent change of heart. It could well be that there has been no change of heart and the recent inactivity is no more than a consequence of the pressures being caused by the Brexit negotiations, which reports indicate are absorbing a major proportion of the UK Government's resources. Whether this is the case or not, there is no doubt that the UK Government is showing considerable interest in achieving a situation that when this country withdraws from the European Union, and even when it is in a state of transition, that the parallel provisions of the EU Charter of Fundamental Rights resulting from the Amsterdam (1998) and Lisbon (2009) Treaties have as limited application as possible. While not forgetting that there are important distinctions between the protection provided by the Charter and Convention Rights, the energy being devoted to restricting the ambit of the Charter rights does suggest we would be right to be on our guard to ensure that after Brexit our protection of the human rights of our citizens are no less effective than they were before our decision to leave the European Union.

I have no hesitation in welcoming the publication of this volume of essays by many of those who, like myself, admired the long-time efforts of Clemens Nathan to improve the protection of human rights. It would be a betrayal of his efforts and those of many other campaigners like him if we allowed the United Kingdom again, as it was in the past, justifiably to be described as "an elective" or "elected dictatorship" (Lord Hailsham, Dimbleby Lecture 1976).

The Rt Hon Lord Woolf, CH

Contents

Foreword

When the infamous photos of Nazi concentration and extermination camps were published in *Life* magazine in May 1945, awareness about the atrocities committed by the Nazi regime rose around the world. This was a defining moment in history, as international public opinion was confronted with the brutality of those events. From these 'human wrongs' emerged an unprecedented social and political will to prevent mass atrocities and uphold a set of common entitlements for all human beings: human rights.

The horrors of the crimes against humanity committed during World War II strengthened the conviction of the international community to create a new international platform mandated to promote and defend peace. Within the tradition of the Legal Pacifism of the nineteenth century and building on the founding principles of the League of Nations, the United Nations was born. To advance its objectives, the new organisation developed the Universal Declaration of Human Rights (UDHR) as "a common standard of achievement for all peoples and all nations." Common, because it embodied human aspirations deeply rooted in different cultures across the globe. At the same time, unique, as it was the first codification of legal rights for all human beings without discrimination, and it encompassed entitlements relating to all spheres of life and dimensions of human personality.

Ever since, the UDHR has served to uphold the humanist values of universal equality and freedom, supporting decolonisation, good governance and the struggle against discrimination. Yet much ground remains to be covered, as is evident by the destruction and destitution encountered in many parts of the world.

The effort to transform the 'ideals' enshrined in the Universal Declaration into reality relies, as this publication eloquently reminds us, on two interrelated and mutually reinforcing processes; namely, the learning about human rights and the confrontation of the most egregious of human wrongs. This combination of knowledge and memory can heal the wounds of the past and create the defences of peace by inspiring commitment to universal values, empathy, compassion and vigilance. Essential to this endeavour, as stressed in this publication, is the elimination of all forms of discrimination and exclusion and a holistic approach that treats all human rights – civil, cultural, economic, political and social – as part of an indivisible, interrelated and interdependent whole.

This vision lies at the heart of the existence of the United Nations Educational, Scientific and Cultural Organisation (UNESCO). UNESCO contributed to the elaboration of the UDHR in 1947 by exploring the philosophical basis in different cultures of human rights as legal entitlements. It was also the first UN agency to endorse the UDHR as a reference point for its programme activities and to commit to disseminating relevant information through mass communication programmes and teaching materials in schools. Building on this legacy, UNESCO mobilises its soft power to defend the principles of respect for human dignity and social justice in all its areas of competence. The alignment to universal values is the foundation of our work in promoting access to quality education for all, of which global citizenship and intercultural education are fundamental components. It underpins the efforts to foster press freedom, media pluralism and the safety of journalists, as well as enhanced youth participation and partnerships for inclusive and sustainable cities. Drawing on the intellectual and moral solidarity of humankind, UNESCO promotes responses to the threats of sectarianism, exclusion and violent extremism that are anchored in the respect for cultural diversity, participation and dialogue. Within UNESCO's mandate to "build lasting peace in the minds of men and women," we are committed to tackling the artificial dichotomy of 'us' and 'them.'

There could not be a more appropriate conclusion for this volume than the inspiring reflection on hope by President Jimmy Carter: "We have faced similar challenges before and we have seen incredible progress." In the same spirit, Martin Luther King Jr. reminded his audience that, "only when it is dark enough, can you see the stars," while President Vaclav Havel advocated for hope as a state of mind, believing that, "It is not the conviction that something will turn out well, but the certainty that something makes sense, regardless of how it turns out." These messages are reinforced by the adoption of the 2030 Agenda for Sustainable Development – a commitment to upholding common standards set by the UDHR and the body of international human rights law vested with the pledge of 'leaving no one behind.'

While we celebrate the 70th anniversary of the UDHR, it is critical that we reflect on the 'rights' and 'wrongs' of the human family as a stepping-stone for taking wiser choices in the future that fully uphold the inherent dignity of all human beings. Instrumental in this effort will be a genuine form of hope that I call upon every one of us to cherish:

> All human beings are born free and equal in dignity and rights.
>
> From Article 1, Universal Declaration of Human Rights (December 1948)

Audrey Azoulay, Director-General of UNESCO

Figure 1 The Universal Declaration of Human Rights was adopted by the United Nations General Assembly at its third session, on 10 December 1948, as Resolution 217 at the Palais de Chaillot in Paris, France. It has since been translated into over 500 languages.

The Drafting Committee consisted of nine members: Eleanor Roosevelt (US), Dr Peng-chun Chang (China), Charles Malik (Lebanon), William Hodgson (Australia), Dr Hernan Santa Cruz (Chile), René Cassin (France), Alexandre Bogomolov (USSR), Charles Dukes (UK) and John P. Humphrey (Canada).

The full Declaration can be found in the Appendix.

Image courtesy of the British Library.

Figure 1 in public domain www.bl.uk/collection-items/universal-declaration-of-human-rights

In honour of Clemens N. Nathan (1933–2015)

Contemporary Human Rights Challenges: The Universal Declaration of Human Rights and its Continuing Relevance has been developed and published in honour of Clemens Nathan, for whom human rights was a passion. The book has grown out of a memorial seminar on the Universal Declaration of Human Rights (UDHR) held at The Athenaeum in London in 2016, a year after Clemens' death, with speakers examining different areas of the Universal Declaration that were particularly reflective of Clemens' work. Dr Carla Ferstman, Alexander Goldberg and The Right Reverend The Lord Williams all spoke at the seminar and are also editors of or contributors to this volume of essays on *Contemporary Human Rights Challenges*. They have been joined by other authors, many of whom had a connection with Clemens through his work in the advancement of human rights and interfaith fields.

At that seminar, The Right Reverend The Lord Williams spoke eloquently about the qualities that Clemens brought to discourse on human rights:

> We have to find imaginative ways of living together as communities. We have to find, again and again, new ways of securing individual liberties without overriding community identities. We have to find ways in which the state can express, articulate, and embody its own limitations without sacrificing or compromising universal rule of law or the universal right of redress. And in order to think those things through, we need more and more people who have precisely that quality of cosmopolitan vision, civilised sensibility, and moral passion that was so evident in Clemens Nathan.[1]

Clemens' values were shaped by the historical context of his time. Born in Hamburg, Germany in 1933, he and his family moved to England three years later to escape Nazi persecution. The transformation from German child to English gentleman, from Jewish refugee to a central figure of the Anglo-Jewish establishment, took hard work and determination and was a key narrative in Clemens' life story. A strong sense of his own roots and a commitment to his Jewish identity never left him; the importance of making a contribution to communal Jewish life was both a pleasure and a duty, but he was also driven to look beyond this communal life to work for wider society. Increasingly, his outlook became an international one as he sought to apply his skills and knowledge to international problems.

Clemens' interest in human rights undoubtedly grew out of a response to his early history. As well as taking a direct role in the work of securing reparations for victims of the Holocaust, he increasingly saw the need to communicate the history and experience of reparations in order to facilitate the work of others, both in this field and beyond – principally, academics, politicians and activists – and he did this by organising conferences, giving talks and publishing research, always looking for opportunities to create synergy by bringing different disciplines and ideas together. Above all it was by sheer strength of personality – a creative force to 'make things happen' – that he found a way of bridging many worlds (Anglo-Jewish, international Jewish, interfaith and international human rights), in so doing showing how people from all walks of life can come together to make significant change to our societies. This was always done with good humour and sprightly individualism.

Clemens' career was in the textile industry, working as a textile agent and technologist principally for British, European and American mills (as well as a significant involvement in the development of the Israeli textile industry through an association with the Shenkar College of Engineering and Design). Though this work will not be covered in this article, his experience of this international industry gave him an insight that was also to influence his interest in international human rights. He described his shock at some of the bad treatment of workers he witnessed in his visits to textile plants in developing as well as developed countries and how he sought to use his influence diplomatically with the factory managers to facilitate change.[2] As a textile agent and businessman as well as a senior figure in the Textile Institute, he understood the complex issues involved in balancing profit with factory conditions and workers' rights, so that his views grew out of direct real-world experience rather than theoretical or abstract principles.

As a frequent traveller for the Cunart Company, the firm he led from the age of 24 following the death of his father, he was able to combine textile work with an ever-increasing voluntary work strand. As Joint Chair of the Consultative Council of Jewish Organisations (CCJO) and President of the Anglo Jewish Association (AJA), he represented Jewish interests at the United Nations in Geneva and New York as well as at the Council of Europe and UNESCO.

He also joined the effort to seek a small measure of justice for Holocaust victims, serving as a Board Member of the Conference on Jewish Material Claims Against Germany (the Claims Conference based in New York) for over a decade, including a role as Chairman of its Nominating Committee. Here he was involved in negotiations with Germany regarding direct payments to Nazi victims[3] and, increasingly, its funding to aid elderly victims through a range of social, welfare and care programmes. There were also talks with Austria about its obligations, as well as for the children who fled on the Kindertransport.

One of Clemens' particular interests was the relationship between religion and human rights, which led him to write the book *The Changing Face of Religion and Human Rights: A Personal Reflection* in 2009. Such interests also spurred him to become an advocate of interfaith work, notably by becoming the first Chairman (1998–2003) of The Centre for the Study of Jewish-Christian Relations (now the Woolf Institute) in Cambridge, which is devoted to teaching, research and dialogue among the three Abrahamic faiths.

However, his interest in human rights was much broader, and an analysis of the outputs of the Clemens Nathan Research Centre (CNRC), which he founded in 2007, shows that the conferences and associated publications (CNRC developed and sponsored ten international conferences and published or contributed to over 20 publications) covered topics addressing many of the Articles of the UDHR. For example, as well as several conferences and publications on reparations and the right to redress in the international context,[4] conferences were held on the role of the media, international development and foreign policy, maternal mortality and the workings of the UN Human Rights Treaty System,[5] demonstrating that his interest touched on many areas of the Declaration.

Clemens found personal inspiration from René Cassin (1887–1977),[6] one of the co-authors of the Universal Declaration and whom he knew personally, to use the experience of the Holocaust to work for change for all humanity. Clemens was a young man when he first met Cassin and was on the board of the CCJO under Cassin's chairmanship (and which Cassin had founded in 1946 – one of the first non-governmental bodies to receive consultative status at the United Nations).

After Clemens gave a speech at the CCJO in Paris on the persecution of Jews in the Soviet Union in 1972, Cassin invited Clemens to present at a conference[7] highlighting the lack of freedom of minority groups in the Soviet Union. Clemens' subsequent reading of a speech by Vladimir Bukovsky (a Jewish dissident on trial in Moscow) was broadcast throughout the Soviet Union by Liberty Radio. Many years later, on a visit to Israel, he met some Georgian immigrants who told Clemens that they had heard his speech being broadcast, and it had given them the hope that they would one day experience freedom, confirming Clemens' long-held belief that the actions of one individual could make a material difference in the lives of others. Giving others cause for hope felt like a precious outcome in itself. This was a seminal moment for Clemens and the start of his many activities in the field of human rights. Years later, he put this belief into practice by being a founding inspiration in the establishment of the London based non-governmental organisation 'René Cassin' which focuses on how Jewish values can contribute in the fight for human rights and by offering educational opportunities for young people to encourage them to enter this area.

Clemens' work ethic always embodied this belief in the power of individual actions – an understanding of history, political theory, philosophy, use of direct action, or involvement in politics – all have their role;[8] but for him, networking and communicating, creating forums and events where such dialogue can take place was key.[9] Clemens wrote: "if we share our own experiences and attempt to see issues from different viewpoints around the world, we can make progress."[10]

Thus he put into practice his belief that people from different communities could learn from his personal experience and the experience of the Jewish community.

Clemens saw our diversity as humanity's strength and that human rights should be viewed in a social and civil context so that we can all develop and flourish. As Clemens himself observed, he was,

> committed to human rights that respect the differences of people everywhere and see the absolute imperative for humanity to work together. I am happier viewing rights as obligations of one human being to another, a responsibility to others rather than the right of individuals.[11]

Clemens was both an optimist and a realist. He knew that the task was huge, but he also knew that we must not desist from undertaking it. By our own actions, using our own set of skills, keeping faith with fair and liberal values and, above all, nurturing and sustaining loving and respectful human relationships, we must continue to strive for a better world.

Together with our sister Jennifer, we are delighted to see how this book has come to fruition. We feel sure our father would have welcomed with enthusiasm the book's fresh outlook on the Universal Declaration 70 years after its adoption and would have enjoyed reading the essays of this eminent group of authors, ranging from scholars and practitioners to leaders, such as the 104th Archbishop of Canterbury and the 39th President of the United States of America, reflecting on the past and examining the challenges ahead.

Liz Ison and Richard Nathan

Notes

1 *Memorial Seminar Proceedings in Honour of Clemens N. Nathan: Contemporary Reflections on the Universal Declaration of Human Rights*, 4th May 2016, The Athenaeum, Pall Mall, London.
2 Preface of Nathan, 2009: xiii.
3 His paper 'Rehabilitation for the Jewish victims of the Holocaust: Sixty Years of the Claims Conference, the Scope of Reparations, and the Changing Nature of Rehabilitation' was published posthumously in the *International Human Rights Law Review* (Nathan, 2016).
4 For example, conference on *Reparations for Victims of Genocide, Crimes Against Humanity and War Crimes: Systems in Place and Systems in the Making*, The Peace Palace, The Hague, The Netherlands, 2007.
5 Bayefsky, 2002.
6 As described in his 2010 pamphlet, *René Cassin: An Appreciation.*
7 Clemens' talk was entitled 'A Review of Some of the Main Trends Affecting Jews During the Last Year in the USSR 1971–1972' at the International Symposium on the 50th Anniversary of the Founding of the USSR for the International Committee for the Defence of Human Rights in the USSR, Palais des Congres Bruxelles, 1972.
8 Clemens' family and friends have set up a PhD scholarship in his name at the Centre for German-Jewish Studies at the University of Sussex to facilitate further understanding and research in this field.

9 This is illustrated by the breadth of contributors and topics published in his honour in Stephens and Walden, 2006.
10 Lecture, 'Rwanda, Racism and Understanding Society', West Point Center for Holocaust and Genocide Studies, Philadelphia, USA, 2009.
11 From the concluding chapter of *The Warp and the Weft* (Nathan, 2018).

References

Bayefsky, A.F. (2002). *How to Complain to the UN Human Rights Treaty System.* Leiden: Martinus Nijhoff.

Nathan, C.N. (2009). *The Changing Face of Religion and Human Rights.* Leiden: Martinus Nijhoff.

Nathan, C.N. (2010). *René Cassin: An Appreciation.* Bicester: Words by Design.

Nathan, C.N. (2016). Rehabilitation for the Jewish Victims of the Holocaust: Sixty Years of the Claims Conference, the Scope of Reparations, and the Changing Nature of Rehabilitation. *International Human Rights Law Review*, 5(2).

Nathan, C.N. (2018). *The Warp and the Weft.* Bicester: Words by Design.

Stephens, A. and Walden, R. (2006). *For the Sake of Humanity.* Leiden: Martinus Nijhoff.

Contributors

John Alderdice has been a Liberal Democrat member of the United Kingdom House of Lords for more than 20 years and is a former Chairman of the party in the House. He is Director of the Centre for the Resolution of Intractable Conflict at Harris Manchester College (University of Oxford) and Chairman of the Centre for Democracy and Peace Building (Belfast). As Leader of the Alliance Party of Northern Ireland, he played a significant role in negotiating the 1998 Good Friday Agreement, was the first Speaker of the Northern Ireland Assembly and then one of four international commissioners appointed by the British and Irish Governments to address security normalisation. He was President of Liberal International, the global federation of more than 100 liberal political parties and is now Presidente d'Honneur. Previously a consultant psychiatrist at the Centre for Psychotherapy in Belfast, he is currently a Clinical Professor in Psychiatry at the University of Maryland (Baltimore). His special interest is in religious fundamentalism, radicalisation and violent political conflict.

Audrey Azoulay is Director-General of UNESCO. She was France's Minister of Culture and Communication from February 2016 to May 2017. She has occupied senior positions in France's public broadcasting sector and then served as rapporteur to France's public auditing authority, the *Cour des comptes*, and as a European Commission legislative expert on issues of culture and the media. Ms Azoulay served France's National Cinema Centre (CNC), first as Deputy Audiovisual Director, then as Director of Financial and Legal Affairs and finally as Deputy Director-General. She is a graduate of the *Ecole Nationale d'Administration* and the Paris *Institut d'études politiques.* Ms Azoulay also holds a Masters degree in Business Administration from the University of Lancaster (UK). In November 2017 Audrey Azoulay was appointed to the post of Director-General of UNESCO.

Michael J. Bazyler is Professor of Law and the 1939 Society Law Scholar in Holocaust and Human Rights Studies at Chapman University Fowler School of Law in Orange, California. He is holder of previous fellowships at Harvard Law School and the United States Holocaust Memorial Museum in Washington, DC and at Yad Vashem in Jerusalem (The Holocaust Martyrs' and Heroes' Remembrance Authority of Israel), where he was the holder of the *Baron Friedrich Carl von Oppenheim Chair for the Study of Racism, Antisemitism and the Holocaust.* He is the author of five books and over a dozen law review articles on subjects covering public international law, international human rights law, international trade law and comparative law. His book, *Holocaust Justice: The Battle for Restitution in America's Courts* (New York University Press, 2003, soft cover 2005), was cited by the US Supreme Court, and *Holocaust, Genocide and the Law: A Quest for Justice in a Post-Holocaust World* (Oxford University Press, 2016) was the winner of the National Jewish Book Award in the category of the Holocaust.

Giovanni Boccardi is the Chief of the Emergency Preparedness and Response Unit within the Culture Sector of UNESCO. His responsibilities involve coordinating and supporting the action by the Organisation to assist Member States in preparing and responding to crises related to conflicts or natural disasters. He graduated in Architecture at the University of Rome (Italy) and obtained a Master Degree on Built Environment from the University College of London (UK). He has worked for UNESCO in different positions since 1994, both in the field (Uzbekistan and Jordan) and at headquarters, where he acted as Chief of a Regional Unit at the World Heritage Centre (first Arab States, then Asia and the Pacific), between 2001 and 2011, and then as Focal Point for Sustainable Development, Disaster Risk Reduction and Capacity Building, until 2014.

Jimmy Carter (James Earl Carter, Jr.), 39th President of the United States, was educated in the public school of Plains, Georgia, attended Georgia Southwestern College and the Georgia Institute of Technology, and received a BS degree from the US Naval Academy in 1946. In the Navy he became a submariner, serving in both the Atlantic and Pacific fleets and rising to the rank of Lieutenant. In 1962 he won election to the Georgia Senate. He lost his first gubernatorial campaign in 1966, but won the next election, becoming Georgia's 76th governor on January 12, 1971. Jimmy Carter served as President from January 20, 1977 to January 20, 1981. President Carter is the author of 29 books, and in 1982 he became University Distinguished Professor at Emory University in Atlanta, Georgia, and founded The Carter Center. Actively guided by President Carter, the non-partisan and non-profit centre addresses national and international issues of public policy.

Danwood M. Chirwa is Professor of Law and Head of the Department of Public Law at the University of Cape Town, South Africa. He is currently also a member of the board of trustees for the UN Trust Fund on Contemporary Form of Slavery. He is the author of *Human Rights under the Malawian Constitution* (Cape Town: Juta & Co Ltd, 2011), co-editor (with Lilian Chenwi) of *The Protection of Economic, Social and Cultural Rights in Africa: International, Regional and National Perspectives* (Cambridge: Cambridge University Press, 2016) and (with Lia Nijzink) of *Accountable Government in Africa: Perspectives from Public Law and Political Studies* (Cape Town: UCT Press/ United Nations University Press, 2012), and founder and Editor-in-Chief of the *Malawi Law Journal.* He has worked with many non-governmental organisations (NGOs) on matters of social justice, including as a board member with the Open Democracy and Advice Centre (ODAC), the Resources

Aimed at the Prevention of Child Abuse and Neglect (RAPCAN) and the Socio-Economic Rights Institute (SERI), and as Secretary-General of the African Network of Constitutional Lawyers (ANCL). He has published, taught and supervised postgraduate students on economic, social and cultural rights.

Mike Dottridge has focused on the rights of adults and children who experience economic or sexual exploitation since 1995. He worked for two human rights NGOs for 25 years, from 1977 until 2002 (Amnesty International and Anti-Slavery International, where he was director). Since 2002 he has worked independently, undertaking evaluations and institutional learning exercises for both international organisations and NGOs. He is the author of numerous articles and handbooks commenting on aspects of international law concerning slavery, forced labour, child labour and human trafficking or suggesting ways to prevent such exploitation and to protect the victims. He is one of the specialists who advised the United Nations High Commissioner for Human Rights on the High Commissioner's Recommended Principles and Guidelines on Human Rights and Human Trafficking (2002) and was a trustee of the United Nations Fund on Contemporary Forms of Slavery from 2011 until 2016.

Léonie Evers is Associate Project Officer in the Emergency Preparedness and Response Unit of UNESCO's culture sector. She holds a Master's degree in International Relations and International Economics from Johns Hopkins University's School of Advanced International Studies in Washington, DC. Having concentrated in Conflict Management and African Studies, she focused on culture, religion, ethnicity and identity as both drivers of conflict and keys in peace-building. She decided to work for the integration of a concern for culture into humanitarian, peacekeeping and security policies – a resolve that proved timely and was reinforced with the advent of the conflict in Mali and the intentional destruction of several mausoleums in the World Heritage Property of Timbuktu. She deeply believes in education, respect for diversity and tolerance as the keys to sustainable peace.

Carla Ferstman is a Senior Lecturer at the Law Faculty, University of Essex. She is a Canadian qualified barrister and solicitor. She received a DPhil in public international law from the University of Oxford, LL.M from New York University and LL.B from the University of British Columbia. Dr Ferstman has worked in the human rights field for the bulk of her career to date. After a brief period in private practice in Canada, she began working internationally, first for the UN High Commissioner for Human Rights in Rwanda and thereafter, with the International Secretariat of Amnesty International in London. From there, she was appointed Executive Legal Advisor of the Commission for Real Property Claims of Refugees and Displaced Persons in Bosnia and Herzegovina, a mass claims body established pursuant to the Dayton Peace Accords. In 2001, Carla joined REDRESS, the award-winning human rights NGO which pursues justice on behalf of victims of torture and related international crimes, first as Legal Director and from 2004 to 2018 as Director. Dr Ferstman is a member of the experts committee of the Convention Against Torture

Initiative – an inter-governmental initiative to secure global ratification of the Convention Against Torture. She also serves on the board of Trauma Treatment International and the Nuhanovic Foundation.

Alexander Goldberg is a chaplain, barrister and human rights activist. He works as an international consultant on intercultural, interfaith and community relations advisor as Chief Executive of the Carob Tree Project. He is the Jewish Chaplain to the University of Surrey and has recently founded an Arts Chaplaincy. He co-founded René Cassin human rights group and represented them at the UN Human Rights Council. He chairs the Football Association's Faith Network, was the inaugural co-chair of the Faiths Forum for London and served as Chaplain to the Paralympic and Olympic Games in 2012. He regularly contributes to television, radio, online and print media, including BBC Radio 2's Pause for Thought. In 2015, he was appointed a King Abdullah Fellow at KAICIID. He has advised the government at ministerial level on human rights, equality and community issues. His work has been recognised by the International Olympic Peace Truce Committee, Mayor of London and US State Department.

Tony Gray runs a small publishing consultancy in Oxfordshire, Words by Design. Through this he provides publishing services to small independent publishers, charities and NGOs; researches, writes and produces personal biographies, family histories and corporate biographies; and offers publishing assistance to individuals wishing to publish books on a whole range of topics. Over a period of 15 years he worked with Clemens Nathan on a variety of projects, assisting with research, planning conferences and publishing a range of books linked with the Clemens Nathan Research Centre. Tony has a DPhil from Oxford University and has his own research interests in human rights, family history and the philosophy of religion.

Charles Hamilton has worked at the UK Equality and Human Rights Commission since 2011. He leads the Commission's work to promote understanding of the importance of human rights, and to safeguard and enhance the human rights legal framework. His professional interests include European and international human rights mechanisms, freedom of expression, LGBT equality, and human rights communication and education. Before joining the Commission he spent six years in a variety of roles at the Office of Fair Trading. He holds an MA in Human Rights from University College London, and lives in Essex with his wife and daughter.

Rebecca Hilsenrath was appointed Chief Executive Officer to the UK Equality and Human Rights Commission in October 2015, before which she held the role of Chief Legal Officer. Rebecca originally practised law at Linklaters and then worked for a number of years as a government lawyer. She was then appointed CEO of LawWorks, a national charity facilitating free legal advice to community groups and individuals in need. She is currently a non-executive director of the Office for Legal Complaints, the board of the Legal Ombudsman. Rebecca has also established two schools, set up the National Pro Bono Centre in Chancery Lane and has sat on the boards of a number of charities and advice agencies. In 2012, she was listed by *The Times* among the 100 most influential lawyers in the country and in 2017 received an honorary doctorate from BPP University in recognition of contributions to the legal profession.

Liz Ison is the younger daughter of Clemens Nathan (to whom this book is dedicated) and his late wife, Rachel. After studying English Literature at Cambridge University, Liz qualified as a speech and language therapist and subsequently lectured, researched and published in the field at University College London. She obtained her PhD there with a thesis based around a multi-year study tracking children's speech and language development. Liz then worked as a government researcher at the Department for Education. Alongside her current role at charity The Reader, she writes, edits and blogs on topics ranging from family and social history to cookery and literature. She lives in London with her husband and three children.

Francesca Klug has been a human rights activist, academic and advocate for over 30 years. Most recently she was Director of the Human Rights Future Project at London School of Economics, where she remains a Visiting Professor. Formerly a Senior Research Fellow at King's College Law School, she assisted the UK government in devising the Human Rights Act. Francesca is a former Chair of Freedom from Torture and the British Institute of Human Rights, is an Academic Expert at Doughty Street Chambers and a member of *Political Quarterly*'s Editorial Board. She is also on the Advisory Boards of the Pears Institute for the Study of Antisemitism and the human rights NGO, *René Cassin*. She has been a Commissioner on the independent Commission on Religion and Belief in British Public Life, a Special Adviser to the Joint Committee on Human Rights and a Commissioner on the statutory Equality and Human Rights Commission (EHRC).

Rashida Manjoo is a Professor in the Department of Public Law, University of Cape Town, South Africa, and a Visiting Professor at Queen Mary University London. Until July 2015, she held the position of United Nations Special Rapporteur on Violence Against Women, its Causes and Consequences, a post she was appointed to in 2009 by the UN Human Rights Council. Professor Manjoo is the former Parliamentary Commissioner of the Commission on Gender Equality, an institution created by the Constitution of South Africa, with a mandate to oversee the promotion and protection of gender equality. She has also been involved in social context training for judges and lawyers, where she has designed both content and methodology. She has over four decades of experience in social justice and human rights work both in South Africa and abroad, and her research and teaching has focused on the intersectional nature of discrimination, with a particular focus on the interaction of interpersonal, communal, institutional and structural factors that negatively impact the interdependence and indivisibility of human rights.

Richard Nathan, the son of Clemens Nathan (to whom this book is dedicated) and the late Rachel Nathan, is a Director and Principal of Bosquet Capital, a specialist advisory firm. Richard is also a Non-Executive Director and Director of several media, publishing and technology companies. He began his career in international news journalism, subsequently moving into commercial publishing and media, and has worked for Kyodo News, *Nature* and Macmillan in London, New York and Tokyo. He was educated in the UK and Japan and is a fluent Japanese speaker. He has authored books on Japan and its economy and regularly writes articles on Japanese culture, publishing and literature.

Kristen L. Nelson is Of Counsel to a boutique Los Angeles law firm focusing on civil litigation, international business and family law and is the Assistant Managing Editor of the European Court of Human Rights module for Oxford Reports on International Law. She was the Project Manager and Lead Researcher on a multi-year Holocaust real property restitution study commissioned by the Prague-based European Shoah Legacy Institute (ESLI) and has extensive experience in litigating high-stakes atrocities and asset recovery cases in US courts. Kristen has a JD from Pepperdine University School of Law and a Master of Laws in Human Rights from the University of Hong Kong.

Michael Newman is Chief Executive of the Association of Jewish Refugees (AJR), which represents and supports Holocaust refugees and survivors in Great Britain. He is a member of the UK delegation to the International Holocaust Remembrance Alliance (IHRA). As well as being an advisor on Holocaust-era restitution issues, guiding Holocaust survivors and refugees, and their families, with applications for compensation and the recovery of Holocaust-era assets, he worked with the UK government to create the position of UK Envoy for Post-Holocaust Issues and now advises incumbent Lord (Eric) Pickles. Michael is a Trustee of the Anglo-Jewish Association (AJA), which supports Jewish students to attend higher and further education, and which is a founding member and director of the Claims Conference. Previously, Michael was a consultant to the International Commission on Holocaust Era Insurance Claims (ICHEIC) and was a researcher at the Holocaust Educational Trust.

Bertrand G. Ramcharan was Professor at the Geneva Graduate Institute, Chancellor of the University of Guyana, UN High Commissioner for Human Rights (Ag.), Commissioner of the International Commission of Jurists and Member of the Permanent Court of Arbitration. A Barrister-at-Law of Lincoln's Inn, he has a PhD from the LSE. He is the author of several books, including *Contemporary Human Rights Ideas* and *Preventive Diplomacy at the United Nations.*

Nigel Rodley (1941–2017) was Chair of the Human Rights Centre at the University of Essex. He had been Legal Adviser at Amnesty International from 1973 onwards and the founding Head of Legal and Intergovernmental Organisations Office. He became a Professor of Law at Essex in 1994 and was Dean of Law from 1992 to 1995. From 1993 to 2001 he served as United Nations Special Rapporteur on Torture. From 2001 to 2016 he was a Member of the UN Human Rights Committee, serving as its Chairperson from 2013 to 2014. He was President of the International Commission of Jurists at the time of his death. In 1998 he was knighted for services to human rights and international law. Other honours included an honorary LLD from Dalhousie University. He was also a joint recipient of the American Society of International Law's 2005 Goler T Butcher Medal for distinguished work in human rights. In 2008 he was appointed an Honorary Fellow of the Faculty of Forensic and Legal Medicine of the Royal College of Physicians.

Eva Sobotka is Head of Sector Consultation and Cooperation at the EU Agency for Fundamental Rights. She has been responsible for developing the very first Fundamental Rights Forum 2016 and currently coordinates the Agency's cooperation with governments, national parliaments, national human rights bodies and civil society. Her areas of expertise include civil society, Roma inclusion, combating antisemitism, learning from the Holocaust, human rights and civic education and combating racism and religious intolerance. Over the last 20 years, she has worked variously as human rights expert with the EU institutions, governments, World Bank, Open Society Institute, and directed the regional office of the American Friends Service Committee in Hungary. She has been a mentor in the International Women Forum and engages in promotion of opportunities for women in leadership.

Rodrigo Uprimny is a lawyer with a Master's degree (DEA) in sociology of development from the University Paris I (IEDES) and a PhD in Economy from Amiens University. He was a Professor and now a Professor Emeritus at the National University of Colombia, and has been a visiting professor at several universities. He was an assistant magistrate and temporary replacement at the Constitutional Court and is Co-Judge of that Court and of the Council of State. He is a member of the International Commission of Jurists and the UN Committee on Economic, Social and Cultural Rights (2015–2018). He is also a columnist for *El Espectador*. Rodrigo was formerly Director of Dejusticia and is currently coordinator of the Drug Policy Line. His areas of interest are especially economic, social and cultural rights (ESCR), transitional justice, judicial system and drug policy. He has published several books and articles on these issues, as author or co-author.

Laura van Waas is Co-Director of the Institute on Statelessness and Inclusion, as well as Assistant Professor at Tilburg Law School. Dr van Waas' PhD manuscript, *Nationality Matters* (Intersentia, 2008), is widely used as a reference for understanding international statelessness law by researchers and practitioners all over the world, as is *Nationality and Statelessness under International Law*, which she edited together with Alice Edwards (Cambridge: Cambridge University Press, 2014). In more than a decade of working on statelessness, Laura has carried out a wide array of research and teaching projects, both within academia and for the UN Refugee Agency. She has conducted studies for, among others, Plan International, the OHCHR, Open Society Foundations, the Women's Refugee Commission, the US Department of State, the European Parliament and the Norwegian Refugee Council.

George R. Wilkes is the founding Director of the Religion and Ethics in the Making of War and Peace Project, based at the University of Edinburgh since 2010. A member of the International Society for Military Ethics in Europe (Euro-ISME) and the Network of International Humanitarian Law Lecturers and Researchers, Dr Wilkes is also on the international steering committees of Relief and Reconciliation for Syria and the Jewish Law Association. He has had a long involvement with post-conflict dialogue and human rights organisations. From 2005 to 2010, he was a Fellow at St Edmund's College, Cambridge, and has lectured at Cambridge, Edinburgh, Leuven and Birmingham universities.

Rowan Williams was born in Wales and studied theology at Cambridge and Oxford, researching the history of religious thought in early twentieth-century Russia and the Russian emigration. After several years as a university teacher, he served for ten years as Bishop of Monmouth in Wales, including three years as Archbishop of Wales, then for another ten years as Archbishop of Canterbury. He has long-standing interests in interreligious dialogue and in the relation of faith communities and society. He is the author of many theological works and a collection of essays, *Faith in the Public Square* (2012), as well as four collections of poetry. Since 2012 he has been Master of Magdalene College, Cambridge.

Lorna Woods is Professor of Internet Law in the Law School at the University of Essex and a member of the Human Rights Centre there. Formerly a practising solicitor in a TMT practice, she has extensive experience in the fields of media policy, communications regulation as well as data protection, privacy and freedom of expression. She has published widely in these areas in both academic journals and practitioner works. Recent publications include 'Social Media: it is not just about Article 10' in Mangan and Gillies (eds.), *The Legal Challenges of Social Media* (Cheltenham: Edward Elgar, 2017) and 'Automated Number Plate Recognition: data retention and the protection of privacy in public places' (2017). Current projects include a contribution to Cole and Boehm (eds.), *GDPR Commentary* (Cheltenham: Edward Elgar, forthcoming).

Harry Woolf was called to the Bar in 1955 and from 1973 to 1974 was junior counsel, Inland Revenue. During this time he represented the Revenue in the majority of their leading cases before the High Court, Court of Appeal and the House of Lords. In 1974 Lord Woolf was appointed first Treasury Counsel (Common Law), a post which he held for five years. Lord Woolf was appointed to the Queen's Bench Division of the High Court of Justice in 1979, as Lord Justice of Appeal in 1986 and a Lord of Appeal in Ordinary in 1992. Between 1996 and 2000 he held the position of Master of the Rolls, and in 2000 was appointed Lord Chief Justice of England and Wales, a position from which he retired in September 2005. In 2003, Lord Woolf was appointed a non-permanent judge of the Court of Final Appeal of Hong Kong, acting as the overseas judge in that Court until 2012. From 2006 to 2012, he was the first President of the Qatar Financial Centre Civil and Commercial Court, (2006–2012). Lord Woolf was awarded a Companion of Honour (CH) in the Queen's Birthday Honours List 2015.

Introduction by the editors

Carla Ferstman, Alexander Goldberg, Tony Gray, Liz Ison, Richard Nathan and Michael Newman

The Universal Declaration of Human Rights (UDHR) was adopted by the United Nations General Assembly 70 years ago, on 10 December 1948 (the full text of the UDHR is reproduced at the end of this volume). The Declaration epitomised the aspirations of the immediate post-war period and seized upon the collective desire to chart a new path based on universal respect for common values and recognition of the inherent dignity of the individual. With the embers of war still burning, the UDHR boldly asserted the universality, indivisibility and interdependence of all human rights, the fundamental principles of equality and non-discrimination as well as a communitarian vision of mutual respect and solidarity. It signified a bold, moral shift in consciousness. While not formally binding, the Declaration was designed to inspire a new code of behaviour and to serve as a blueprint for later binding treaties and national laws – in its own words, a "common standard of achievement for all peoples and all Nations."

The Declaration is an iconic and visionary text, but at the same time it is a product of the imperfect time in which it was drafted. A good part of the world was still under colonial rule. There was limited mutual respect for diversity in legal and political systems and disparities among cultures, ideologies, languages and religions. There were significant gaps in wealth and opportunity and deep imbalances between the recognition of the rights of men and women. Those and many other limitations continue to frame our understanding of the meaning, role and purpose of human rights and their relative importance in a world weighed down by power, politics, poverty, conflict and division.

The belief in the power of human rights as a positive regulating force is a key inspirer for this collection of essays, which assess the impact of human rights in several areas of life. We have been motivated by the optimism of the UDHR drafters and their later adherents whom, we argue, were anything but naïve. The drafters exhibited a fatalistic and prescient optimism – a pragmatic recognition that adherence to fundamental principles of universal human rights and dignity was and continues to be a necessary precondition for the human race to survive and to thrive in pluralistic societies and in a complex and increasingly inter-connected world. The hope for the human rights project is not a product of fervour or dogma. Professor Bertrand Ramcharan, former UN High Commissioner for Human Rights, explains that "the only moral glue that can unite humanity remains the Universal Declaration of Human Rights." We are fated to hope and human rights because we are wed to the present and to the future. We simply must be.

As Lord Woolf reminds us, "human rights, as they did in the past, will need the support of champions." In this, we have been inspired by the life and advocacy work of Clemens Nathan, a philanthropist and humanitarian whose memory serves as the catalyst for this book. The themes of dignity and hope, on which he talked often, pervade this collection of essays.

We have benefitted tremendously and are so grateful to the vanguards, thought-leaders, human rights practitioners and academics who have graciously agreed to lend their unique perspectives to this publication. The engagement of such a diverse group of experts attests to the influence of human rights discourse in so many domains, and we hope this has helped to enrich the text.

Others have written on the UDHR drafting process,[1] the precursors or antecedents to the Declaration and its philosophical underpinnings,[2] or have sought to define and clarify the meaning of the different articles.[3] Our approach has been mainly to explain the significance of the Declaration in practice – to consider areas in which the text has helped or hindered us in the practical realisation of human rights and to explore the extant gaps and challenges with which the human rights movement continues to struggle. We have not sought to cover all 30 articles of the UDHR within this one volume but instead to highlight those articles that bring into acute focus the issues and lessons of the past as well as contemporary perspectives on our fundamental human rights.

There have been important advances in protections, including the recognition of the obligations to respect, protect and fulfil human rights and the progressive understanding of the role of non-state actors. Yet clearly key blind spots remain. Many of the ideals the Declaration espouses have continued to be subject to debate and are regularly thwarted in all parts of the world. Some of the themes we explore in this book include:

1) The significant disparities between and within countries and regions, which impede the realisation of rights for all. Despite the laudable statement in Article 1 of the Declaration that "All human beings are born free and equal in dignity and rights," access to rights depends far too often on relative privilege defined by gender, race, class, wealth and where one is born.
2) The difficulty to keep pace with the practical and ethical challenges posed by modern technological advances, including cyber-warfare and information technology.
3) The extent to which the human rights framework has accounted for the evolution of public-private divides is a theme, which repeats throughout

the text, and is taken up by Professor Rashida Manjoo and Dr Carla Ferstman. The changing landscape of human rights actors, including the importance of securing both individual and group rights, is a constant referent in reflections by Lord Alderdice, Lord Williams, Professor Francesca Klug, Dr George R. Wilkes and Alexander Goldberg. The complexity of how the world now operates means that there are now many more actors beyond the state which have the capacity to violate human rights, including private security companies, terror cells, corporations, the media and inter-governmental and non-governmental organisations. The human rights framework is only slowly adapting to capture these facets.

4) The impact of environmental degradation and climate change on natural habitats, causing competition over dwindling resources. These factors have contributed to poverty, increased inequities and conflict and have fuelled the mass movement of people across borders and continents. The human rights framework has more to do to address practically the causes or consequences of displacement, a challenge referred to by both Professor Ramcharan and Dr Laura van Waas.
5) The work of the UN and other multilateral projects as agents for peace and promoters of human rights has been thwarted by selective application, political malaise and bureaucratisation. Equally, the resurgence and intensification of nationalism and xenophobia in many countries and regions has undermined the collective security agenda and impeded international solidarity. As noted by Professor Klug, "A backlash against the post-war human rights architecture, with its universal, transnational ethic, is gaining momentum; not least amongst some of the democracies which played a crucial role in its creation."
6) War, oppression and systemic violence are constant features of the international landscape. As is noted by Michael Newman, "Stemming from a response to the atrocities of the Holocaust and the Second World War, the Declaration itself has not been enough to prevent further genocide in disparate areas of the world. The crimes perpetrated by the Khmer Rouge in Cambodia, against the Tutsis in Rwanda and against Muslims in Bosnia are three indelible stains on the post-war international community that has repeatedly called for 'never again'."

The extent to which the 30 articles of the Declaration have been enforced by governments and other actors on the international plane is not the litmus test we have used to assess the relevance of the text in the modern day. How one responds to the usual challenges of implementation depends on where one is situated on the pendulum of pessimism or optimism. While the gaps in enforcement can serve to de-legitimise the rules, the continued battle to secure basic human rights in all parts of the world underscores our collective responsibility to keep fighting. Not only must we keep our heads up above the parapet, but we must also be resolved to commit to a long-term vision of human rights protection that will never follow a simple or steady path of progressive successes.

Lord Alderdice explains in his chapter on terrorism that,

> It is crucial in such times that we maintain our commitment to human rationality and human rights, but we must understand that they do not in themselves represent a sufficient understanding of the human condition, how we function as individuals and groups, and how we can evolve and progress to greater peace, stability and reconciliation in our world.

Human rights is a long-term, messy project, but it cannot be understood in isolation. Lord Alderdice gives hope to the possibility that,

> we may also be standing on the threshold of a major step forward in our understanding of humanity; a paradigm shift that takes us beyond a rather legalistic, rationalistic, linear approach to human rights and into the complexity of large group relationships. We must work creatively on taking such a next step. Not only our rights and freedom but our very survival as a species may depend upon it.

As President Jimmy Carter implores us,

> we must accommodate changing times, but cling to principles that never change. . . . If we are to revitalise a global human rights movement, we must work to strengthen our societies' commitments to peace and human rights so that future generations inherit a less violent and more just world.

Sir Nigel S. Rodley (1941–2017)

Our editorial committee was led by Professor Sir Nigel Rodley KBE until his death in January 2017. Sir Nigel had collaborated with Clemens Nathan on several books and conferences, and he agreed to join an editorial group to develop a book marking the 70th anniversary of the Declaration. The volume that you see today has been hugely influenced by Sir Nigel's vision, reflecting his dedication to the international protection of human rights. This vision has underpinned our approach to this book throughout, and we continue to draw inspiration from his life and work. As fellow editors, we are also indebted to Nigel's extensive connections to the pre-eminent academics and practitioners in specific fields of human rights.

For some in the editorial group, it was the first time working with Nigel, but we quickly realised that he was not only brilliant, insightful and a force for good but also a true gentleman. He has made a deep and lasting impact on us all.

Figure 2 René Cassin conceptualised the Declaration as a portico of a Greek temple: having a foundation (general principles), steps (the preamble: the reasons for the Declaration) and four columns (the main body of the Declaration, which covers the rights of the individual; the rights of the individual in civil and political society; spiritual, public and political freedoms; and economic, social and cultural rights). Laid on these columns is the pediment, the last three articles of which dealing with the responsibilities or the links between human beings and society.

Image by Alex Pearl

Figure 2 permission to use given by Alex Pearl

Notes

1 Morsink, 1999; Schabas, 2013.
2 Freeman, 2003.
3 Alfreðsson and Eide, 1999.

References

Alfreðsson, G. and Eide, A. (1999). *The Universal Declaration of Human Rights: A Common Standard of Achievement*. The Hague: Martinus Nijhoff.

Freeman, W. (2003). *Philosophical Theory and the Universal Declaration of Human Rights.* Ottawa: University of Ottawa Press.
Morsink, J. (1999). *The Universal Declaration of Human Rights: Origins, Drafting, and Intent.* Pennsylvania: University of Pennsylvania Press.
Schabas, W. (2013). *The Universal Declaration of Human Rights: The Travaux Préparatoires.* Cambridge: Cambridge University Press.

Section I

Reflections on the Declaration's foundation articles and some cross-cutting themes

1 The foundations

Articles 1 and 2

Bertrand G. Ramcharan

Introduction

The world is in political, economic, social and moral crisis. Poverty, conflicts, terrorism, inequality, bad governance, and gross violations of human rights are pervasive. Climate change and mass movements of people contribute to waves of humanitarian emergencies. The validity of the international order is under challenge by powerful states, some of which advocate 'sovereign rights' over individual rights. 'Strongmen' have assumed power in key countries. Religious violence causes untold suffering. Though it remains a difficult task 70 years after the UDHR was adopted, the only moral glue that can unite humanity remains the UDHR. And the heart of the Declaration resides in its Articles 1 and 2.

Articles 1 and 2, building on the human rights provisions of the UN Charter, laid the foundations of the contemporary international legal order and are of the greatest importance legally, philosophically and from the perspectives of international public policy. Even though the Declaration, as such, was professedly considered a moral rather than a legal document, Articles 1 and 2 had implicit legal status and made 'instant international customary law' because of the 'higher value' of the self-evident truths contained in Article 1, the fact that the non-discrimination provisions in Article 2 reiterated and expanded on the Charter's non-discrimination legal obligations, and because of the consensus that flowed into these articles.

Writing in 1967, René Cassin recalled that the Universal Declaration had opened with "*a categorical affirmation of a higher value* which makes life itself worthwhile: that all human beings are endowed with an inherent dignity and a common heritage of liberty, equality of rights and full membership in the brotherhood of man."[1] Writing in the same publication, Louis Sohn concluded that in a relatively short period the Universal Declaration had become a part of the constitutional law of the world community and, "together with the Charter of the United Nations, it has achieved the character of a world law superior to all other international instruments and to domestic laws."

In adopting Articles 1 and 2 the General Assembly announced to the world that the future governance of humanity must be on the basis of the principles contained in these two articles. Tore Lindholm correctly assessed that Article 1 provided the "indispensable normative basis by way of which the representatives of a plurality of religious, moral traditions, and ideologies may establish not only a political compromise but a non-exclusive and stable moral agreement on human rights."[2] Morsink thought that, "These are not mere Enlightenment reflexes; they are deep truths rediscovered in the midst of the Holocaust and put on paper again shortly thereafter."[3]

The clarity and force of the provisions of Articles 1 and 2 bear out their historic legal, philosophical and policy significance: all human beings, Article 1 proclaimed, are born free and equal in dignity and rights. They are endowed with reason and conscience and should act towards one another in a spirit of brotherhood. Everyone, Article 2 declared, is entitled to all the rights and freedoms set forth in the Declaration without distinction of any kind, such as race, colour, sex, language, religion, political or other opinion, national or social origin, property, birth or other status. Morsink highlighted that the article reiterated the Charter's non-discrimination principle; the prohibited grounds of discrimination were expanded; and a strong effort was made to extend the principles of equality and non-discrimination to the peoples of non-self-governing territories.[4]

In what follows I consider the vision of the drafters, discuss the legal and philosophical significance of Articles 1 and 2, elucidating the contents of eight concepts that appear in the two articles (human beings, free, equal, dignity, rights, reason, conscience, brotherhood), and then look at policy and normative developments undertaken in implementation of the two articles since the Universal Declaration was adopted 70 years ago.[5]

The vision of the drafters

When the Commission on Human Rights began drafting the Declaration in 1947, René Cassin, the French representative, advocated that two or three fundamental principles be incorporated in the future Declaration: (a) the unity of the human race or family; (b) the idea that every human being has a right to be treated like every other human being; and (c) the concept of solidarity and fraternity among men.[5] On Articles 1 and 2 specifically, Cassin, speaking later in the General Assembly just prior to the adoption of the Universal Declaration, thought that the Declaration had to begin with a statement of the framework within which all the rights that followed were contained. Article 1 represented that framework.[6] It would cause the most impression on public opinion – a declaration of principles which might meet with general agreement, despite all differences of doctrine. It was a statement of vital importance.[7]

Charles Malik of Lebanon suggested that the Commission base itself on four principles: (a) the human person is more important than the racial, national or other group to which he may belong; (b) the human person's most sacred and inviolable possessions are in his mind and his conscience, enabling him to perceive the truth, choose freely and to exist; (c) any social pressure on the part of the state, religion or race involving the automatic consent of the human person is reprehensible; and (d) the social group to which the individual belongs may, like the human person himself, be wrong or right. The person alone is the judge. Speaking later in the General Assembly, Malik underlined that the Declaration had been constructed on a "firm international basis wherein no regional philosophy or way of life was permitted to prevail."[8]

Peng Chun Chang of China advocated a declaration that would accord with the spirit and atmosphere of the post-war era and submitted that the document should reflect freedom from want.[14] Hernán Santa Cruz of Chile advocated a charter of human rights, giving it not only legal but also real human content. This charter should be a spiritual guide for humanity, enumerating the rights that must be respected everywhere.[6] Articles 1 and 2 reflected these and similar visions of the drafters.

Legal and philosophical significance

Through Articles 1 and 2, the United Nations was in effect recognising the existence of new legal obligations for the future governance of humanity. The normative obligations of Governments henceforth would be:

- To recognise in their constitutional, legal and governance systems the freedom, dignity, equality and fundamental human rights of every person on the planet.
- To legislate for, and uphold, the principle of equality and non-discrimination for every human being.
- To recognise and apply the foregoing normative precepts to the inhabitants of non-self-governing territories.
- To govern on the basis of the principles of international solidarity and cooperation.

In arguing that Articles 1 and 2 contained instant international customary law, we are aware that, as pointed out by Morsink, "The view that the Declaration had no legal and only moral force was the nearly unanimous view of the delegations involved in the drafting."[9] However, it may be considered that the issue of the legal status of specific provisions is one for objective determination, item by item, in light of the provisions of international law regarding the formation of international customary law. One should have in mind here the decision of the International Court of Justice in cases such as the North Sea Continental Shelf Cases.[10]

Cassin was of the view that the Universal Declaration was, "an authoritative interpretation of the Charter of the United Nations." The non-discrimination principle of the Charter contained binding legal obligations on governments. In short, even while adopting a document meant in principle to be a moral rather than a legal one, the General Assembly was, by virtue of the provisions of general international law on treaty and customary obligations, in fact implicitly recognising norms of instant international customary law contained in Articles 1 and 2.

On the philosophical significance of the provisions of Articles 1 and 2, a group of philosophers approached by UNESCO to help think through the philosophical aspects of a future declaration concluded that it was possible to achieve agreement across cultures concerning certain rights that "may be seen as implicit in man's nature as an individual and as a member of society and to follow from the fundamental right to live."[11]

At the first meeting of the drafting committee of the Commission on Human Rights, when it considered the initial draft prepared by John Humphrey and the Secretariat, Col. Hodgson asked, "What was the 'philosophy' behind the paper? What principles did they adopt; what method did they follow? Is it their own idea; is it a collection of various principles?" Humphrey replied that he could not oblige Colonel Hodgson, "for the simple reason that [the draft] is based on no philosophy whatsoever." He had been asked to compile a list of rights for discussion purposes, and that was what he had done.[12]

During the discussions, the Chinese representative commented that Article 1 rested on the basis of eighteenth-century philosophy. That philosophy was based on the innate goodness of man. In declaring human rights for human beings, the drafters sought to protect everyone with human attributes: a thinking being capable of consciousness (experience of thoughts and sensations), with memory, beliefs, hopes and emotions, able to perform actions, which makes them moral agents responsible for what they do.[13]

The foundation concepts

On the concept of a '*human being*,' Simon Blackburn has written that from Plato to Aristotle, "our capacities for reason have been seen as the crowning glory of humanity: the bit that sets us apart from other, 'lower' animals, and is even a special mark of divine favour."[14] It was expressly recognised during the drafting of the Declaration that the words "all human beings" had been used precisely in order that both men and women might be included.[15]

When Cassin's refinement of the initial draft by Humphrey was considered by the Drafting Committee, he reiterated that the Declaration should base universal rights on the "great fundamental principle of the unity of all the races of mankind." He later wrote that the main difficulty in framing the introductory 'General Principles' was "to find a formula that did not require the Commission to take sides on the nature of man and society, or to become immured in metaphysical controversies, notably the conflict among spiritual, rationalist, and materialist doctrines of the origin of human rights."[16]

On the concept of being *free*, this idea was linked with the Charter's concept of self-determination, which would give rise to the momentous decolonisation movement and which would lead to a transformation of the world through recognition of the rights of all colonial and dependent peoples to freedom and self-determination. The drafters sought to register that human beings, by their very nature, should be free to develop to the fullness of their potential, with freedom to think, being in charge of themselves, without being subjected to slavery or subjection, without being in bondage to another, having personal rights and social and political liberty. The concept of freedom was universal, applying to all countries and peoples across the globe, to minority as well as majority populations, to women as well as men, to children, to minorities and indigenous peoples.

On the concept of *equality*, Bernard Williams has noted of the idea of equality: "It is their common humanity that constitutes their equality." While the idea of equality has been challenged by some prominent philosophers such as Robert Nozick, the international community, in the UN Charter, the Universal Declaration and subsequent normative instruments, has, as a matter of international public policy, elevated the principle of equality into a norm of *jus cogens* in international law.

Kantian ethics had laid stress on the equal right of all human beings to treatment as ends in themselves as a foundation of all morality.[17] During the drafting of the Declaration, Hernan Santa Cruz (Chile) considered that Article 2 aimed above all at giving expression to one of the basic provisions of the Charter. The United Nations had been founded principally to combat discrimination in the world.

The concept of *dignity* signifies worth and estimation. In modern moral philosophy, especially that of Kant, dignity is considered as a universal attribute, an offshoot of the capacity for self-consciousness and practical reason. The entrenchment of human dignity as a universal human rights norm was one of the great normative innovations of the 1940s. During the drafting, dignity as a right had been challenged by the representative of South Africa. Mrs Roosevelt replied that the word *dignity* had been considered carefully by the Human Rights Commission, which had included it in order to emphasise that every human being is worthy of respect.[18] The Commission had decided to include it in order to emphasise the inherent dignity of all mankind.[19]

Turning to the concept of *a right*, Kant thought that the fundamental moral right is to be treated as an end in oneself, and reason alone justifies and grounds this right.[20] The Charter and the Universal Declaration began a process under which human rights norms are discussed, distilled and proclaimed in consensual processes in authoritative international organs such as the UN General Assembly. The International Bill of Human Rights and the broader collection of United Nations human rights instruments are the outcomes of this process. This, in the stirring words of the late Louis Henkin, is an 'Age of Rights.'

The concept of *reason* signifies the intellectual faculty characteristic of human beings by which conclusions are drawn from premises. Brand Blanshard's definition of reason, in *Reason and Analysis*,[21] as "the faculty and function of grasping necessary connections", has been considered too narrow.[22] Some consider reason to be the faculty by the exercise of which we can perceive, or arrive at, truths of some particular kind. Reason signifies the careful weighing of arguments and evidence.

The concept of *conscience* signifies a moral sense of right or wrong as regards things for which one is responsible; a faculty or principle pronouncing upon the moral quality of one's own actions or motives; reason or fairness signifies "the consciousness humans have that an action is morally required or forbidden."[23]

The concept of *brotherhood* signifies fraternal tie. During the drafting process, Mr Kayali (Syria) commented that the word *brotherhood* was an expression of the ideal moral relationship which should exist between men and meant that all men should behave to others as they would wish others to behave to them.[24] Mr Anze Matienzo (Bolivia) thought that there was no intention of claiming that human beings were perfect. The draft declaration was designed to set a goal for mankind. It should inspire men to transform into realities the principles it proclaimed.[25]

Normative and policy implementation

The United Nations has done much for the normative and policy implementation of the two articles and their eight concepts. First, on the centrality of *human beings*, the International Court of Justice has emphasised the principle of humanity in peacetime as well as during armed conflicts. The United Nations has sought to improve the conditions of life for children, women, indigenous peoples, minorities and those living under slavery or at risk of enslavement or being trafficked. Caring for humanity is the rationale for all these activities. It will be essential, in the future, to uphold the principle that while religion or belief may influence the private sphere, the international law of human rights governs the public sphere.

Second, on the concept of humans being born *free*, colonialism has been eradicated save for some remaining vestiges; self-determination is a fundamental principle of international law; *apartheid* is no more; and there is growing recognition that people may live their lives as they choose and according to their orientations.

Third, on human beings born *equal*, the inherent dignity and the "equal and inalienable rights of all members of the human family" were recognised in the UDHR's opening lines as the "foundation of freedom, justice and peace in the world." The UN Charter was the first international instrument to mention equal rights of men and women in specific terms. The claim to equality, the late Sir Hersch Lauterpacht held, "is in a substantial sense the most fundamental of the rights of man. . . . It is the starting point of all other liberties."[2]

The International Convention on the Elimination of Racial Discrimination, the Convention on the Elimination of Discrimination against Women and the Convention on the Rights of the Child, among others, are sentinels in the defence of equality. The jurisprudence of the UN Human Rights Committee, the Committee on the Elimination of Discrimination against Women (CEDAW) and the Committee on the Rights of the Child reinforce the edifice of equality. With more and more people commingling world-wide, the principle of non-discrimination will have an even greater role in the future.

The prohibition of discrimination has become a norm of positive law, as has been recognised by the International Court of Justice, which has declared that to establish and to enforce distinction, exclusions, restrictions and limitations exclusively based on grounds of race, colour, descent or national or ethnic origin, which constitute a denial of fundamental human rights, is a flagrant violation of the purposes and principles of the Charter.

Fourth, on human beings born equal in *dignity*, the proclamation of the right to development, the launching of successive development decades, the Millennium Development Goals, the Sustainable Development Goals, and other efforts have been essentially focussed on the quest for the vindication of human dignity world-wide. Norms and machinery for the protection of minorities and indigenous populations are also premised on the protection of human dignity.

Fifth, on human beings born free and equal in *rights*, the International Bill of Human Rights, the more elaborate international human rights code, Charter-based and treaty-based machineries, all attest to the continuing quest for the universal realisation of human rights. Numerous problems of implementation still exist, but the quest for universal realisation and protection continues.

Seven decades later, one may ask about the fate of the human rights project launched in the 1940s. Basing ourselves on the three parts of the International Bill of Human Rights, the moral authority of the Universal Declaration is high, and the authority of the Universal Declaration has been repeatedly reaffirmed in solemn consensual international statements of the world community, including the UN Millennium Declaration. Some parts of the Universal Declaration have attained the status of international customary law.

On the second part of the International Bill of Human Rights, numerous additional human rights treaties and other normative instruments have been adopted since 1948, elaborating on the provisions of the Universal Declaration. We thus have today a veritable international code of human rights, with instruments such as the Convention on the Rights of the Child attaining near universal ratification.

It is the third part of the International Bill of Human Rights that has been, and remains, problematic: measures of implementation. Unfortunately, gross violations of human rights are still taking place in many parts of the world, and many countries lack adequate and effective national protection systems.

During the period of the Cold War, the principal adversaries sought to protect their friends and to admonish their adversaries. The principled international protection of human rights suffered. When the former colonies and dependent territories came into the United Nations they pushed, in the 1960s, for the UN to deal with gross violations of human rights in the non-independent countries and in *apartheid* South Africa. Thus began a process whereby the UN, particularly its Commission on Human Rights, would discuss gross violations of human rights publicly, establish fact-finding exercises into allegations of gross violations, adopt resolutions condemning gross violations, and sending envoys to countries for contacts within the framework of confidential petitions procedures. The Commission on Human Rights also appointed a number of fact-finders into broad-based or country-based violations, which are collectively known as the UN human rights special procedures.

When UN investigative and other protection procedures came to be used to examine the human rights records of developing countries themselves, they used their voting majorities in the UN to stifle the Commission on Human Rights and its fact-finders. Dissatisfaction with the operations of the Commission on Human Rights led to its replacement in 2005 by a UN Human Rights Council whose practice is to favour approaches of dialogue and consensus over straight-talking when dealing with situations of gross violations of human rights. The developing countries have a majority on the Human Rights Council and use that majority to block condemnations of governments for gross violations of human rights – save in some instances. This is a problem in the operations of the UN Human Rights Council.

The Human Rights Council does have a new procedure whose long-term results are still to be seen. This is its Universal Periodic Review (UPR) process under which every country, once every four-and-a-half years, submits a report on its efforts to implement UN human rights norms and participates in a review process with its peers on the Council. For the time being, the process is still very diplomatic, and its ground rules do not allow for scrutiny of gross violations of human rights inside the country being reviewed.

The UPR process is proceeding on the basis of the UN human rights norms and could thus contribute to the entrenchment of universality. The process could, in the long term, lead to the establishment or strengthening of national protection systems, but while questions are sometimes asked about the role of national human rights institutions, this has not been systematic so far. The UPR process could, in the long term, make an important contribution in encouraging the development and strengthening of national protection systems.

In the meantime, gross violations of human rights continue to take place world-wide, and national protection systems are deficient or non-existent in many countries, while the international protection of human rights remains in its adolescence, notwithstanding the existence of human rights treaty procedures, the UN Human Rights Council and the Office of UN High Commissioner for Human Rights.

Sixth, human beings should act towards one another with *reason*. The continuing quest is to uphold this principle. Its validity is as important as when it was proclaimed. It will be crucial, in the future, to emphasise the principle we put forward earlier, that religion or belief is a matter for the private sphere and that the public domain must be governed by the reasoning of international human rights.

Seventh, human beings should act towards one another in *conscience*. Amnesty International made its name campaigning for prisoners of conscience and against torture. Conscience must guide the world in the decisions that are made in respect of people fleeing for their safety and people being persecuted in the name of religion or belief.

Eighth, people should act towards one another in a spirit of *brotherhood*. Caring for millions of refugees and displaced persons has been a concrete manifestation of the spirit of brotherhood and sisterhood. The quest to eliminate extreme poverty in many parts of the world is a continuing challenge to the spirit of brotherhood and sisterhood. The principle of human solidarity, which René Cassin so faithfully championed, remains a stirring call to human brotherhood and sisterhood.

Conclusion

As this chapter is being written, the world is witnessing repeated acts of inhumanity committed by terrorists and others against innocent people. The world needs to re-establish and enforce a governing consensus. That consensus must reside in Articles 1 and 2 of the Universal Declaration. The Vienna Declaration on Human Rights (1993) put the matter well: "The universal nature of these rights and freedoms is beyond question."[26] In the Millennium Declaration, world leaders resolved "to respect fully and uphold the Universal Declaration of Human Rights; to strive for the full protection and promotion in all our countries of civil, political, economic, social and cultural rights for all."[27] Governments should mean what they say!

Notes

1 Cassin, 1967: 1. Italics added.
2 Lindholm, 1999: 62–63.
3 Morsink, 1999: 39.
4 Morsink, 1999; see also Skogly, 1999.
5 See, generally, Glendon, 2002; Lauren, 2013; Malik, 2000; Morsink, 1999; and Normand and Zaidi, 2008.
6 A/C.3/SR. SR 96, reproduced in Schabas, 2152.
7 A/C.3/SR.SR 97, reproduced in Schabas, 2161.
8 Glendon, 2002: 165.
9 Morsink, 1999: 295.
10 International Court of Justice, 1969.
11 Glendon, 2002, ch 5.
12 Glendon, 2002: 58.
13 See on this Mumford, 2012, chapter 7, 'What is a Person?', especially 65–66.
14 Blackburn, 2009: 53.
15 A/C.3/SR. 98, reproduced in Schabas, 2169.
16 Glendon, 2002: 67–68.
17 Blackburn, 2016.
18 Glendon, 2002: 146.
19 A/C.3/SR 98, reproduced in Schabas, 2169.
20 Blackburn, 2016.
21 Blanshard, 1962.
22 Warnock, 1967.
23 Blackburn, 2016.
24 A/C.3/SR 99, reproduced in Schabas, 2184.
25 A/C.3/SR 98, reproduced in Schabas, 2173.
26 Vienna Declaration and Programme of Action, 1993, Declaration, paragraph 1.
27 United Nations Millennium Declaration, 2000: paragraph 25.

References

Blackburn, S. (2009). *What Do We Really Know? The Big Questions of Philosophy.* London: Quercus.

Blackburn, S. (2016). *The Oxford Dictionary of Philosophy.* 3rd ed. Oxford: Oxford University Press.

Blanshard, B. (1962). *Reason and Analysis*. London: Routledge.

Cassin, R. (1967). Twenty Years After the Universal Declaration: Freedom and Equality. *Journal of the International Commission of Jurists*, Special Issue 1968, International Year for Human Rights, pp. 1–16.

Glendon, M. (2002). *A World Made New*. New York: Random House Trade Paperbacks.

International Court of Justice. (1969). *North Sea Continental Shelf Cases*. [online] Available at: www.icj-cij.org/files/case-related/51/5537.pdf [Accessed 25 Aug. 2017].

Lauren, P. (2013). *Evolution of International Human Rights*. 2nd ed. Philadelphia: University of Pennsylvania Press, Inc.

Lindholm, T. (1999). Article 1. A New Beginning. In: G. Alfreddson and A. Eide, eds., *The Universal Declaration of Human Rights. A Common Standard of Achievement*. The Hague: Martinus Nijhoff, pp. 41–74.

Malik, H. (2000). *Charles Malik and the Universal Declaration*. Oxford: Charles Malik Foundation and the Centre for Lebanese Studies.

Morsink, J. (1999). *The Universal Declaration of Human Rights*. Philadelphia: University of Pennsylvania Press.

Mumford, S. (2012). *Metaphysics: A Very Short Introduction*. Oxford: Oxford University Press.

Normand, R. and Zaidi, S. (2008). *Human Rights at the UN: The Political History of Universal Justice*. Bloomington: Indiana University Press.

Schabas, W. (2013). *The Universal Declaration of Human Rights: The Travaux Préparatoires*. Cambridge: Cambridge University Press.

Skogly, S. (1999). Article 2. In: G. Alfreddson and A. Eide, eds., *The Universal Declaration of Human Rights. A Common Standard of Achievement*. The Hague: Martinus Nijhoff, pp. 75–87.

United Nations Millennium Declaration. (2000). United Nations Millennium Declaration. New York: United Nations. www.un.org/millennium/declaration/ares552e.htm

Vienna Declaration and Programme of Action. (1993). New York: United Nations.

Warnock, G. (1967). Reason. In: P. Edwards, ed., *The Encyclopedia of Philosophy Vol.7*. London: Palgrave Macmillan, pp. 83–85.

2 Not alone – the origins, significance and legacy of Article 29

Francesca Klug

> Everyone has duties to the community in which alone the free and full development of his personality is possible.

Four days before the British government triggered Article 50 of the Treaty of Lisbon in March 2017, initiating the process for leaving the European Union, a caller to the BBC Radio 4 flagship phone-in show, 'Any Answers', blamed human rights for the woes befalling the UK.[1]

The caller was adamant that the UK's 1998 Human Rights Act (HRA) was responsible for the rise in immigration widely credited as driving 'Brexit' (the referendum result in favour of Britain exiting the EU). This Act, which incorporates most of the Articles in the European Convention on Human Rights (ECHR) into domestic law, was portrayed as preventing judges from deporting those who are "preaching hatred" and threatening security. "We need to consider the rights of the society as a whole, not just the rights of the individual", the caller insisted.

This human rights sceptic might have been surprised to learn that had the drafters of the UDHR heard him, they would broadly have agreed with his last assertion. "Everyone has duties to the community", proclaims UDHR Article 29, and this requires clearly defined "limitations" to be placed on the exercise of individual rights, as "determined by law".

A bolt from the blue?

When the UDHR was adopted on 10 December 1948, Article 29 must have appeared like a bolt from the blue, apparently disembodied from the bulk of the Declaration which preceded it. Following directly after the assertion that, "Everyone is entitled to a social and international order in which the rights and freedoms" in the UDHR "can be fully realised" (Article 28), references to individual duties and limits on rights might have appeared to contradict, or at least fatally weaken, this rousing affirmation of a new world order.

What were the lawyers, NGOs and state delegates who had lobbied for a UN Bill of Rights, during and immediately after World War II, to make of this? With virtually no international mechanisms to hold states to account when they abused their own citizens, these campaigners fought long and hard for individuals to be protected from persecution and annihilation by their own governments. In the wake of a global conflagration which had produced unprecedented atrocities and (what was newly defined as) genocide,[2] how were human rights defenders to interpret such a counter-intuitive commandment aimed not at states, but at the very individuals that the Declaration was drafted to protect? Was Article 29 to be understood merely as a sop to governments who feared the radical nature of the first global instrument to assert that all individuals everywhere had inviolable rights? Was it only a rhetorical flourish to appease those with philosophical objections to individual rights, from faith leaders to Marxists? Or was it just a tactical after-thought to ensure maximum buy-in at the UN from states with belief systems that were very different from those of Western liberal democracies? In other words, given the non-legally binding nature of the UDHR, was Article 29 intended to be no more than a chimera, with no likely lasting impact at all?

The debates and deliberations of the drafters suggest that Article 29 was no mere after-thought designed to sugar-coat the Declaration for public consumption. In fact, they were at times intensely preoccupied with the responsibilities human beings owe to each other, the wider society and the international community. There is a back story to this. Two years after World War II, a little known, but remarkable, symposium of philosophers and writers was published by UNESCO. Giants in their field, including Harold Laski, Aldous Huxley and Mahatma Gandhi, contributed their reflections on the meaning and nature of rights, and their inter-relationship with duties, to a Committee of Experts in Paris.[3] The following year their deliberations were presented to the drafters of the founding document of the modern international human rights movement: the UDHR.

How influential the UNESCO Symposium was on the UN delegates charged with scoping the first leg of what became known as the 'International Bill of Rights' is unclear,[4] but their focuses frequently overlapped. Various other factors contributing to this interest in individual duties and limitations on rights, included: the communitarian philosophies of delegates from China, India, Egypt and some other Middle Eastern countries; religious sensitivities to the need for human obligations to sit alongside rights as expressed by adherents of the world's major religions; Soviet and Socialist anti-individualism; and 'statist' concerns not to unleash too libertarian a document on the world, which the governments that the delegates represented would come to regret.

A product of its time

The coupling of rights with responsibilities was hardly new. The Preamble to the 1789 French Declaration of the Rights of Man and Citizen asserted that it was a "perpetual reminder" of both "rights and duties" (although there was no equivalent reference in the American Bill of Rights two years later). Thomas Paine, the English radical who witnessed the French Revolution, recorded that some members of the French National Assembly queried the absence of a Declaration of Duties, to which Paine responded:

> A declaration of Rights is, by reciprocity, a declaration of Duties also. Whatever is my right as a man is also the right of another; and it becomes my duty to guarantee as well as possess.[5]

But viewing the UDHR through the lens of the European Enlightenment (as is not uncommon amongst critics and supporters alike) inevitably paints a distorted picture.[6] Not only did the UDHR receive input from 57 states representing diverse religious and political systems,[7] but as the UN delegates themselves were sometimes at pain to stress, their Declaration was a product of its own time, including 'lessons learnt' from the immediate and more distant past. The Chinese delegate, Peng Chun Chang, advised against producing a document which would be "out of time with the spirit and atmosphere of the post war era".[8] The drafters were not only asking how human beings can escape state tyranny and gain control over their own lives in the manner of their Enlightenment predecessors, but also how a sense of mutual moral responsibility can be inculcated in all human beings everywhere. This was now understood to be indispensable to prevent flagrant breaches of human rights that were not just conducted by remote states but by tangible human beings, whether under orders or otherwise, and which can take place in multiple locations, wherever there are gross imbalances of power. As the legal historian Brian Simpson observed in his landmark study of the ECHR, "those who had experienced occupation knew . . . that under German occupation . . . those who ill-treated the population were, not infrequently, their own fellow citizens".[9]

This insight – which is distinct from the state-directed targets of the American and French bills of rights – is reflected in the different sets of actors who are appealed to in the UDHR, all referenced in its Preamble. These include "every individual and every organ of society" charged with promoting "respect for these rights and freedoms" as well as "member states" responsible for the "observance" of them. Article 29 can only be understood in the context of this layered audience.

An ethical framework

Although the UDHR, despite external and internal pressures to the contrary, was not intended to be legally enforceable, neither was it aimed to be a document of pious sentiments with little impact. On the contrary, it strove to use its moral – in lieu of legal – authority to influence global affairs. Eleanor Roosevelt, the President of the United Nations Commission on Human Rights (UNCHR) – the body tasked with overseeing the draft – argued that the absence of legal mechanisms "made it all the more necessary" for the Declaration to exercise "the greatest possible force of moral persuasion".[10]

The mission was to produce what the French delegate, René Cassin, described as "the first document about moral value adopted by an assembly of the human community".[11] As a corollary, the drafters displayed a profound interest in the fundamental nature and characteristics of human beings. In January 1947, at the very first session of the UNCHR, the Lebanese delegate, Charles Malik, asserted that when we say "human rights" we are "raising the fundamental question: what is a man?"[12] Despite substantial disagreements, reflecting their different backgrounds and the orientations of the states they represented, the delegates shared a common starting point: in a document proclaiming individual rights, the question of what human beings owed to others could not be ducked.

Unlike the UNESCO symposium, however, the UN's Declaration was never intended to be a purely intellectual endeavour. The ambition of the drafters was nothing short of re-setting human relations within and between states. This was to be based on an asserted belief in the value of human dignity, defiantly declared in the aftermath of catastrophic events that many of the delegates had witnessed, and in some cases directly experienced. Assistant Professor of Religion, Jenna Reinbold, describes their goal as the creation of "a secular narrative capable of wielding the authority of a religious one".[13]

In an assertion that gives credence to Reinbold's characterisation, Chang remarked,

> the aim of the United Nations was not to ensure the selfish gains of the individual but to try and increase man's moral stature. It was necessary to proclaim the duties of the individual, for it was a consciousness of his duties which enabled man to reach a high moral standard.[14]

The priority and status to be given to such duties was earnestly debated. Some state delegates argued for a list of individual responsibilities but others asserted that this was unnecessary provided that duties are rooted in what humans owe to each other. Some delegates felt strongly that these obligations should be aired up front in the Preamble, others in an article of their own at the end of the Declaration. This is where they landed, but the affirmation in Article 1 that "all human beings" are "endowed with reason and conscience and should act towards one another in a spirit of brotherhood" can be understood as the twin provision to Article 29, bookending the UDHR with an ethical framework within which other provisions should be interpreted.

More vexed was the question: who did individuals owe duties to? Was it the state, society or other individuals? Charles Dukes, the UK representative, argued that it would be "useless to try to define the liberties of the individual without taking account of his obligations towards the State",[15] but the majority of delegates concluded that it would be inappropriate to assert such duties in the world's first human rights declaration. Dukes' assertion missed the point anyway. The drafters were not focused on what people owed their governments, whose legitimacy (as the Preamble states) depended on "human rights" being "protected by the rule of law". Their purpose was to inculcate human beings with a moral sense to hold states to account when they turned on minorities or other vulnerable communities, as they had witnessed with the Nazi and fascist regimes that had just been defeated.

A communitarian vision

A further point often missed is the communitarian vision embedded in Article 29, which is essential to understanding its scope and impact. The carefully chosen words, exhaustingly explored by the delegates, expressed not just one but two intertwined ideas. Individuals have responsibilities to the wider society in which they live, not for ideological or religious reasons necessarily, but because they live in communities which '*alone*' provide the means through which the "full and free development of [their] personality", and hence humanity, "is possible".[16] Returning to the bookended ethical framework in which the UDHR's substantive articles were embedded, this sense of responsibility to others explains how "the conscience of mankind" has been "outraged" by the "barbarous acts"[17] which led to the demands for an International Bill of Rights in the first place.

The inclusion of the word 'alone' was supported by 23 votes with 5 against. The UK delegate explained that this word "stressed the essential fact that the individual could attain the full development of his personality only within the framework of society".[18] This emphasis on the wider community, largely absent in the Enlightenment Declarations of Rights which preceded the UDHR, was partly a product of the more collectivist time in which it was written and the communitarian influences of its drafters. Whilst on-going colonial rule by Western powers meant that most of sub-Saharan Africa was completely unrepresented amongst the delegates, the UDHR bore the marks of Latin American Socialists, European Social Democrats, Marxist Soviets, a Chinese Confucian, Middle Eastern Muslims, a Lebanese and European Christians, a Hindu and a Jew. Cassin asserted that, "the human being was above all, a social being", warning against "the danger of putting too little importance upon social rights".[19] This perspective was mainly reflected in the economic, social and cultural rights discussed elsewhere in this book, but Article 29 stands as a rebuke to the social authoritarians and collectivist Marxists who to this day persist in dismissing human rights as a fatally individualistic framework.[20] It reads almost as a direct reply to Marx's famous assertion that:

> None of the so-called rights of man . . . go beyond egoistic man . . . that is, an individual withdrawn into himself, into the confines of his private interests . . . and separated from the community.[21]

It is because Article 29 offers the possibility of rehabilitating the idea of fundamental human rights from this cross-centuries and cross-cultural critique that Johannes Morsink, one of the pre-eminent authorities on the drafting of the UDHR, has argued that the word 'alone' may well be "the most important single word in the entire document".[22]

Lawful limitations on rights

Without Article 29's second clause linking "duties to the community" to "limitations" in the exercise "of rights and freedoms", the ethical sentiments and communitarian vision it outlined would have remained abstract and theoretical. It is this subsequent clause which grounds them, first by establishing that there must be limits to the manifestation of rights if the wider community is to be protected, and second by linking these limitations to the collectivist framework already declared. The Dutch delegate explained that it was a natural extension to the debate on Article 29 to establish that "the rights of the individual were not absolute" and that it was therefore "necessary to define the restrictions demanded by respect for the rights of other individuals and different social groups".[23] In other words, there is little purpose in granting individuals human rights if the cost is the demise of the community in which, Article 29 asserted, they 'alone' can live and flourish.

The limitations on rights that are listed in clause 2 are a further reflection of this communitarian philosophy. Limits on rights must not only be "determined by law" – affirming 'the rule of law' – but be "solely" for the purpose of securing "due recognition and respect for the rights and freedoms of others", for "the just requirements of morality", "public order" and – significantly – "the general welfare in a democratic society". Erica-Irene Daes, the former UN Special Rapporteur on discrimination and minorities, described "this provision" as "of a moral nature in the sense that it lays down a general rule for individual behaviour in the community to which the individual belongs".[24]

Terms like 'morality' and 'general welfare' are obviously loose and subject to wide and contrasting interpretations, depending on the orientation of different states and individual philosophies. Mindful of this, a number of delegates called for a further qualification reflected in the third clause of Article 29: "These rights and freedoms may in no case be exercised contrary to the purposes and principles of the United Nations". Cassin explained that this was to clarify that "the individual belonged to the international community as well as to his own national society".[25] Article 29 did not just cement the *ethical* framework of the UDHR, but its *universal* scope.

Influence and impact

The influence and impact of Article 29 has been far wider and deeper than the absence of a UDHR enforcement mechanism would suggest. When the twin UN Covenants, the other two legs of the 'International Bill of Rights', were ratified in 1976,[26] their Preambles likewise asserted that "the individual" has "duties to other individuals" as well as "the community to which he belongs". Reproducing the UDHR's communitarian framework in the interpretative provisions of these legally binding treaties (which is what Preambles affectively are) reaffirmed the significance of the UDHR's ethical approach, which was thereafter not to lie buried in the penultimate article of the UDHR.

The *American Convention on Human Rights* (ACHR), ratified in 1978, has a short chapter on 'personal responsibilities',[27] which partially resembles Article 29, whilst the 1981 African Charter on Human and Peoples' Rights uniquely enumerates duties owed by individuals to others, the family and the state.[28] In stark contrast to the absolute protection of free speech in the 1791 American Bill of Rights, the ACHR also explicitly prohibits "advocacy of national, racial or religious hatred"[29] whilst both the ECHR and International Covenant on Civil and Political Rights (ICCPR) refer directly to the "duties and responsibilities" attached to exercising free expression.[30] The 1984 UN Convention on the Rights of the Child similarly cites the "rights and duties" of parents and carers and their "common responsibilities". In 1993 the UN General Assembly adopted a new Declaration which further elaborated on the responsibilities of individuals but mainly in the context of promoting human rights, as required by the UDHR's Preamble.[31]

Yet the second clause of Article 29 has had the most direct and lasting effect. It can fairly lay claim to be the midwife of the qualifications and limitations characteristic of all subsequent international and regional human rights treaties. Spawned by the UDHR, most of these contain a similar set of limitations to those catalogued in Article 29, albeit in the case of the ECHR the list is both longer and more proscriptive (largely at the behest of the UK lawyers who played a prominent role in drafting it). Such limitation clauses have led judicial bodies (like the European Court of Human Rights (ECtHR)) to develop the ground-breaking 'doctrine of proportionality'. This establishes the circumstances in which it is legitimate and necessary for states to set proportionate boundaries to the exercise of rights in individual cases – a concept as pivotal to the global evolution of human rights as any substantive provision.[32] Judicial case law has in turn provided a guide as to where the exercise of fundamental liberties might hurt others; for example, by citing free expression as a justification for hate speech or encroaching on individuals' privacy.[33] Through this route the obligations of individuals and private bodies to other human beings, and to the wider community, have been outlined.

As legally enforced instruments ratified by states, governments are held directly responsible for ensuring that individual responsibilities are maintained under international human rights law. This has given impetus to the evolving legal doctrine of 'positive obligations' on states to interfere between private parties where necessary to uphold the human rights of individuals. In the case of Mrs Eweida, for example, an employee of the private company British Airways, the ECtHR held that in failing to protect a Christian employee's desire to wear a visible cross at work, the UK government had breached its 'positive obligation' to safeguard her right to manifest her religious beliefs.[34]

It is through this route that human rights law has provided protection to victims of crime, abuse and harassment, in defined circumstances, leading to significant advances for victims and witnesses.[35] There is a direct lineage between the philosophy in Article 29, which recognises that individuals have duties to other human beings and to the community in which they live, and this landmark jurisprudence.[36]

A modern dilemma

The Article 29 framework has been severely tested in recent years, especially through national debates which have taken place all over the world on the limits of free expression in the light of religious sensibilities. Never was this more so than during the so-called cartoon controversy that engulfed Europe and the Middle East in 2005/6. On 30 September 2005, the Danish newspaper, *Jyllands-Posten*, published twelve cartoons, some depicting the Prophet Mohammed as a terrorist with a bomb, apparently linking Islam with terrorism. Journalists at the paper initially claimed that the cartoons were printed in response to their perception of increasing self-censorship, but according to culture editor, Flemming Rose, when death threats followed, "it became an issue of . . . the fundamental right of free speech".[37]

This was a period of heightened tensions following the '9/11 attacks' and Western military interventions in Iraq and Afghanistan. By the end of January 2006, protests which began in Denmark spread across the Middle East and the wider world, reportedly resulting in at least 200 deaths globally. After the French satirical magazine *Charlie Hebdo* republished the cartoons on 9 February, adding some of its own, passions were further inflamed. When, nine years later, at least twelve people were killed after gunmen stormed *Charlie Hebdo*'s central Paris office in January 2015, commentators traced this back to the publishing of the Danish cartoons and subsequent portrayals of the Prophet.

Both *Charlie Hebdo* and *Jyllands-Posten* were cleared of any offences for publishing the cartoons.[38] Indeed, the Danish Regional Public Prosecutor discontinued his investigation on the basis that the publication concerned a subject of public interest, citing free expression as a factor in this decision.

UN human rights bodies took a different view. *Doudou Diène*, Special Rapporteur on 'contemporary forms of racism, racial discrimination, xenophobia and related intolerance', cited xenophobia and racism in Europe as the root of the controversy, effectively criticising the Danish government for inaction after the publication of the cartoons.[39] The then UN High Commissioner for Human Rights, Louise Arbour, expressed "regret" over "any statement or act that could express a lack of respect for the religion of others".[40] The implications were that self-restraint can be necessary to prevent the demonisation or denigration of racial and religious minorities in certain contexts, and that this is not necessarily inconsistent with a free and uncensored press. Exercising the right to free expression in a manner that shows "respect for the religion of others", in other words, does not require published material to be banned except in exceptional circumstances, but it can involve refraining from speaking – or indeed drawing – to protect others in the community. What the Danish journalists called "self-censorship" takes on a different meaning when it is not the state or other sources of power that are being attacked but vulnerable minorities whose core identity, and sometimes lives, are at stake.

This approach – traceable to UDHR Article 29 and further developed in subsequent human rights treaties and case law – reflects lessons learnt from the Holocaust, further reinforced by the Rwandan genocide and Bosnian massacres. Free speech, the cornerstone of a democratic society, can also be used to deny, or even obliterate, the rights of others. Words and pictures can spur whole populations to hate and persecute minorities. This may not have been clear in the Europe of the Enlightenment, but the post-war human rights framework encompasses the *totality* of this perception.

Conclusion

The caller to the radio phone-in show, referenced at the beginning of this chapter, was of course not alone in his interpretation of human rights. In objecting to their apparently individualistic, libertarian impact, he echoed the views of former British Prime Minister, David Cameron. From the outset, his stated reason for advocating the repeal of the UK's Human Rights Act was that it had "helped to create a culture of rights without responsibilities".[41] This policy is still a live issue. The current Prime Minister, Theresa May, favoured withdrawal from the ECHR over leaving the EU in the build-up to the 2016 referendum,[42] and indicated during the 2017 General Election that the repeal of the HRA is unfinished business that could be revisited after the UK has exited the EU.[43]

The 70th anniversary of the UDHR is an opportunity to remind human rights advocates and critics alike that the depiction of international human rights as anti-communitarian is as inaccurate as it is misleading. The drafters of the Declaration wrapped the rights they enumerated within an ethical framework of human beings owing obligations to each other, affirming state limitations on individual rights, where necessary, for the common good. Within this context, Article 29 kick-started the evolution of human rights thinking to encompass the actions of private individuals in certain circumstances, bringing terrorism, domestic violence and child abuse within the ambit of human rights law by charging states with 'positive obligations' to address such wrongs.[44]

The drafters of the UDHR could not have predicted the current revival of nationalism and xenophobia all over the world. A backlash against the post-war human rights architecture, with its universal, transnational ethic, is gaining momentum; not least amongst some of the democracies which played a crucial role in its creation. With international terrorism, as much as states, responsible for 'crimes against humanity', in the twenty-first century,[45] Article 29 has the capacity to inject new life into the global vision of human rights, keeping them relevant for the challenges of the modern world.

Notes

1 Any Answers with Anita Anand, BBC Radio 4, 25 March 2017.
2 UN Convention on the Prevention and Punishment of the Crime of Genocide, 1948.
3 Human Rights. Comments and interpretations. A symposium edited by UNESCO, 1949. Not all the contributors were physically present at 'the symposium'.

4 The other two legs of the 'International Bill of Rights' are the UN's International Covenant on Civil and Political Rights and International Covenant on Economic, Social and Cultural Rights, both ratified in 1976.
5 Paine, 1984: 114.
6 Morsink, 1999: 283. See also Klug, 2015: 36.
7 Virtually the whole of sub-Saharan Arica was unrepresented at the UN in 1948 due to colonisation. Today 193 states are represented at the UN.
8 ECOSOC, 1947.
9 Simpson, 2010: 601.
10 Eleanor Roosevelt, quoted in Morsink, 1999: 295 note 5. The UDHR has been cited so often in case law over the last seven decades that it is now generally accepted that some of its provisions have become part of 'customary international law'.
11 Ibid, 33.
12 Quoted in Glendon, 2000: 2.
13 Reinbold, 2017.
14 ECOSOC, 1948.
15 ECOSOC, 1947.
16 Article 29, Clause 1.
17 Preamble, UDHR.
18 Quoted in Morsink, 1999: 248 note 5.
19 Ibid, 5.
20 Klug, 2000: 52–55.
21 Marx, 1844. See also Waldron, 1987: 53.
22 F Corbet, quoted in Morsink, 1999: 248 note 5.
23 LJC Beaufort quoted in Morsink, 1999: 249.
24 Daes, 1990: 19.
25 Morsink, 1999: 251 note 5.
26 See note 3.
27 The ACHR is a regional human rights treaty open to all members of the Organisation of American States. It is the equivalent to the ECHR for the Americas.
28 See also Martinez, 2003.
29 ACHR Article 13.5.
30 ECHR Article 10 (2); ICCPR Article 19 (3).
31 Declaration on the Right and Responsibility of Individuals, Groups and Organs of Society to Promote and Protect Universally Recognised Human Rights and Fundamental Freedoms, 1998.
32 See, for example, the series of cases which considered when it is 'necessary' and 'proportionate' in 'a democratic society' to place limitations on religious dress (Eweida and others v United Kingdom [2013]).
33 E.g., Erbakan v Turkey (2006) outlines the principle of proportionate limits to free speech which "incite or promote . . . hatred based on intolerance," whilst Peck v UK (2003) All ER (D) establishes justified limits to freedom of expression involving the disclosure of CCTV images to the media.
34 See note 23.
35 E.g., X&Y v Netherlands (1985); Whiteside v UK (1994); Osman v UK (1999); Z v UK (2001); E v UK (2003); Rantsev v Cyprus and Russia (2010).
36 See Klug, 2015, note 5, 201.
37 Naser Khader and Flemming Rose: Reflections on the Danish Cartoon Controversy, 2007.
38 Charlie Hebdo was acquitted in court of charges that it incited hatred.
39 Diène, 2006.
40 Arbour, 2005.

41 Cameron, 2006.
42 The Guardian, 2016.
43 Forward Together, Conservative Party Manifesto, June 2017.
44 Keir Starmer, the former Director of Public Prosecutions, has stated that the victims of crime have been the overwhelming beneficiaries of the UK'S Human Rights Act: Starmer, 2014.
45 After the '9/11 attack,' Mary Robinson, UN High Commissioner for Human Rights, declared it to be a 'crime against humanity', Klug, op cit, note 5, 47.

References

Arbour, L. (2005). Letter to the Organisation of the Islamic Conference (OIC). *The Brussels Journal.* 28 July 2006 [online journal] www.brusselsjournal.com/node/1224

Cameron, D. (2006). *Balancing Freedom and Security – A Modern British Bill of Rights.* www.theguardian.com/politics/2006/jun/26/conservatives.constitution

Daes, E. (1990). *Freedom of the Individual under the Law: A Study of the Individual's Duties to the Community and the Limitations on Human Rights and Freedoms Under Article 29 of UDHR.* Geneva: United Nations.

Daily Telegraph. (2016). Theresa May to Fight 2020 Election on Plans to Take Britain Out of European Convention on Human Rights After Brexit Is Completed.

Declaration on the Right and Responsibility of Individuals, Groups and Organs of Society to Promote and Protect Universally Recognised Human Rights and Fundamental Freedoms. (1998). [online] Geneva: United Nations. Available at: http://Declaration on the Right and Responsibility of Individuals, Groups and Organs of Society to Promot . . . [Accessed 5 Dec. 2017].

Diène, D. (2006). *Report of the Special Rapporteur on Contemporary Forms of Racism, Racial Discrimination, Xenophobia and Related Intolerance on the Situation of Muslim and Arab Peoples in Various Parts of the World.* [online] Geneva: United Nations. Available at: www.refworld.org/docid/45377b040.html [Accessed 5 Dec. 2017].

E v UK [2003]763 36 (EHRR), p. 31.

ECOSOC. (1947). *ECOSOC Paper.* E/CN/4/SR.14. Geneva: United Nations, p. 4.

ECOSOC. (1948). *ECOSOC Paper E/800, 98th Meeting of the 3rd Committee of the UN General Assembly.* Geneva: United Nations, p. 87.

Erbakan v Turkey [2006]§ 56 (European Court of Human Rights).

Eweida and Others v United Kingdom [2013] IRLR 231 (European Court of Human Rights).

Glendon, M. (2000). Introduction. In: H. Malik, ed., *The Challenge of Human Rights, Charles Malik and the Universal Declaration.* Oxford: Charles Malik Foundation.

The Guardian. (2016). "UK Must Leave European Convention on Human Rights," says Theresa May.

Human Rights. (1949). *Comments and Interpretations.* A symposium edited by UNESCO. New York: Columbia University Press.

Klug, F. (2000). *Values for a Godless Age: The Story of the UK's New Bill of Rights.* London: Penguin.

Klug, F. (2015). *A Magna Carta for All Humanity: Homing in on Human Rights.* London: Routledge.

Martinez, M. (2003). *Human Rights and Human Responsibilities: Final Report of the Special Rapporteur.* E/CN.4/2003/105. [online] Geneva: United Nations. Available at: http://hrlibrary.umn.edu/demo/HumanRightsandResponsibilities_Martinez.pdf [Accessed 5 Dec. 2017].

Marx, K. (1844). *On the Jewish Question.* Paris: Deutsch-Französische Jahrbücher.

Morsink, J. (1999). *The Universal Declaration of Human Rights: Origins, Drafting and Intent.* Pennsylvania: University of Pennsylvania Press.

Naser Khader and Flemming Rose: Reflections on the Danish Cartoon Controversy. (2007). *Middle East Quarterly.* [online], XIV(4), pp. 59–66. Available at: www.meforum.org/1758/naser-khader-and-flemming-rose-reflections-on [Accessed 24 Aug. 2017].

Osman v UK [1999]87/1997/871/1083 (ECHR), p. 193.

Paine, T. (1984). *Ways and Means, Rights of Man [1791].* London: Penguin.

Peck v UK [2003] 44647/98 (ECHR).

Rantsev v Cyprus and Russia [2010] 25965/04 (ECHR).

Reinbold, J. (2017). *Seeing the Myth in Human Rights.* [online] OpenDemocracy. Available at: www.opendemocracy.net/openglobalrights/jenna-reinbold/seeing-myth-in-human-rights [Accessed 24 Aug. 2017].

Simpson, A. (2010). *Human Rights and the End of Empire: Britain and the Genesis of the European Convention.* Oxford: Oxford University Press.

Starmer, K. (2014). Tom Sargant Memorial Lecture. *Justice,* 15 October 2014.

UN Convention on the Prevention and Punishment of the Crime of Genocide. (1948). Geneva: United Nations.

Waldron, J. (1987). *Nonsense Upon Stilts: Bentham, Burke and Marx on the Rights of Man.* London: Methuen.

Whiteside v UK [1994] 76A (DR), p. 80.

X&Y v Netherlands [1985] 8 (EHRR), p. 235.

Z v UK [2001]29392/95 (ECHR).

3 Terrorism and the development of thinking on human rights

John Alderdice

Terrorism is a crime, but this can mask the fact that it is primarily a tactic of asymmetric warfare, often used by those who are less powerful against those who are, at least in formal terms, more powerful. The purpose of the terrorist is to use the creation of powerful feelings of fear to leverage greater impact. Those who are the victims of a terrorist attack are not the targets of the campaign. The tactic aims to provoke governments and others in power to lose their moral authority by over-reacting against the community the terrorists claim to represent, to undermine the sense that the government has the capacity to protect those for whom they have responsibility and, crucially, to damage the sense that those in authority have 'right' on their side. Over the last century the development of those measures of public morality that we call human rights has been intimately related to the reactions of governments to the use of terrorism against them.

It was a terrorist act, the assassination of Ferdinand, Archduke of Austria, on 28 June 1914, that was the trigger for the first truly global conflict, and the result was not just horrible violence but the dissolution of the old world order in Europe and beyond. During the nineteenth century the understanding and use of terrorism had been developed by revolutionary anarchists as an effective tool in their campaign to subvert governance. By the early twentieth century, support for their underlying ideals and principles had waned, but the other movements then espoused what appeared to be an effective tactic for undermining those in power. The terrorist attack in Sarajevo in 1914 unleashed horrors that were inflicted and experienced on an unprecedented scale and resulted not only in the wholesale destabilisation of the imperial world order of the time, but also impacted massively the intellectual life of the Western world.

The optimistic political and intellectual liberalism and rationalism that had emerged centuries before from the Reformation and the Enlightenment had received a serious blow. Faith in human rationality had led to extraordinary progress in science and technology, and would continue to do so, not least in medicine, transport and communication, but it had received a profound setback. Enlightenment thinkers had hoped that a few generations of education in rationality would be a sufficient curb on human aggression and violence and would result in the peaceful and stable progress of humanity. World War I put a serious question mark against those optimistic assumptions. Initially it was hoped that the problems that had led to Germany, with probably the best, most rational and orderly education system in the world, engaging in such destruction were political in nature and could be addressed by the application of more democratic principles. If human rationality had not contained human aggression, surely it was a problem of the old imperial political context and order, and a new democratic constitution for Germany and international cooperation through the League of Nations would prevent a recurrence.

However, the application of human rationality to governance in Germany's new 'Weimar' Republic and in international cooperation through the League of Nations did not resolve the problem. Despite improvements in the management and infrastructure of Germany, there was catastrophic inflation and a rise in political extremism that resulted in a second and even more appalling global conflict.

If human education in rationality, applied to socio-economic and political development, did not prevent the disastrous violence of world wars, then perhaps a new universal rules-based approach might succeed. The result was the replacement of the League of Nations by the United Nations to bring countries together, the creation of the Bretton Woods institutions to address the challenges of economic instability, the running of the Nuremberg Trials to make clear that there would be no impunity for crimes against humanity which were not acceptable even in times of all-out war, and very importantly the setting out of a new secular code of global 'commandments' in the UDHR.

The thirty articles of the UDHR started with a statement of belief in Article 1:

> "All human beings are born free and equal in dignity and rights," it said, followed by the insistence that, "They are endowed with reason and conscience and should act towards one another in a spirit of brotherhood."

These foundational beliefs were followed in Articles 2 to 21, and in 27, by a set of potentially justiciable civil and political rights. Articles 22 to 26 went further, setting down social and economic rights, which were described in legalistic terms, but actually required economic and political implementation. And finally Articles 28 to 30 insist on a social and international order and a set of responsibilities and prohibitions that are necessary for the implementation of the rights set down earlier.

Despite Article 1, what the creation of this Declaration recognised was that the freedom and dignity that every individual should be able to enjoy depended not only on human rationality, but also on conscience and the moral imperative of a spirit of brotherhood, and it was very clear that conscience and the spirit of brotherhood had failed in Europe for a calamitous second time in a generation. The human rights that had been declared by the humanists and liberals of the eighteenth and nineteenth centuries would not be guaranteed merely by an appeal to a rational moral conscience. The new UDHR was adopted by the new global body of nation states and was imbedded in an international rules-based system and embodied in the new international institutions which it was hoped would ensure its implementation.

The decades that followed gave grounds for hope that humanity had learnt its lesson and that a new age had begun, guided by universal values that went beyond religion, nationality or culture and was founded on this new body of universal law, based on human rights, which gave the possibility of a new international culture of lawfulness. International courts began to hold to account those found guilty of crimes against humanity. Countries that had been former enemies over many centuries came together, first in Europe and then in other regions, to form transnational unions which cooperated on economic, legal, cultural, scientific and political challenges, as well as the emerging global threats to the environment. Real progress was made on tackling infectious diseases and reducing poverty and hunger. The end of the Cold War saw serious efforts to reduce the stockpiles of nuclear weapons and limit their further proliferation to new states. To some, especially in the West, it really began to look as though a new golden age was dawning.

On Tuesday, 11 September 2001, another terrorist attack of devastating significance occurred. It was not that this was the first major terrorist attack since the pre-war campaigns of the old anarchists, though it was colossal in terms of the numbers killed and injured, but it was symbolically massive, too. Since World War II there had been many terrorist campaigns as the colonies sought their freedom from imperial control, and some that were also part of the vicarious struggle between the US and the USSR during the so-called Cold War, but since then there had been other warning signs of something new. Ancient feuds in the Balkans, frozen for decades within the sphere of influence of the USSR, started to re-emerge as the old Soviet system dissolved, but United Nations forces were unable to prevent the subsequent massacres, even when they were present. In Africa too, genocidal horrors challenged the hope that in such situations even the most fundamental rights could be protected by the international community. Even as so-called second generation or socio-economic rights were being pressed, new rights and responsibilities were being promulgated. 'Group rights' establishing how ethnic or religious minorities and first nation peoples should be treated were added to the canon of human rights, and the new doctrine of the Responsibility to Protect was endorsed by all the member states of the United Nations in 2005. If one was to judge by what was agreed on paper at a global level, enormous progress was being made.

However, away from chambers of the international institutions and the libraries of global agreements, a different story was unfolding. Many people and communities around the world did not feel that their human rights as individuals and as groups were actually being protected, nor did they believe that peaceful democratic politics was showing any evidence that matters would be satisfactorily addressed in that way. As a result, some countries had been experiencing the return of terrorism, and not only in historically unstable regions such as the Middle East.

In my own part of the United Kingdom, with all its history of parliamentary democracy, high intellectual and educational achievement, relative prosperity and its role as a signatory (and sometimes author) of international human rights commitments, all was not well. Since 1968 a terrorist campaign had been fought by the Irish Republican Army (IRA) with the aim of breaking Northern Ireland away from the United Kingdom to create an independent communist republic. Republicans insisted that the partition of Ireland had only been maintained through systematic injustices and the disregard of the rights of its Catholic Nationalist people. There were civil rights marches in 1967, but when these were confronted with pro-British protestors and violent loyalist mobs, the guns which had been silent for some years came back out again, and physical force republicanism returned to the tactic of terrorism which it had employed in the past, although now with an expanded arsenal and tactics upgraded from the outbreaks of violence in earlier centuries and in the War of Independence in the early twentieth century.

The initial reaction of Northern Ireland's Protestant Unionist regional administration in Belfast, and subsequently the British Government in London, to this recurrence of politically motivated violence was largely a security response. However, the more the local police force, later backed by the British Army, tried to crack down on the terrorism and violence, the more the terrorists built support in some pockets of the Catholic Nationalist minority community. When the guns and bombs appeared in earnest, the political concessions that were offered seemed to be too little too late. Soon the British Government found itself agreeing to the temporary suspension of some human rights, in particular the introduction of executive detention without trial, known locally as 'internment'. This polarised the community further and acted as a powerful recruiting sergeant for the IRA in the Catholic Nationalist community. It took years for the British Government to learn the lesson that while there is a security role in combatting terrorism, the prorogation of human rights in counter-terrorism is often wholly counter-productive, especially in open democratic societies. Once the Government had openly breached some human rights by the use of internment, even in what could be regarded as extenuating circumstances, it became vulnerable to the accusation that it had breached others. And not only did other major breaches occur, but claims of human rights abuses also became part of the propaganda struggle of the terrorist organisations against the Government.

Northern Ireland was sliding back into a deep historic feud and remained there for a generation. All attempts at normal political negotiation, social and economic development and incremental human rights improvements failed to end the terrorist campaign. The police and army chiefs repeatedly told the Government, and some even said publicly, that they would continue to do their job and contain the situation, but that there was no military or security solution to the problem of terrorism. It was, they said, a political problem that would have to be addressed politically. Those who were responsible for public order and security had realised that terrorism was not just ordinary violent crime.

Of course, terrorism is criminal activity, but while the 'ordinary' criminal engages in crime for personal benefit, tries to ensure that no-one finds out that he did it, and regards his conviction and punishment as a disaster, the terrorist generally seeks and gets no personal material benefit, ensures that the public knows that his organisation carried out the atrocity, and regards the failure of his cause as the ultimate catastrophe, not the compromise of his own welfare or even the loss of his own life. The failure of policing and security attempts to resolve the problem of terrorism, and an understanding that we were dealing with a different motivation for a different kind of crime in Northern Ireland, eventually led us to try to find a new way of analysing and understanding the problem of terror in order to find a new way of dealing with it.

Human rationality was important, but it had to be applied to understanding the non-rational part of the human condition – that part which feels so passionately about values, principles, culture and identity that people are prepared to sacrifice their social and economic welfare, and even their lives and those of their children, in a struggle that is not in their best socio-economic and power interests. It also became clear that while the civil and political rights of individuals, the social and economic rights of communities, and the inclusion and protection of minorities were all vital in a peace process that had any hope of bringing the terrorist campaign to an end, human rationality and human rights were not sufficient tools to bring peace. It was necessary to start paying attention to human relationships; not the relationships between individuals or within families, but the relationships of the various large groups that made up our divided people.

We identified three sets of relationships – between Protestant Unionists and Catholic Nationalists within Northern Ireland, between the people of the North and the people of the South of Ireland, and between Britain and Ireland. The Irish Peace Process was then constructed on the basis of an examination of these three sets of disturbed historic relationships. The political representatives of the IRA terrorists said that they were only engaging in the violence because they could not find any other way to deal with the deep unfairness they felt and the history of humiliation and disrespect for their people and their culture. If there could be a new way of righting these wrongs and building new relationships characterised by respect for human rights in all its fullness, and achieved through a new process of engagement and dealing with the legacy of the hurts of the past, then perhaps a new beginning was possible. While this process has followed a long and winding road with many hurdles and setbacks, it has ultimately been successful in helping the people of Ireland leave behind a belief in the use of violence and physical force and instead commit to democratic politics and a human rights–based rule of law.

However, on 11 September 2001, as I watched the unfolding atrocities in New York, Arlington and Stoney Creek, Pennsylvania live on my television screen at home in Belfast, I immediately sensed that something I recognised was under way but of an entirely different order of magnitude. We had known terrorism and political violence for over 30 years, and experience told me that in addition to the individual casualties who had lost their lives and others whose lives would be changed forever in the US attacks, there would be an unspoken victim – the liberal commitment to a human rights–based approach to communal problems. This attack on the United States of America on its home territory in such a devastatingly symbolic fashion would almost certainly result in a fierce and violent response, as was intended by the terrorists who planned and executed the attack. Although successive US administrations had been involved in the Irish Peace Process, and had made very considerable contributions to it, even as I watched the television screen and heard details of what was happening, my heart sank as I feared that these attacks, which were so destructive of the lives and human rights of those in New York, at the Pentagon and elsewhere, would almost certainly result in pressure for powerful punitive responses which would test the limits of human rights elsewhere and change the global dynamic from progress towards greater openness, freedom and human rights to an emphasis on security based on physical force. While in our province we were learning lessons about what worked and what did not work in addressing terrorism, I could not help fearing that the counter-productive reactions that I had seen as a teenager in Northern Ireland would now be unleashed in a fierce reaction to the 9/11 attacks, despite us having learned repeatedly at home that this was precisely the purpose of the terrorists.

We did not have long to wait. The terrorists maintained that they were resorting to the use of terrorism as a tactic because they had learnt from experience to have no faith in the instruments of international human rights law and politics to achieve the betterment of their people in their region. In turning to the tactic of terrorism, they were breaching the criminal law, but they claimed that they were doing so in the service of what they regarded as a higher law on behalf of their people, values, religion, culture and identity. As they struck back at the terrorist networks, the major global powers increasingly disregarded the instruments, institutions and processes of the United Nations and human rights law. Military interventions were based on United Nations Security Council resolutions if they could be achieved, but not getting UN Security Council agreement was not regarded as a prohibition. The justification for some of the military interventions soon came to be seen, at home and abroad, as dependent on untrustworthy information and even dishonesty. The use of extraordinary rendition and inhuman and degrading treatment were no longer seen as 'beyond the pale' for some Security Council members when dealing with terrorism. The term *terrorism* was increasingly used as a morally loaded descriptor rather than as the identification of a specific tactic of asymmetric warfare. The labelling of violent actions as terrorism became a justification in itself for any kind of aggressive military or other actions even, and perhaps especially, when they contravened human rights provisions.

One of the singular strengths of the UDHR is precisely that these rights are meant to apply to every single human being, wherever they are in the world and independent of domestic pressures or political system. Within states, however, there is not only a legislature that sets down what is the law, but also a policing service that can move freely throughout the jurisdiction to investigate alleged breaches of the law, a justice system that makes judgements as to guilt or innocence and hands down sentences, as well as a penal system to administer the sanctions on those found guilty. Not all of these key functions of a justice system apply fully in the case of international human rights law, and increasing the number and complexity of human rights instruments, without having effective implementation, has brought the system into disrepute and left some people feeling that in the absence of redress they must eventually take matters into their own hands and respond with passionate and destructive anger.

Human rights enthusiasts have also felt that ensuring that a new right is adopted by international agreement is always a step towards its full recognition and implementation. However, it is here that the limits of human rationality and human rights become apparent and the importance of human relationships and the psychology of large groups make their presence felt. If the statement of a human right does not lead within a reasonable time to its implementation, then the whole notion of human rights begins to be undermined. The addition of too many rights, introduced too quickly, and sometimes in conflict with each other, can produce a reaction against human rights as an approach. As a result, people may turn to terrorism to address the wrongs that they feel human rights promised but failed to resolve. On the other hand, those opposed to the terrorists and the changes they want to see come to feel that so much focus on the rights of terrorist suspects and the communities from which they emerge becomes an obstacle to the recognition of the rights of the communities who are the victims of the terrorist campaigns, and they demand that their responsible governments take more and more strident action in what appears to be a fight for survival against an existential threat.

In successfully frustrating the authority of the state and of the international institutions of cooperation and by demonstrating the complexity of the implementation of the rights of every individual and community, terrorists have provoked increasing restrictions on rights and freedoms. They have dented the hopes for social and international order expressed in Article 28, diminished the rights and freedoms, as well as the sense of respect and community, set down in Article 29, and succeeded in diverting governments from their commitment to fully maintain and develop the human rights and freedoms set out in the UDHR.

It is crucial in such times that we maintain our commitment to human rationality and human rights, but we must understand that they do not in themselves represent a sufficient understanding of the human condition, how we function as individuals and groups, and how we can evolve and progress to greater peace, stability and reconciliation in our world. We need to appreciate emotions not only as feelings, but as part of the way that we think. Terrorism does not just frighten us. It also affects the way we think and act. As we struggle to address these challenges, we may find ourselves depressed and distressed that the progress we thought we had made seems so vulnerable to dissolution. However, we should reflect that while during relatively peaceful, stable periods our understandings tend to proceed by incremental evolutionary development, it is usually in times of crisis when our whole way of thinking and 'being-in-the-world' is challenged so that it becomes possible and indeed necessary to take a leap into a whole new way of understanding.

As was the case a century ago, our reactions to terrorism may be contributing to us slipping into a third global conflict, but we may also be standing on the threshold of a major step forward in our understanding of humanity – a paradigm shift that takes us beyond a rather legalistic, rationalistic, linear approach to human rights and into the complexity of large group relationships. We must work creatively on taking such a next step. Not only our rights and freedom but our very survival as a species may depend upon it.

Section II

The rights of the individual

(Articles 1–11)

Introduction to Section II

Carla Ferstman

This section of the book focuses on what has become known as the first column of the Declaration – individuals' rights and freedoms *qua* individuals. These rights, including rights to life, liberty and personal security; the prohibition of slavery, torture and arbitrary arrest and detention; rights to legal recognition, equality before the law, and effective remedies for violation of fundamental rights, have a strong and arguably predominant placement in the UDHR. They are concerned mainly with protecting individuals from unfairness, abuse of power and aggression directed at them mainly, though not exclusively, by the state.

At the time of the drafting of the Declaration, this group of rights was relatively well-recognised and reflected in a variety of legal systems around the world. This was particularly the case with prohibitions such as slavery and torture, described respectively by Dottridge and Ferstman. As such, the pillar on individual rights did not engender too much debate among the drafters, though its relative weight vis-à-vis other, more collective rights was perhaps more contested. Nevertheless, this pillar, like all other pillars of the Declaration, was influenced significantly by the then-recent horrors of World War II. For instance, Dottridge notes the importance of the atrocities committed against forced labourers in Germany, Japan and elsewhere, to the framing of the UDHR article on slavery. Similarly, Ferstman notes that Nazi medical experiments in concentration camps were in the minds of the drafters when developing the article on the prohibition of torture, and Bazyler and Nelson explain the role of the mass theft of property in the framing of Article 8 of the UDHR – the right to an effective remedy.

As with all aspects of the Declaration, the articles in this first pillar were drafted in language which is a product of its time. In the 70 years since the Declaration's adoption, our thinking about the nature and content of rights, how and why rights are violated and what is required to guarantee their protection and enforcement has been subject to continued change. The chapters in this section of the book explore these evolutions, focusing on issues such as the role of 'neutral' language in circumscribing or containing individuals' rights. This is a theme picked up by Hilsenrath and Hamilton in their consideration of the failure of the UDHR to make explicit reference to sexual orientation or gender identity. It is also picked up by Manjoo, who explains in her chapter that the framing of the UDHR in gender-neutral terms, "does not take specificity into account." She argues that, "The consequence is that the particularity of women's experiences and realities, including the ways in which women experience discrimination and/or are denied equality, or suffer specific violations because of their gender, is rendered largely invisible." This she argues, "can then lead to *de facto* discrimination and the achievement of formal as opposed to substantive equality." This is an area where there has been development following the adoption of the UDHR, with the adoption of a number of specialist treaties and declarative texts both at the universal and regional levels.

The chapters in this section also consider the progressive recognition that acts taking placing in 'the private sphere' impact on the realisation of rights and engage states' positive obligations as the principal guarantors of the rights of their own citizens. The UDHR focuses on acts directly attributable to states, though human rights has progressively been understood to include state responsibility to act with due diligence in responding to and preventing violence committed by private actors. These extensions are considered in Ferstman's and Manjoo's chapters.

Another theme explored in the chapters is the wide gaps which remain between the 'haves' and the 'have-nots' which underpin vulnerability, discrimination and marginalisation and impede equal access to individual rights. In this respect, there is a constant interplay between the multiple forms of discrimination experienced by different sectors of society, the failure to realise economic, social and cultural rights and the capacity to implement civil and political rights. It is typically the most marginalised within societies and the individuals who are most socially and economically disadvantaged whose civil and political rights are least capable of being realised. This theme is explored by Dottridge, who recounts that when reporting to the UN Human Rights Council in 2017, the Special Rapporteur on contemporary forms of slavery indicated that discrimination (particularly against people of 'low' caste status, indigenous people and other minority groups, and also against migrants) and lack of trust in criminal justice systems continued to impede access to justice for victims of slavery, practices similar to slavery, servitude and forced labour. Similarly, as Manjoo notes in respect of discrimination and violence against women, the factors contributing to rights violations consist of "multiple concentric circles, each intersecting with the other." She explains that:

> These circles include structural, institutional, interpersonal and individual factors. The structural factors include macro-level social, economic and political systems; institutional factors include formal and informal social networks and institutions; interpersonal factors include personal relationships between partners, family members and within the community; and, individual factors include personality and individual capacities to respond to violence.

The declarative force of the UDHR can ring hollow if in the 70 years since the text's adoption too little has been achieved to enable individuals to exercise practically their rights and to enforce the prohibitions. The challenge of enforcement is a constant theme of the authors in this section of the book; simply declaring certain conduct to be illegal or impermissible is not enough to prevent its occurrence. However, the authors' analyses go further by also considering the important ways in which the UDHR has spear-headed the development of more specialist treaties and declarative texts (see chapters by Dottridge, Manjoo and Ferstman), later interpretive and implementation frameworks (see Bazyler and Nelson), as well as the progressive recognition of new categories of rights holders. For example, as Hilsenrath and Hamilton note, the Declaration, "has had a significant direct and indirect impact on LGBTI equality, most notably through the various legal instruments which have sprung from it at the global, regional and domestic levels."

4 Article 3

Everyone [including women] has the right to life, liberty and security of person

Rashida Manjoo[1]

Introduction

This chapter examines Article 3 of the UDHR and asserts that the realisation of the right to life, liberty and security of the person is not a reality in the lives of women in many countries of the world. It focuses particularly on the ultimate act of violence against women, i.e., the issue of gender-related killings of women. The manifestations, causes and consequences are briefly discussed, as well as the accountability deficit in respect of this human rights violation. This particular phenomenon is a reflection of the failure in addressing the numerous manifestations in a continuum of violence, which ultimately results in the killings of women. In addition, the absence, at the international level, of specific legally binding obligations on states to respond to, protect against and prevent violence against women broadly does contribute to the impunity challenge. The chapter concludes that the rights articulated in Article 3 of the UDHR are being violated in most countries, despite some positive legislative and programmatic developments at the national level.

Rather than being identified as a new form of violence, gender-related killings are the extreme manifestation of existing forms of violence against women. Such killings are not isolated incidents which arise suddenly and unexpectedly, but are the ultimate act of violence which is experienced in a continuum of violence. Women subjected to continuous violence, and living under conditions of gender-based oppression and threat, are always on 'death row, always in fear of execution.' This results in the inability to live, and is a major part of the death process when the lethal act finally occurs.[2] The discrimination and violence which is reflected in gender-related killings of women can be understood as multiple concentric circles, each intersecting with the other. These circles include structural, institutional, interpersonal and individual factors. The structural factors include macro-level social, economic and political systems; institutional factors include formal and informal social networks and institutions; interpersonal factors include personal relationships between partners, family members and within the community; and individual factors include personality and individual capacities to respond to violence.[3]

The principles of dignity, equality, freedom, justice and peace underpin the UDHR. Article 2 of the UDHR states: "Everyone is entitled to all the rights and freedoms set forth in this Declaration, without distinction of any kind, such as race, colour, sex, language, religion, political or other opinion, national or social origin, property, birth or other status." Thus the UDHR applies equally to *everyone* without distinction, which means that no individual may be discriminated against or hindered from enjoying her or his human rights. Non-discrimination is one of the crucial values in the work for the realisation of human rights, and this aspirational goal is reflected in many countries' constitutions. Of relevance to the issue of gender-related killings of women, the UDHR includes the right to life, liberty and security of the person in Article 3, and the right not to be subjected to torture or to cruel, inhuman or degrading treatment or punishment in Article 5. In linking Articles 3 and 5 to Article 2, it is clear that these rights apply to all women and girls, without distinction, which is crucial for a life free of all forms of violence, thereby reinforcing the norms on the promotion and protection of equality and non-discrimination rights of women.

The UDHR is framed in general terms and facially it can be considered a gender-neutral document that does not take specificity into account. The consequence is that the particularity of women's experiences and realities, including the ways in which women experience discrimination and/or are denied equality, or suffer specific violations because of their gender, is rendered largely invisible. Violence against women is a systemic, widespread and pervasive human rights violation, experienced largely by women because they are women. The concept of gender neutrality is framed in a way that understands violence as a universal threat to which all are potentially vulnerable and from which all deserve protection. This ignores the reality that violence against men does not occur as a result of pervasive inequality and discrimination, and also that it is neither systemic nor pandemic in the way that violence against women indisputably is. The global shift to neutrality in the sphere of violence against women favours a more pragmatic and politically palatable understanding of gender, that is, as simply a euphemism for 'men and women,' rather than as a system of domination of men over women. Violence against women cannot be analysed in isolation of the individual, institutional and structural factors that demand gender-specific approaches to ensure an equality of outcomes for women. Attempts to combine or synthesise all forms of violence into a gender-neutral framework tends to result in a depoliticised or diluted discourse, which abandons the transformative agenda that is needed.

Violence against women has been affirmed, in many human rights instruments and by human rights bodies, as a violation of the rights and fundamental freedoms of women. The killing of women constitutes a violation of, amongst others, the rights to life, equality, dignity and non-discrimination, and not to be subjected to torture and other cruel, inhuman or degrading treatment or punishment. For example, through its general recommendations, the Convention on the Elimination of All Forms of Discrimination against Women and the General Assembly's Declaration on the Elimination of Violence against Women address violence against women, which would include the killing of women, as acts of violence which are prohibited under international law.[4] Furthermore, international humanitarian law proscribes gender-based violence, extrajudicial executions of women and forbids attacks on women's personal dignity, in particular humiliating and degrading treatment. UN Treaty bodies and Special Procedures mandate holders have also condemned specific forms of violence, including femicide, honour-related killings, systematic killings, disappearances and witchcraft-related killings of women. These bodies have also raised concerns in relation to the significant obstacles for women in accessing justice, the climate of impunity surrounding such cases and also the systematic failure of states to investigate or provide redress.

The phenomenon of killings of women

Globally, the prevalence of different manifestations of gender-related killings is reaching alarming proportions. Culturally and socially embedded, these manifestations continue to be accepted, tolerated or justified – with impunity as the norm. Vulnerability to violence can be understood as a condition created by the absence or denial of rights. States' responsibility to act with due diligence in the promotion and protection of women's rights is largely lacking as regards violence against women in general and the killing of women in particular. Understanding that violence against women is a manifestation of historically unequal power relations between men and women, a human rights analysis posits that the specific causes of such violence and the factors that increase the risk of its occurrence are grounded in the broader context of systemic gender-based discrimination and other forms of subordination as experienced by women. The following sections highlight some current manifestations of gender-related killings of women.

Killings of women as a result of intimate partner violence

Intimate partner violence is a problem affecting millions of women all over the world, and the overwhelming burden of partner violence is borne by women. Research on intimate partner violence homicide reflects, almost without exception, that females are at greater risk than males and that the majority of female homicide victims are killed by male intimate partners.[5] The United Nations Office on Drugs and Crime research reports also confirm that in many countries intimate partner/family-related homicide is the major cause of female homicides and that female homicide rates are much more likely to be driven by this type of violence than the organised crime-related homicide typology that affects men.[6] As with all forms of intimate-partner violence, intimate-partner femicide is likely to be significantly under-reported. A report of the World Health Organisation estimates that globally between 40% and 70% of female murder victims are killed by an intimate partner.[7] In many countries the home is the place where a woman is most likely to be murdered, whereas men are more likely to be murdered in the street.[8]

Killings of women due to accusations of sorcery/witchcraft

The killing of women accused of sorcery/witchcraft has been reported as a significant phenomenon in countries in Africa, Asia and the Pacific Islands.[9] The pattern of violations includes violent murders, physical mutilation, displacement, kidnapping and disappearances of girls and women.[10] In many countries where women are accused of sorcery/witchcraft, they are also subjected to exorcism ceremonies involving public beating and abuse by shamans or village elders.[11] Both young and elderly women are at risk of sorcery/witchcraft violence and can include widows or other vulnerable elderly women who do not have children or relatives to protect them, women born out of wedlock or women who do not have any standing in the family.[12] A study has found that in some parts of Africa, older women are more vulnerable to sorcery-related killings due to their dependence on others or the property rights that they hold.[13] Perpetrators who torture or kill are almost exclusively men, often related socially or biologically to the victim.[14]

Killings of women and girls in the name of 'honour'

Honour killings take many forms, including direct murder, stoning, women and young girls being forced to commit suicide after public denunciations of their behaviour, and women being disfigured by acid burns, leading to death. Honour crimes are also linked to other forms of family violence and are usually committed by male family members as a means of defending family honour, of controlling women's sexual choices and also limiting their freedom of movement. Punishment is often public in character, and it usually has a collective dimension, with the family as a whole believing it to be injured by a woman's actual or perceived behaviour.[15] UN treaty bodies have expressed concerns that honour-related crimes often go unreported, are rarely investigated, usually go unpunished and when they are punished the sentences are far less than for equally violent crimes without the 'honour' dimension.[16]

Killings in the context of armed conflict

During armed conflict, women experience numerous forms of physical, sexual and psychological violence perpetrated by both state and non-state actors, including unlawful killings.[17] Violence is often used as a weapon of war, to punish or dehumanise women and girls, and to persecute the community to which they belong. Women and girls suffer from operations randomly or strategically targeting and terrorising the civilian population, but also from summary and extrajudicial executions, imprisonment, torture, rape and sexual mutilations for fighting in resistance movements, engaging in the search for and defence of their loved ones or for coming from communities suspected of collaboration.[18] Gender inequality becomes more pronounced in conflict and crisis situations as competing masculine discourses place contradictory demands on women and conflict is instrumentalised as a pretext to further entrench patriarchal control.[19]

Dowry-related killings of women

Dowry-related violence is particularly embedded in religious and cultural traditions of the South Asian region.[20] This term covers the deaths of young brides who are murdered or driven to suicide by continuous harassment and torture perpetrated by the groom's family, in an effort to extort dowry payment, or to demand an increased dowry of cash or goods. The most common manifestation of this practice is the burning of the bride. These incidents are often presented as (and accepted to be) accidents, such as death as a result of an 'exploding stove.'[21] In some cases dowry-related harassment of women has been aggravated by acid attacks, leading to blindness, disfigurement and deaths of women.[22] Experts argue that in addition to law reform, there is a need to address underlying cultural concerns, such as the subordinate status of women within their birth/natal and marital homes, issues of property and ownership within these realms, the control of women's sexuality, the stigma attached to divorce and the lack of support for a woman after she is married.[23]

Killings of Aboriginal and indigenous women

The social, cultural, economic and political marginalisation of Aboriginal and indigenous women globally, along with a negative legacy of colonialism, historic racist government policies and the consequences of political and economic policies, has resulted in extremely high levels of violence within these communities. In cases of killings of Aboriginal and indigenous women, the main failings by the authorities is the failure of police to protect them from violence; to investigate promptly and thoroughly when they are missing or murdered; and the disadvantaged social and economic conditions in which they live, which make them vulnerable to such violence.[24] The Committee on the Elimination of Discrimination against Women (CEDAW) has noted that, "indigenous women and girls face the highest levels of violence, especially at home where indigenous women are thirty five times as likely to be hospitalised as a result of family violence related assaults, as compared to non-indigenous females."[25] The Committee has also expressed its concern regarding the "hundreds of cases involving Aboriginal women who have gone missing or been murdered in the past two decades have neither been fully investigated nor attracted priority attention, with the perpetrators remaining unpunished."[26]

Extreme forms of violent killings of women

The growing socio-political phenomena of gangs, organised crime, drug dealers, human and drug trafficking chains, massive migration and the proliferation of small arms has had a devastating impact on women's lives, particularly in the region of Central America and also in Mexico. Organised crime groups and gangs have multiplied and have created an internal system of control of local territories and of communities. They have established an open market for a profitable arms trade, which allows them to position themselves as the main providers of private security for drug cartels, entrepreneurs and the elite. The northern triangle of Central America has the highest rates of homicide in a non-conflict context, with rising levels in the rates of killings of women.[27] Many of the murdered women come from the most marginalised sectors of society: they are poor, from rural areas, of ethnic origin, sexual workers or *maquila* workers, with young women between 16 and 24 years old being the most vulnerable group. Many murders exhibit evidence of sexual assault, signs of brutality and the use of firearms. Femicide is considered the second highest cause of death of women of reproductive age in Honduras.[28]

Killings as a result of sexual orientation and gender identity

Gender-based killing due to sexual orientation and gender identity is a phenomenon that has been recently, albeit insufficiently, documented. Lesbian, gay, bisexual, transsexual, transgender, intersex and queer persons (LGBTIQ), and also activists working in this sector, are targeted because they do not conform to stereotypes of gender sexuality and/or identity, thus becoming victims of homophobic crimes. Although limited statistics are available, civil society reports suggest that violence, motivated by hatred and prejudice, is a daily reality for many. It is "characterized by levels of serious physical violence that in some cases exceed those present in other types of hate crimes."[29] Manifestations include violence and abuse of police power, sexual violence in prisons, murders fuelled by hate, as well as other forms of discrimination. As noted by some academics, there is a paradox in the advancement in the protection of individuals' sexual rights on the one hand, and the increasing escalation of homophobic crimes on the other hand.[30] LGBTIQ persons, including women,

> are especially vulnerable to many kinds of violent crime, from killings in private homes to killings in public spaces known as 'social cleansing', extortion by blackmailers who threaten to reveal their identity to the public, and abuse from officials, especially the police, who sometimes arrest them.[31]

Particular challenges to secure the right to life, liberty and security for women

The challenge of gender neutrality in laws, policies and programmes can lead to *de facto* discrimination and the achievement of formal as opposed to substantive equality. This then impacts the focus and attention to human rights violations that disproportionately impact women. In addition, cultural practices that are harmful and degrading to women, killings in the name of honour, female genital mutilation, witchcraft-related killings, intimate partner violence and female infanticide, among others, contribute to the inability to secure the right to life, liberty and security of women. The lack of attention to the problem gives rise to the lack of safety, failure to investigate, prosecute and afford reparation (including guarantees of non-recurrence), thereby fostering a cyclical pattern of violence. This cycle normalises violence against women, empowers the perpetrators, who are conditioned to believe that they are above the law, and it also makes victims more vulnerable, as in many cases speaking out may be either futile and/or lead to more risk.

Individual, institutional, communal and structural factors also limit the effectiveness of human rights realisation, which can be linked to the gender-neutral framing of international human rights instruments, including the UDHR. Feminist academic literature has exposed the shortcomings and challenges of international human rights law, both in its origin and in its more modern development, with regard to respecting, protecting and fulfilling women's human rights. The invisibility regarding the widespread and pervasive human rights violations (as reflected in the violence against women sphere) in concrete human rights terms, has been attributed to the male domination of the human rights sector and also the male-centric approach in the development of international human rights law.[32] This has led to women being seen as synonymous with the family and the family being seen as part of the private sphere. Such views have resulted in the differential treatment accorded to women's lives, realities and their experiences of human rights violations, due to both the protection of the family unit, as well as patriarchal notions linked to the viewing of women as wives, mothers, victims and the property of men.

Standard-setting has led to normative developments in the UN and regional human rights documents – but the prevalence rates and practices on the ground belie the notion that such normative developments are leading to effective remedies at the national level. The UDHR and most human rights frameworks which subsequently followed focus on acts directly attributable to states, though this has progressively evolved through the interpretative work of UN treaty bodies through their general recommendations/ comments, their concluding observations on States Parties reports, and their findings and recommendations in the communications process. This has led to a deeper understanding of state responsibility to act with due diligence in responding to and preventing violence against women, including the violent acts of private actors, as well as state officials, who are not the direct perpetrators of the violence but who fail to protect against and prevent harm due to their practices in handling such cases. The notion of transformative remedies, as being essential in the quest to ensure accountability and guarantees of non-repetition, are also part of evolving developments. Ground-breaking jurisprudence in the regional human rights system, through cases such *Opuz v Turkey* (European Court of Human Rights)[33] and the *Cotton Fields v Mexico* (Inter-American Court of Human Rights)[34] have also contributed to such developments. The enduring challenge is that of rhetoric in normative development versus reality on the ground.

Continuing challenges

While states have initiated various preventive programmes, there are numerous gaps in states' efforts. Challenges include: lack of overall societal transformation, inadequate provision of access to justice, the absence and/or insufficiency of the rights-based discourse when addressing the killings of women, and the blindness to structural inequalities and the complex intersecting relations of power in the public and private spheres, which form part of the root causes of sex and gender discrimination. The lack of adequate assessment of risk, the lack of enforcement by the police and the judiciary of civil remedies and criminal sanctions, and the absence or inadequate provision of services such as shelters also exacerbates the risk of women of being abused and murdered, as often women have no choice but to continue living with their abusers.[35] Women's rights activists have also identified other challenges, including the difficulty of translating social realities into claims based on rights, the narrow interpretation of rights within an international legal order and the prevalence of discriminatory cultural stereotypes in the administration of justice.

The formulation of rights-based claims by women remains an important strategic and political tool for women's empowerment and for addressing human rights violations. Unfortunately, normative and institutional weakness results in impunity in cases of gender-related killings of women, as the norm is the inadequacy of legislative frameworks, the lack of respect for the rule of law, corruption and the poor administration of justice. A holistic approach for the elimination of all forms of violence against all women would require that systemic discrimination, oppression and marginalisation of women must be addressed at the political, legal, operative, judicial and administrative levels.[36]

Conclusion

The largely unfulfilled promise of Articles 3 and 5 of the UDHR in relation to women and their right to life, liberty and security of the person, as well as the prohibition of torture or cruel, inhuman or degrading treatment, is a reality that one cannot deny, considering the prevalence of numerous manifestations of violence against women that are widespread and pervasive. Despite the values and rights that are included in the UDHR, a document that is almost 70 years old, the normative developments to date on the issue of violence against women have been slow, with non-binding soft law developments within the UN system being the practice. There is no comprehensive specific UN convention framework on violence against women, with the non-binding 1993 Declaration on the Elimination of Violence against Women (DEVAW) being the only internationally accepted consensus document. The interpretative work of treaty bodies has contributed to providing standard-setting in the sphere of violence against women. Unfortunately, this has not been sufficient to change national-level practices through the acceptance of international standards.

The lack of specific legally enforceable standards impacts attempts to ensure appropriate responses and also accountability for acts of violence against women. Although many states have acknowledged violence against women as a widespread and systematic human rights violation, and are working to differing degrees on eradicating it, the normative gap within international law is a barrier to holding states accountable for the failure to respect, protect and fulfil the human rights of women. An international Convention on the Elimination of Violence Against Women or an Optional Protocol to the Convention on the Elimination of All Forms of Discrimination Against Women would contribute towards ensuring that states are held accountable to standards that are legally binding; it would provide a clear normative framework for the protection of women that is applicable globally; and it would have a specific monitoring body to substantively provide in-depth analysis of both general and country-level developments. A legally binding international instrument would provide a protective, preventative as well as an educative function.

The right to life, liberty and security of women requires acknowledging that violence against women impairs and nullifies women's realisation of all human rights; it prevents women from participating in their communities as full and equal citizens; it reinforces male dominance and control; it supports discriminatory gender norms; and it maintains systemic inequalities between women and men. These factors in turn preserve and perpetuate conditions that enable violence against women to continue. Full, inclusive and participatory citizenship requires that violence against women be seen as a barrier to the realisation of all human rights, and consequently to the effective exercise of citizenship rights. Citizenship is characterised by meaningful participation, autonomy and agency through one's membership in a community – a community that is not necessarily defined by nationality – but one that consists of an indivisible and interrelated set of rights, and corresponding obligations on states to respect, protect and fulfil such rights. The realisation by women of UDHR Article 3 rights may lead to giving life to the Preamble of the UDHR, which holds that "the recognition of the inherent dignity and of the equal and inalienable rights of all members of the human family is the foundation of freedom, justice and peace in the world."

Notes

1 This chapter draws on my 2012 report to the UN Human Rights Council, which addresses the topic of gender-related killings of women (UN Doc. A/HRC/17/16).
2 Shalhoub-Kevorkian, 2003 at 581.
3 See generally Moser, 2001.
4 See Article 4(c) of the Declaration on the Elimination of Violence against Women, UN General Assembly resolution 48/104 of 20 December 1993, U.N.Doc.A/RES/48/104 (1994).
5 See generally Heise and Garcia-Moreno, 2002; (Campbell, 1992); and (Gauthier and Bankston, 2004).
6 United Nations Office on Drugs and Crime, 2011.

7 Heise and Garcia-Moreno, 2002.
8 Supra note 6.
9 United Nations, 2012, Chapter 8, Victim Groups, at para. 46.
10 OHCHR, n.d.
11 Supra note 9.
12 Zocca and Urame, 2008.
13 Galloway, 1995.
14 Supra note 10.
15 See Secretary-General, United Nations, 2006 and Baydoun, 2011.
16 See generally reports of the Committee against Torture, the Special Rapporteur on extrajudicial executions and the CEDAW Committee.
17 Report of the Secretary-General, supra note 15.
18 Manjoo, 2010.
19 Ertürk, 2007.
20 Agnes, 2011.
21 News.bbc.co.uk, 1999.
22 Law Commission of India Report, 2009.
23 Kishwar, 2005.
24 McIvor and Day, 2011.
25 CEDAW Committee, 2010.
26 CEDAW Committee, 2008.
27 UNDP, 2009.
28 Sánchez, 2011.
29 See Human Rights First, 2008.
30 Lemaitre, 2009.
31 Lemaitre, 2009 at p. 80.
32 See generally Charlesworth, Chinkin and Wright, 1991, and (Charlesworth and Chinkin, 2000).
33 Opuz v Turkey (2009).
34 CEDAW Committee, 2005, Para 286.
35 Casas and Vargas, 2011.
36 Manjoo, 2011.

References

Agnes, F. (2011). Gender Based Killings – A South Asian Perspective. *On file with author.*

Baydoun, A. (2011). Killing of Women in the Name of Honour: An Evolving Phenomenon in Lebanon. *Paper on file with author.*

Campbell, J. (1992). If I Can't Have You, No One Can: Power and Control in Homicide of Female Partners. In: J. Radford and D. Russell, eds., *Femicide: The Politics of Woman-Killing*. New York: Twayne.

Casas, L. and Vargas, M. (2011). *The Response of the State to Domestic Violence. Revista de Derecho*, XXIV, 131–151.

CEDAW Committee. (2005). *Report on Mexico Produced by the Committee on the Elimination of Discrimination Against Women Under Article 8 of the Optional Protocol to the Convention, and Reply from the Government of Mexico.* [online] Geneva: United Nations, para 286. Available at: www.refworld.org/docid/4a54bc0e1a.html [Accessed 5 Dec. 2017].

CEDAW Committee. (2008). *CEDAW Committee, Concluding Observations to Canada* UN. Doc. CEDAW/C/CAN/CO/7. [online] Geneva: United Nations, CEDAW/C/CAN/CO/7, para 31. Available at: www.refworld.org/docid/494ba8ce0.html [Accessed 5 Dec. 2017].

CEDAW Committee. (2010). *Concluding Observations to Australia*. CEDAW/C/AUS/CO/7, 2010, para 40. [online] Geneva: United Nations. Available at: www2.ohchr.org/english/bodies/cedaw/docs/co/CEDAW-C-AUS-CO-7.pdf [Accessed 5 Dec. 2017].

Charlesworth, H. and Chinkin, C. (2000). *The Boundaries of International Law*. Manchester: Manchester University Press.

Charlesworth, H., Chinkin, C. and Wright, S. (1991). Feminist Approaches to International Law. *The American Journal of International Law*, 85(4), p. 613.

Ertürk, Y. (2007). *Report of the Special Rapporteur on Violence against Women, Its Causes and Consequences, Mission to Turkey*. A/HRC/4/34/Add.2. Geneva: United Nations.

Galloway, S. (1995). *Femicide Project. OHCHR. Report by Country*. Zimbabwe: Women in Law and Development in Africa (WiLDAF).

Gauthier, D. and Bankston, W. (2004). "Who Kills Whom" Revisited: A Sociological Study of Variation in the Sex Ratio of Spouse Killings. *Homicide Studies*, 8(2), pp. 96–122.

Heise, L. and Garcia-Moreno, C. (2002). Violence by Intimate Partners. In: E. Krug, L. Dahlberg, J. Mercy, A. Zwi and R. Lozano, eds., *World Report on Violence and Health*. Geneva: World Health Organization.

Human Rights First (2008). *Violence Based on Sexual Orientation and Gender Identity Bias*. Hate Crime Survey. [online] New York: Human Rights First, p. 1. Available at: www.humanrightsfirst.org/wp-content/uploads/pdf/fd-080924-lgbt-web2.pdf [Accessed 5 Dec. 2017].

Kishwar, M. (2005). Destined to Fail: Inherent Flaws in the Anti Dowry Legislation. *Manushi*, 148.

Law Commission of India Report. (2009). *The Inclusion of Acid Attacks as Specific Offences in the Indian Penal Code and a Law for Compensation for Victims of Crime*. 226. [online] Law Commission of India. Available at: https://indiankanoon.org/doc/87066215/ [Accessed 5 Dec. 2017].

Lemaitre, J. (2009) Love in the Time of Cholera: LGBT Rights in Colombia. *Sur Journal*. [online], 6(11). Available at: https://ssrn.com/abstract=1706721 [Accessed 30 Nov. 2017].

Manjoo, R. (2010). *Report of the Special Rapporteur on Violence Against Women, Its Causes and Consequences*. [online] Geneva: United Nations. Available at: www2.ohchr.org/english/bodies/hrcouncil/docs/14session/A.HRC.14.22.pdf [Accessed 5 Dec. 2017].

Manjoo, R. (2011). *Report of the Special Rapporteur: Multiple and Intersecting Forms of Discrimination and Violence against Women*. [online] Geneva: United Nations. Available at: www2 ohchr.org/english/bodies/hrcouncil/docs/17session/A-HRC-17-26.pdf [Accessed 5 Dec. 2017].

McIvor, S. and Day, D. (2011). Gender-Motivated Killings of Aboriginal Women and Girls Canada. *On file with author*, 2011.

Moser, C. (2001). The Gendered Continuum of Violence and Conflict. In: C. Moser and F. Clark, eds., *Victims, Perpetrators, or Actors? Gender, Armed Conflict and Political Violence*. London: Zed Books.

News.bbc.co.uk. (1999). BBC News | South Asia | Bride Burning 'kills hundreds'. [online] Available at: http://news.bbc.co.uk/1/hi/world/south_asia/431607.stm [Accessed 30 Nov. 2017].

OHCHR. (n.d.). Gender-Motivated Killings of Women Accused of Sorcery & Witchcraft a Form of Femicide: Papua New Guinea Casel. *Paper prepared for Expert Group Meeting*, 12 October 2011, pp. 9–10.

Opuz v Turkey [2009] 33401/02 (ECHR).
Sánchez, J. (2011). *Impunidad: Un grito sin respuesta. Informe final femicidios en Honduras.* Honduras: Tribuna de Mujeres Contra los Femicidios.
Secretary General, United Nations. (2006). *In-Depth Study on all Forms of Violence Against Women.* [online] Geneva: United Nations. Available at: https://documents-dds-ny.un.org/doc/UNDOC/GEN/N06/419/74/PDF/N0641974.pdf?OpenElement [Accessed 5 Dec. 2017].
Shalhoub-Kevorkian, N. (2003). Reexamining Femicide: Breaking the Silence and Crossing "Scientific" Borders. *Signs: Journal of Women in Culture and Society*, 28(2), pp. 581–608.
UNDP. (2009). *Abrir espacios para la seguridad ciudadana y el desarrollo humano.* Colombia: Informe sobre Desarrollo Humano para América Central. IDHAC.
United Nations. (2012). *Handbook Compiling Observations and Recommendations of the UN Special Rapporteur on Extrajudicial Executions.* Geneva: United Nations.
United Nations Office on Drugs and Crime. (2011). *2011 Global Study on Homicide.* Vienna: United Nations Office on Drugs and Crime.
Zocca, F. and Urame, J. (2008). *Sorcery, Witchcraft and Christianity in Melanesia.* Goroka, Papua New Guinea: Melanesian Institute.

5 Articles 2 and 7

Equality and the Universal Declaration of Human Rights: progress and challenges for Lesbian, Gay, Bisexual, Transgender and Intersex (LGBTI) equality

Rebecca Hilsenrath and Charles Hamilton

Introduction

How might the UDHR look if it had been written today? Specifically, how might its authors have dealt differently with issues of sexual orientation and gender identity? Of course it is an impossible question to answer: the UDHR is a product of a particular period of history. Its Preamble notes its origin in the 'barbarous acts' which had so recently 'outraged the conscience of mankind'. The unparalleled crimes of the Nazis and their allies made pressing and clear the need to codify universal rights.

LGBTI[1] people, in particular gay men, were singled out for vicious persecution by the Nazis. Though fewer than the Jewish victims of the Holocaust, the gay men murdered in concentration camps and elsewhere number at least in the thousands.[2] Neglected from the official reparations and many of the mainstream accounts of Nazi atrocities in the immediate post-war period, gay Holocaust survivors continued to experience persecution for decades after the war (consensual same-sex relationships were not decriminalised in Germany until the late 1960s), with their war-time suffering not widely acknowledged or memorialised until later still.

These atrocities are beginning to fade from living memory. In the coming years, we will lose the last of the eyewitnesses to the Holocaust (the last surviving person sent to a Nazi concentration camp for being gay died in 2011),[3] and it will become more difficult to rebut revisionism or outright denial about the events of those years, especially as such claims are made increasingly and powerfully via new online media. All of this potentially makes it harder to counter criticism of the structures that were set up in response, such as the United Nations (UN), Council of Europe (CoE) and European Union (EU). We are therefore indebted to the visionaries who seized a unique moment and set down our universal rights in the aftermath of the war.

This chapter assesses the UDHR's legacy for equality and non-discrimination in relation to sexual orientation and gender identity, at the global level, at the regional (continental) level and in domestic jurisdictions with a focus on the United Kingdom. It examines the pace of change since 1948, as well as progress still to be achieved – in the legal, policy and social spheres. Whilst seeking to avoid the pitfall of discussing hierarchies of rights, it considers the influence of various factors, including religion.

The UDHR and equality

While space constraints preclude a full analysis, it is nevertheless worth briefly considering the legacy of the UDHR for gender as well as LGBTI equality, including with regard to the relative starting points for these strands, the contrasting ways in which the UDHR has directly and indirectly impacted on them, and some of the reasons for these differences. After all, these are not unrelated issues: attitudes toward sexual orientation and gender equality, both then and now, are bound up in broader concepts of gender roles and gender identity. The Nazis' obsession with traditional male and female roles and relationships was one reason why they felt so threatened by homosexuality[4] – and was not entirely isolated from wider Western attitudes at the time. Yet, notwithstanding the systemic and everyday disadvantages faced by women then and (albeit to a lesser extent) now, women's rights in the UK and elsewhere undoubtedly enjoyed a much higher degree of respect and protection than did LGBTI rights in 1948. Whereas at that time same-sex relationships enjoyed no legal protection and were criminalised across much of the world, the wider global acceptance of women's rights allowed for the explicit recognition of gender equality in Article 2 of the UDHR.

Chief among the architects and visionaries behind the UDHR was Eleanor Roosevelt, whose address to the UN General Assembly on the adoption of the UDHR expressed the hope that "this Universal Declaration of Human Rights may well become the international Magna Carta of all men everywhere".[5] Her language, with 'men' as a synonym for 'people', is jarring to the modern ear – all the more so considering that the actual text of the Declaration espouses equality (and gender neutrality) quite well. The 'foundation blocks' of the UDHR, Articles 1 and 2, which provide the focus for this chapter, rest on this principle of equality, as well as on dignity, liberty and brotherhood. Its gender neutrality marked significant progress on similar passages in some Enlightenment texts from which the UDHR's authors had drawn inspiration:[6]

> All human beings are born free and equal in dignity and rights. . . . Everyone is entitled to all the rights and freedoms set forth in this Declaration, without distinction of any kind, such as race, colour, sex, language, religion, political or other opinion, national or social origin, property, birth or other status.[7]

The UDHR's recognition of 'other status' as being worthy of protection means that the definition of discrimination contained in Article 2 is not exhaustive. As such, this left open the possibility of later recognition in human rights law of LGBTI rights in a way unlikely to have been envisaged by its authors,[8] though in the face of strong resistance in many quarters. The Vienna Declaration and Programme of Action acknowledges the reality of resistance by noting that, whilst the significance of historical, cultural and religious backgrounds must be borne in mind, it is the duty of the states to promote and protect all human rights and fundamental freedoms.[9] The same non-exhaustive term is used in several legally binding descendants of the UDHR, including the International Covenant on Civil and Political Rights (ICCPR, Articles 2 and 26), the European Convention on Human Rights (ECHR, Article 14) and the UN Convention on the Rights of the Child (CRC, Article 2).

The UDHR's Article 7 also provides for a broad conception of equality:

> All are equal before the law and are entitled without any discrimination to equal protection of the law. All are entitled to equal protection against any discrimination in violation of this Declaration and against any incitement to such discrimination.[10]

Progress to date on LGBTI equality – both in international systems and national contexts – has been slow to arrive. Not only have activists faced challenges in addressing homophobia and transphobia, and deeply engrained cultural constructs of masculinity and femininity and the 'nuclear family' (the cultural context in which the Nazi persecutions took place and, indeed, in which the UDHR was drafted), but instances of competing rights and interests are complex to address, and have arguably been used by some to exaggerate the extent of the conflict.[11] The growing body of human rights and equality law, however, is gradually moving beyond the traditional grounds of discrimination specifically referred to in the UDHR.

LGBTI rights at the UN level

Although the wording of Article 7 provides a comprehensive and inclusive right to equality, it seems unlikely to have crossed the minds of its authors that LGBTI rights would come to be recognised as human rights protected in law. Yet, despite the legal and societal norms of the time when it was written, and the lack of explicit reference to sexual orientation or gender identity in the UDHR, there is now a substantial weight of international human rights law behind LGBTI rights. The Yogyakarta Principles are a set of binding principles that show how international human rights law applies to issues of sexual orientation and gender identity. They are the result of an initiative in 2006 by a group of leading international human rights experts to record comprehensively the basis in international law for the protection of sexual orientation and gender identity rights. They are explicitly intended as an expression of existing legal principles, rather than the creation of new norms,[12] in particular affirming human rights law reflected in international and regional treaties, such as Articles 1 and 2 of the UDHR.[13] The

Jurisprudential Annotations prepared by Michael O'Flaherty (who also served as Rapporteur to the meeting in Yogyakarta where the principles were formulated) contain exhaustive references to numerous legal instruments, judgements of international courts and decisions of UN committees which confirm and uphold LGBTI rights.[14] Nevertheless, with their unequivocal calls for an end to all anti-LGBTI and discriminatory laws and practices, the Principles remain very far from being universally acceptable to all governments, let alone all people.

Global disharmony concerning the rights of LGBTI people means that they continue to be excluded from the explicit protection of international human rights instruments, and this shows little sign of imminent change. Consistent opposition from some states and regions stands in the way of progress towards a dedicated UN Convention on LGBTI issues. It also prevented the creation of a UN independent expert on LGBT rights until recently when, in November 2016, Vitit Muntarbhorn was appointed as the first UN Independent Expert on the Protection against Violence and Discrimination based on Sexual Orientation and Gender Identity. This was a long-awaited victory for the recognition, against fierce opposition, of LGBTI rights at the UN level. The debate at the Human Rights Council illustrated the UDHR's potential to be treated as all things to all people, with both the supporters and opponents of the mandate citing the UDHR in their arguments, and both sides citing the principle of universality in human rights.[15]

However, the UN human rights system – which is made up of UN Charter-based bodies, treaty monitoring committees and mandated independent experts – is not inflexible in practice. The Universal Periodic Review has been an important vehicle for addressing LGBTI issues via the UN system,[16] as have some of the softer mechanisms, although these are contentious topics at the global level.[17] Decision-making concerning refugees has also included LGBT rights within the anti-discrimination provisions of UN instruments.[18] Article 33 of the Convention relating to the Status of Refugees[19] provides protection from expulsion for individuals where their life or freedom would be threatened on account of their membership in a particular social group. The UN human rights system has interpreted 'particular social group' to include refugees who fear persecution on account of their sexual orientation or gender identity. Significantly, the existence of criminal laws, such as sodomy laws, can be persecutory per se and are sufficient to identify a particular social group of those affected asylum seekers.[20]

The UDHR and LGBTI rights in regional systems

Although the UDHR is generally (though not universally) regarded as not being justiciable, it was the basis for later binding treaties including crucially the ECHR, whose jurisprudence must be considered part of the UDHR's legacy. One of the chief creators of the ECHR, the Briton David Maxwell Fyfe (later a Conservative Cabinet Minister as Lord Kilmuir), is often lauded as a hero in human rights circles. He served as a prosecutor of Nazi war criminals at Nuremberg, and used his first-hand experience of the catastrophic disregard for human rights to inform his leading role in the drafting of the ECHR. He successfully advocated for the ECHR to be legally binding on states, and jurisprudence under the ECHR he helped craft now firmly incorporates LGBTI rights. In Europe, progress in the law, policy and public perceptions surrounding LGBTI rights can therefore be traced in part to the UDHR via the ECHR.[21] The landmark ECtHR cases of Dudgeon and Goodwin[22] were instrumental in advancing significant areas of LGBT law in the UK (respectively, the decriminalisation of homosexuality in Northern Ireland and legal recognition of gender reassignment under the Gender Recognition Act 2004), while in Germany an intersex individual used the ECHR to successfully sue a surgeon for unnecessary medical interventions.[23] More recently, the ECtHR case of Oliari[24] addressed the absence of official recognition for same-sex partnerships in Italy. Whereas the cases of Dudgeon, Goodwin and Oliari were decided on the basis of Article 8 (Private life), several other significant ECtHR cases have made specific use of the 'other status' provision in Article 14,[25] copied from the UDHR.

The ECHR also has legal force through its incorporation into the fundamental principles of EU law. It is through these mechanisms that the rights of LGB refugees, indirectly derived from the UDHR, have been a live point of interest in the courts, particularly during the current European refugee crisis, where the issue of 'concealment' of one's sexual orientation in the face of a real threat of persecution has evolved.[26] For example, the Court of Justice of the European Union has held that,

> requiring members of a social group sharing the same sexual orientation to conceal that orientation is incompatible with the recognition of a characteristic so fundamental to a person's identity that the persons concerned cannot be required to renounce it. . . . The fact that [the applicant] could avoid the risk by exercising greater restraint than a heterosexual in expressing his sexual orientation is not to be taken into account.[27]

Despite this purposive interpretation, though, the gender identity of trans asylum seekers and refugees, for example in detention centres and shared housing allocation, is often overlooked with serious consequences.

Outside Europe, human rights progress also owes something to the UDHR. For example, the 1963 Organisation of African Unity Charter was the first regional instrument to deal with human rights on the continent, by explicitly endorsing the UDHR in its preamble. The African Charter on Human and Peoples' Rights (the African Charter), adopted in 1981 as a result of mounting domestic and international pressure to address extreme human rights abuses, brought about a real step-change in the recognition of individuals' rights. Although the Commission was established to ensure implementation of the rights enshrined in the African Charter adopted in 2014 a resolution on protection against violence and other human rights violations against persons on the basis of their real or imputed sexual orientation or gender identity, neither the Commission nor its judicial enforcement mechanism (the African Court on Human and Peoples' Rights, ACHPR) has yet issued a decision on a sexual orientation or gender identity discrimination complaint. At the Organization of American States, the Inter-American Commission on Human Rights created a specialised unit within its Executive Secretariat to promote the rights of LGBTI persons and established a new rapporteurship on the subject, which became fully operational in February 2014. The Inter-American Court on Human Rights has slowly begun to adjudicate LGBTI cases, deciding in 2016 that Ecuador discriminated against a military police officer on the basis of sexual orientation when he was discharged from service for having breached the army's rules of military discipline, which prohibited sexual acts between persons of the same sex.[28] In another case, the Inter-American Court determined that sexual orientation cannot be used to deny custody rights. In that case, Karen Atala was denied custody rights over her three daughters because she is a lesbian living with a same-sex partner.[29]

Comparative domestic experience

Although a full assessment is not possible, it is difficult to overstate the scale of worldwide disparities at the level of national law and practice. Alongside developments such as the recognition of the right to same-sex marriage by the US Supreme Court,[30] there are areas of grave concern about LGBTI legal rights and their realisation. The Office of the UN High Commissioner for Human Rights (OHCHR) reports widespread prejudice, abuse and extrajudicial killings.[31] Seventy-one countries still criminalise homosexuality, with 13 of these imposing the death penalty.[32] Russia has passed laws prohibiting gay 'propaganda', and there have been several attempts to introduce legislation in Uganda imposing the death penalty for homosexuality. Reports in summer 2017 of police in Chechnya rounding up gay and bisexual men and subjecting them to torture and inhuman or degrading treatment shocked people around the world. In some instances, healthcare providers refuse to provide much-needed care to LGBTI people because of personal or religious beliefs. Most governments still deny trans people the right to legally change their name and gender from those that were assigned to them at birth.

The rapid progress in the West, coupled with stagnation and regression in parts of the developing world, amounts to a polarising of attitudes and practices, which reinforces a perception that LGBTI rights are a Western imperialist concept. Yet there is a strong argument that homophobia, not LGBTI rights, stems from imperialism, with some states such as Jamaica and India retaining discriminatory colonial-era laws long after the demise of the British Empire. LGBTI rights campaigners have highlighted the influence of evangelical Christians from the United States on legislators in Uganda. The picture is never clear-cut. Take, for example, South Africa, whose 1996 constitutional prohibition on discrimination and legalisation of same-sex marriage placed it at the global forefront of equality, and where Archbishop Desmond Tutu has equated the struggle for gay rights with the struggle against apartheid[33] – but where nevertheless homophobic violence including 'corrective' rape is widely reported. Another example of the diversity in approach can be found in Botswana, where the High Court upheld a transgender person's right to change the gender marker in their passport.[34] In August 2017, Canada joined a number of countries[35] by enabling citizens to opt for gender-neutral category 'X' for the purposes of their passports, and in October 2017 an activist gained permission to bring High Court proceedings in the UK on the same issue.

It cannot be denied that a lot of opposition to gay rights stems nominally or actually from religious belief, and it is inescapable, for example, that many of the opponents of Vitit Muntarbhorn's appointment were representatives of countries with majority Muslim or conservative Christian populations. However, attitudes to LGBTI rights within religions are far from universal (see the example of the UK below, which also discusses attitudes toward LGBTI rights in Christianity), and it is likely that to different degrees in all religions there is a spectrum of acceptance and intolerance, and a level of incongruence between established doctrine and popular views. A number of majority Muslim countries have decriminalised same-sex sexual activity, and some have anti-discrimination laws that protect LGBTI people. There are movements within Islam calling for more LGBT rights, and several examples of openly gay imams and gay-friendly mosques in France, the USA, South Africa and Australia. Nevertheless, the vast majority of Muslims globally oppose homosexuality.[36] These distinctions also vary by nationality, with somewhat higher levels of tolerance among Muslim communities in secular Western countries.[37] Great variations exist also within Judaism, from a general prohibition and disapproval of homosexuality (with some exceptions) in Orthodox Judaism to widespread acceptance, and approval of same-sex marriage, in Reform Judaism, with many shades of opinion, doctrine and practice in between.

The UK context

Through cases such as Dudgeon and Goodwin cited earlier, the progress on LGBT equality in the UK, from criminalisation and immense disadvantage to widespread acceptance and same-sex marriage in less than 50 years, can in part be traced to the UDHR, via the ECHR. Maxwell Fyfe, whose indirect legacy mentioned earlier includes the LGBTI rights jurisprudence under the ECHR that directly affected UK law, made a further inadvertent but major contribution to the advancement of gay rights in the UK. Though evidently a homophobe (not unusually for his time), as Home Secretary he established the Wolfenden Committee, which went on to recommend the decriminalisation of homosexuality.[38]

Research has found public attitudes towards LGB people in the UK to be positive and to have improved greatly over time,[39] in a period where gay people have become more visible and same-sex marriage has become less remarkable (these developments are further discussed later). At the same time, Britain has become somewhat less tolerant of people who look different or who have different religious practices. Evidence shows that discrimination rises where there are limited resources, and during this period we have seen the impact of austerity on prejudice. On the other hand, a conflated antipathy toward immigrants of any origin, together with religions which manifestly prohibit same-sex relationships, may have contributed to the increasing secularisation and intolerance of religion, which could lead to an increase in acceptance of LBGTI communities.

Although in terms of outcomes it lags behind LGB equality, transgender equality and legal recognition have improved in the UK in recent years. The Gender Recognition Act 2004 requires a holder of a gender recognition certificate to be treated 'for all purposes' according to their affirmed legal gender. The Equality Act 2010 prohibits discrimination and protects those who propose undergoing, are undergoing or have undergone gender reassignment. The Human Rights Act (incorporating as it does Articles 8 and 14 of the European Convention) and the Data Protection Act 1998 provide additional protection for the privacy of trans people.

The drivers of greater acceptance may be complex and varied (the earlier section touched on some aspects and drivers of different prejudices), but the example of civil partnerships and same-sex marriage in Britain appears to be a clear example of legislation driving rapid attitudinal change. Civil partnerships, once controversial, helped to normalise same-sex relationships in the public consciousness. When combined with the fact that predictions of societal breakdown failed to materialise, this made it very difficult to find any rational grounds on which to oppose the natural extension to marriage equality. Such a shift in attitudes, accompanied – or caused – by major legislative reform, may have occurred much earlier in the case of gender, but it is worth considering what lessons it might provide when seeking to address prejudice, both in the UK and elsewhere.

Across Britain a number of faiths and denominations (including Reform and Liberal Judaism, Quakers and Unitarians) chose to opt into performing same-sex marriages, even when, in England and Wales, the primary legislation for same-sex marriage specifically excluded certain denominations. A February 2017 vote in the General Synod also indicated that the Church of England may be moving towards changing its official stance on same-sex marriage[40] (although recent history suggests that it would not do so without a conservative backlash and the threat of schism). In May 2017 the Church of Scotland instructed officials to consider changes to church law that would allow ministers to preside over same-sex marriage ceremonies, whilst the Kirk assembly called on Church leaders to "take stock of its history of discrimination at different levels and in different ways against gay people and to apologise individually and corporately and seek to do better". There are signs of (modest) movement within Roman Catholicism too, with some of the Pope's recent statements.[41] Whilst certain exemptions exist in equality law (affecting, for example, how religious denominations may exclude certain groups from particular roles), there is no fundamental conceptual or legal hierarchy in treatment between religion or belief and sexual orientation or gender identity, at least in the UK. Where religion and sexual orientation collide, the differences can appear irreconcilable.

Some of the recent UK case law (Ashers' Bakery, Ladele, McFarlane, Preddy & Hall)[42] taken together might give the impression that the UK courts will favour non-discrimination of gay people over the manifestation of religion. However, all of those cases, while different, centred on how the law deals with the right to receive a publically available service free from discrimination. No legal or moral principle, and no judgement, places sexual orientation above or below religion. The difference lies less in any hierarchy of rights and more in reducing the circumstances where a requirement in equality law amounts to a disproportionate interference on the right of a service provider to manifest their religion.

Despite the progress, it would be wrong to paint an entirely rosy picture of LGBTI rights in the UK. Pockets of discrimination remain even in mainstream media, for example with a *Daily Mail* headline recently gaining notoriety for appearing to base its criticism of a High Court judge in part on his being 'openly gay'.[43] Our research has reported some evidence about domestic violence and sexual violence being more likely to be experienced by LGB people (as well as young people, women and disabled people) compared to other groups, and the evidence shows an increase in LGBT-related hate crime in recent years.[44] There are also settings in which some people report feeling the need to conceal their sexual orientation.[45] It would also be wrong to consider the LGBTI community as a monolithic group with uniform experiences. There are still major challenges and differing rates of progress across the UK, for example, the Gender Recognition Act requires a pathologisation of transgender identities for the purposes of obtaining a gender recognition certificate, and Northern Ireland has not yet legalised same-sex marriage.

Whereas civil partnerships show that legislation can drive social attitudes, the other side of the same coin is that attitudes can lag behind the law. This is particularly the case in relation to trans and intersex people, who are far less visible than LGB people. This is partly because trans and intersex people are less common than LGB people, and furthermore because people might know a trans person without knowing that the person is trans because they are unwilling to openly share their trans identity (for example, because of a wish to 'pass' as cisgender or because of a fear of discrimination). The official recognition of trans identity is recent in the UK, which further contributes to a poor understanding among most people, with the common conflation, confusion or stereotyping of different types of gender and trans identity. According to our research, trans people face a lack of visibility and, where disadvantage is encountered, this has very significant impact on life chances.[46] This is coupled with casual transphobic prejudice, as well as more serious discrimination, harassment and violence, in many countries including the UK. Work to address trans equality is further hampered by a lack of data and formal evidence of trans people's experiences, for example when accessing services.[47]

There is further to go on transgender legal rights: as David Locke points out, and the Equality and Human Rights Commission's work supports, the law may not yet adequately protect people who identify as non-binary or do not conform to the gender binary,[48] and do not wish to undergo treatment for gender reassignment. The gender recognition certificate also does not fully account for those who have affirmed a gender without seeking or proposing treatment for reassignment.[49] In addition, intersex people face a number of equalities challenges which are distinct from trans issues, including gaps in legal provisions on the right of bodily integrity, physical autonomy and self-determination, and protection from discrimination.

Conclusion

To answer the impossible question with which we opened, of how different the UDHR might look if drafted today – and specifically how differently it might treat LGBTI equality – the answer is perhaps 'not very'. On LGBTI rights, universal recognition remains so distant that it would be no more possible to agree on explicit protection in an Article 2 if it were drafted today than in 1948. This mixed picture means that, despite its age, the UDHR's provision for equality holds up well as a universal document. From a Eurocentric and twenty-first-century perspective, its omission of LGBTI rights from Article 2 may seem glaring, but there is at present no likelihood that such protection would attract the universal acceptance that makes the UDHR still such a potent force today.

In the same speech in 1948 referred to earlier, Eleanor Roosevelt expressed a view that the Declaration was an imperfect document born of compromise, but nevertheless a great document. It has had a significant direct and indirect impact on LGBTI equality, most notably through the various legal instruments which have sprung from it at the global, regional and domestic levels. Nevertheless, a declining commitment to the importance of international human rights instruments in the West, coinciding as it does with the stalling of rights for many groups, means that the UDHR has never been more significant or more needed.

Notes

1 Lesbian, gay, bisexual, transgender and intersex. This chapter refers repeatedly to this categorisation and to its individual components. It attempts to make clear the differing experiences of individuals within the various groups encompassed by the abbreviation, and seeks – at times perhaps without complete success – to avoid its use as an inaccurate catch-all for diverse sexual orientation and gender identity.
2 Boden, 2011.
3 haaretz.com, 2011.
4 Boden, 2011.
5 YouTube, 2017.
6 For example, the 1776 US Declaration of Independence ('all men are created equal') and France's 1789 Declaration of the Rights of Man and of the Citizen ('Men are born and remain free and equal in rights'). The latter's failure to recognise the rights of women provoked Olympe de Gouge to write her *Déclaration des droits de la femme et de la citoyenne* ('Declaration of the Rights of Woman and the Female Citizen') in 1791, prompting Mary Wollstonecraft to write her 'Vindication of the Rights of Woman' the following year, which in turn inspired countless twentieth- and twenty-first-century feminists and campaigners including Millicent Garrett Fawcett and Ayaan Hirsi Ali.
7 UDHR, Articles 1 and 2.

8 We should acknowledge Roosevelt's status as a 'gay icon' and early champion of LGB dignity, more for her close and public friendships with several high-profile out lesbians than for the unsubstantiated rumours about her own sexual orientation; see Peyser, 2016. Even so, she surely could not have foreseen the advances in LGBTI rights over the past 70 years and, in any case, she was not the UDHR's sole author. This view is also supported by a reading of the travaux préparatoires which record the discussions that informed the drafting of the UDHR (see Schabas, 2013).

9 Vienna Declaration and Programme of Action, paragraph 5.

10 NYU Global Institute for Advanced Study, 2016, discusses the breadth of protection for equality in the UDHR, both through autonomous and accessory rights.

11 Malik, 2008.

12 International Commission of Jurists, 2007.

13 For example, Article 1 of the Yogyakarta Principles states: "All human beings are born free and equal in dignity and rights. Human beings of all sexual orientations and gender identities are entitled to the full enjoyment of all human rights."

14 O'Flaherty, 2007.

15 OHCHR statement: 'Council establishes mandate on protection against violence and discrimination based on sexual orientation and gender identity', 30 June 2016.

16 International Bar Association, 2016, provides a lot of detail on this and on how LGBTI issues generally are dealt with in the UN system.

17 MacArthur, 2015, considers whether international human rights law has made room for the development of sexual orientation and gender identity (SOGI) rights. She concludes that there are some positives (e.g., softer UN mechanisms) but there is still further to go, and advises care and caution and a diverse approach to different aspects of SOGI rights.

18 Anderson, 2009: 133: "Refugee decision-makers have interpreted the anti-discrimination provisions to include homosexuality, as it is acknowledged 'that [LGBT] persons are entitled to all human rights on an equal basis with others.'"

19 United Nations High Commissioner for Refugees, 2010.

20 United Nations High Commissioner for Refugees, 2008.

21 Johnson, 2015.

22 *Dudgeon v United Kingdom* (1981) and *Goodwin v the United Kingdom* (2002).

23 *Völling vs Regional Court Cologne* (2008).

24 *Oliari and Others v Italy* (2015).

25 European Court of Human Rights, 2017.

26 United Nations High Commissioner for Refugees, 2002, paragraph 3. Also, see current applications/cases pending before the European Court of Human Rights: *A.T. v Sweden* (2015), *E.S. v Spain* (2016), *M.T. v France* (2017), and *O.S. v Switzerland* (2017) – all summarised in European Court of Human Rights, 2017.

27 *X, Y and Z v Minister voor Immigratie en Asiel*, 2013.

28 *Homero Flor Freire v Ecuador* (Preliminary exceptions, Merits, Reparations and Costs), 2016.

29 *Atala Riffo and daughters v Chile* (Merits, Reparations and Costs), 2012.

30 In *Obergefell v Hodges* (2015), the court held that both the Due Process Clause and the Equal Protection Clause of the Fourteenth Amendment guarantees the right to marry for same-sex couples in the same manner as it does to opposite-sex couples.

31 Ohchr.org, n.d.i.

32 Carroll and Mendos, 2017: 40: "There are eight states where the death penalty is activated. . . . Further there are another five where interpretation of sharia, or

where black letter law, permits the death penalty technically, but it is not invoked to our knowledge."
33 BBC News, 2013.
34 Reuters, 2017.
35 For example: Australia, Denmark, Germany, Malta, New Zealand and Pakistan.
36 Pew Research Center, 2013.
37 ICM Research, 2015; Pew Research Center, 2017.
38 However, he also led the unsuccessful opposition in the House of Lords to its implementation, and said to a colleague, "I am not going down in history as the man who made sodomy legal". See Kynaston, 2009, 370.
39 For example, NatSen Social Research, 2013.
40 BBC News, 2017.
41 Hale, 2015.
42 *Lee v McArthur & Ors* (2016) [appeal still pending before the Supreme Court], *Ladele v London Borough of Islington* (2009), *McFarlane v Relate Avon Ltd* (2010), *Bull & Bull v Hall and Preddy* (2012).
43 *Daily Mail*, 2016.
44 Equality and Human Rights Commission, 2015, 69–71.
45 Equality and Human Rights Commission, 2016, 101–110.
46 Equality and Human Rights Commission, 2015, 49–64.
47 Equality and Human Rights Commission, 2015, 55 and 98.
48 Trans identity can be 'non-binary' in character, located at a (fixed or variable) point along a continuum between male and female, or 'non-gendered', i.e., involving identification as neither male nor female.
49 Locke, 2016.

References

Anderson, A. (2009). On Dignity and whether the Universal Declaration of Human Rights Remains a Place of Refuge After 60 Years. *American University International Law Review*. [online], 25(1). Available at: http://digitalcommons.wcl.american.edu/cgi/viewcontent.cgi?article=1009&context=auilr [Accessed 12 Dec. 2017].

A.T. v Sweden [2015] Application no. 78701/14 (ECtHR).

Atala Riffo and Daughters v Chile (Merits, Reparations and Costs) [2012] Series C No. 239 (Inter-American Court on Human Rights).

BBC News. (2013). Archbishop Tutu Would Not Worship a Homophobic God. [online] Available at: www.bbc.co.uk/news/world-africa-23464694 [Accessed 12 Dec. 2017].

BBC News. (2017). *Church of England Votes Against Same-Sex Marriage Report*. [online] Available at: www.bbc.co.uk/news/uk-38982013 [Accessed 12 Dec. 2017].

Boden, E. (2011). The Enemy Within: Homosexuality in the Third Reich, 1933–1945. *Constructing the Past*. [online], 12(1). Available at: http://digitalcommons.iwu.edu/constructing/vol12/iss1/4 [Accessed 12 Dec. 2017].

Bull & Bull v Hall and Preddy [2012] Civ 83 (EWCA).

Carroll, A. and Mendos, L. (2017). *State-Sponsored Homophobia – A World Survey of Sexual Orientation Laws: Criminalisation, Protection and Recognition*. 12th ed. Geneva: The International Lesbian, Gay, Bisexual, Trans and Intersex Association.

Daily Mail. (2016). The Judges Who Blocked Brexit: One Founded a EUROPEAN Law Group, Another Charged the Taxpayer Millions for Advice and the Third Is an Openly Gay ex-Olympic Fencer.

De Gouge, O. (1791). *Déclaration des droits de la femme et de la citoyenne ('Declaration of the Rights of Woman and the Female Citizen').*

Dudgeon v United Kingdom [1981] application No. 7525/76 (ECtHR).

E.S. v Spain [2016] Application No.13273/16 (ECtHR).

Equality and Human Rights Commission. (2015). *Is Britain Fairer? The State of Equality and Human Rights 2015.* Manchester: Equality and Human Rights Commission.

Equality and Human Rights Commission. (2016). *Research Report 101: Prejudice and Unlawful Behaviour: Exploring Levers for Change.* Manchester: Equality and Human Rights Commission.

European Court of Human Rights. (2017). *Factsheet: Sexual Orientation Issues.* [online] Available at: www.echr.coe.int/documents/fs_sexual_orientation_eng.pdf [Accessed 12 Dec. 2017].

France. (1789). *Déclaration des droits de l'homme et du citoyen ('Declaration of the Rights of Man and the Citizen').* Paris: French National Assembly.

Goodwin v the United Kingdom [2002] Application No. 28957/95 (ECtHR).

haaretz.com. (2011). Last Homosexual Holocaust Survivor Dies at 98. [online] Available at: www.haaretz.com/news-in-brief-1.377072 [Accessed 12 Dec. 2017].

Hale, C. (2015). The Pope Francis Statement That Changed the Church on LGBT Issues. *Time Magazine.* [online] Available at: http://time.com/3975630/pope-francis-lgbt-issues/ [Accessed 12 Dec. 2017].

Homero Flor Freire v Ecuador (Preliminary Exceptions, Merits, Reparations and Costs) [2016] Series C No. 315 (Inter-American Court on Human Rights).

ICM Research. (2015). *C4 / Juniper Survey of Muslims 2015.* [online] London: ICM. Available at: www.icmunlimited.com/wp-content/uploads/2016/04/Mulims-full-suite-data-plus-topline.pdf [Accessed 12 Dec. 2017].

International Bar Association. (2016). *Sexual Orientation, Gender Identity and Expression, and Sex Characteristics at the Universal Periodic Review.* [online] Available at: http://ilga.org/wp-content/uploads/2016/11/SOGIESCatUPR_report.pdf [Accessed 12 Dec. 2017].

International Commission of Jurists. (2007). *Yogyakarta Principles – Principles on the Application of International Human Rights Law in Relation to Sexual Orientation and Gender Identity.* [online] Available at: www.yogyakartaprinciples.org/wp/wp-content/uploads/2016/08/principles_en.pdf [Accessed 12 Dec. 2017].

Johnson, P. (2015). 'The Choice of Wording Must Be Regarded as Deliberate': Same-Sex Marriage and Article 12 of the European Convention on Human Right. *European Law Review*, 40(2), pp. 207–224.

Kynaston, D. (2009). *Family Britain, 1951–1957.* London: Bloomsbury Publishing.

Ladele v London Borough of Islington [2009] Civ 1357 (EWCA).

Lee v McArthur & Ors [2016] 39 (NICA).

Locke, D. (2016). Identity Politics. *New Law Journal.* [online] Available at: www.newlawjournal.co.uk/content/identity-politics [Accessed 12 Dec. 2017].

M.T. v France [2017] Application No. 61145/16 (ECtHR).

MacArthur, G. (2015). Securing Sexual Orientation and Gender Identity Rights Within the United Nations Framework and System: Past, Present and Future. *Equal Rights Review.* [online]. 15, pp. 25–54. Available at: www.equalrightstrust.org/ertdocumentbank/Securing%20Sexual%20Orientation%20and%20Gender%20Identity%20Rights%20within%20the%20United%20Nations%20Framework%20and%20System%20Past,%20Present%20and%20Future.pdf [Accessed 12 Dec. 2017].

Malik, M. (2008). *'From Conflict to Cohesion': Competing Interests in Equality Law and Policy.* [online] London: Equality and Diversity Forum. Available at: www.equalrightstrust.org/ertdocumentbank/Securing%20Sexual%20Orientation%20and%20Gender%20Identity%20Rights%20within%20the%20United%20Nations%20Framework%20and%20System%20Past,%20Present%20and%20Future.pdf [Accessed 12 Dec. 2017].

McFarlane v Relate Avon Ltd [2010] Civ 771 (EWCA).

NatSen Social Research. (2013). *British Social Attitudes Survey 30th Edition.* [online] London: NatCen Social Research. Available at: www.bsa.natcen.ac.uk/latest-report/british-social-attitudes-30/personal-relationships/homosexuality.aspx [Accessed 12 Dec. 2017].

NYU Global Institute for Advanced Study. (2016). *Article 7: The Equality and Non-Discrimination Provision. Appendix E to the Report of the Global Citizenship Commission.* [online] Open Book Publishers. Available at: www.openbookpublishers.com/shopimages/The-UDHR-21st-C-AppendixE3.pdf [Accessed 12 Dec. 2017].

O.S. v Switzerland [2017] Application No. 43987/16 (ECtHR).

Obergefell v Hodges [2015]135 S. Ct. 2071 (US Supreme Court).

O'Flaherty, M. (2007). *Jurisprudential Annotations to the Yogyakarta Principles.* Nottingham: University of Nottingham Human Rights Law Centre.

O'Flaherty, M. and Fisher, J. (2008). Sexual Orientation, Gender Identity and International Human Rights Law: Contextualising the Yogyakarta Principles. *Human Rights Law Review*, 8(2), pp. 207–248.

Ohchr.org. (n.d.i). Speak Up Stop Discrimination: Combatting Discrimination Based on Sexual Orientation and Gender Identity. [online] Available at: www.ohchr.org/EN/Issues/Discrimination/Pages/LGBT.aspx [Accessed 12 Dec. 2017].

Ohchr.org. (n.d.ii). OHCHR | Council Establishes Mandate on Protection Against Violence and Discrimination Based on Sexual Orientation and Gender Identity. [online] Available at: www.ohchr.org/EN/NewsEvents/Pages/DisplayNews.aspx?NewsID=20220 [Accessed 12 Dec. 2017].

Oliari and Others v Italy [2015] Application Nos. 18766/11 and 36030/11 (ECtHR).

Pew Research Center. (2013). *The Global Divide on Homosexuality.* [online] Washington, DC: Pew Research Center. Available at: www.pewglobal.org/2013/06/04/the-global-divide-on-homosexuality [Accessed 12 Dec. 2017].

Pew Research Center. (2017). *U.S. Muslims Concerned About Their Place in Society, but Continue to Believe in the American Dream.* [online] Washington, DC: Pew Research Center. Available at: www.pewforum.org/2017/07/26/findings-from-pew-research-centers-2017-survey-of-us-muslims)/ [Accessed 12 Dec. 2017].

Peyser, M. (2016). Eleanor Roosevelt, The First Lady of Gay Rights. *Huffington Post.* [online] Available at: www.huffingtonpost.com/marc-peyser/the-first-lady-of-gay-rights_b_7608122.html [Accessed 12 Dec. 2017].

Reuters. (2017). Activists Celebrate Botswana's Transgender Court Victory. [online] Available at: www.reuters.com/article/us-botswana-transgender-court/activists-celebrate-botswanas-transgender-court-victory-idUSKBN1C91OW [Accessed 12 Dec. 2017].

Roberts, C. (2014). *The Contentious History of the International Bill of Human Rights.* Cambridge: Cambridge University Press.

Schabas, W. (2013). *The Universal Declaration of Human Rights: The Travaux Préparatoires.* Cambridge: Cambridge University Press.

United Nations General Assembly. (1993). *Vienna Declaration and Programme of Action*. A/CONF.157/23. [online] Geneva: United Nations. Available at: http://ap.ohchr.org/documents/alldocs.aspx?doc_id=5819 [Accessed 12 Dec. 2017].

United Nations High Commissioner for Refugees. (2002). *Guidelines on Gender-Related Persecution Within the Context of Article 1A(2) of the 1951 Convention and/or Its 1967 Protocol Relating to the Status of Refugee*. [online] Geneva: United Nations. Available at: www.unhcr.org/3d58ddef4.pdf [Accessed 12 Dec. 2017].

United Nations High Commissioner for Refugees. (2008). *Guidance Note on Refugee Claims Relating to Sexual Orientation and Gender Identity*. [online] Geneva: United Nations. Available at: www.refworld.org/pdfid/48abd5660.pdf [Accessed 12 Dec. 2017].

United Nations High Commissioner for Refugees. (2010). *Convention and Protocol Relating to the Status of Refugees*. [online] Geneva: United Nations. Available at: www.unhcr.org/uk/protection/basic/3b66c2aa10/convention-protocol-relating-status-refugees.html [Accessed 12 Dec. 2017].

United States, Declaration of Independence. (1776). *Völling vs Regional Court Cologne* [2008]25 O 179/07 (Cologne).

Wollstonecraft, M. (1792). *Vindication of the Rights of Woman*.

X, Y and Z v Minister voor Immigratie en Asiel [2013] Joined Cases C-199/12, C-200/12 and C-201/12 (Court of Justice of the European Union).

YouTube. (2017). Eleanor Roosevelt on the adoption of the Universal Declaration of Human Rights – 1948. [online] Available at: www.youtube.com/watch?v=F-WktGCFLA0 [Accessed 14 Aug. 2017].

6 Article 4

No-one to be held in slavery or servitude: provisions that are not as redundant as many had assumed

Mike Dottridge

Article 4: no longer redundant

At the end of World War II, slavery remained a legal institution in only a handful of states in the Arabian peninsula. When these countries nominally abandoned the practice in the 1960s and 1970s, the international community assumed that classical slavery had been abolished, although it was aware that forced labour imposed by government officials continued, alongside some cases of acute economic exploitation by private employers. It was not until after the end of the Cold War, in particular when publicity focused on Eastern European women being exploited elsewhere in Europe, that the international community woke up to the reality that exploitation bearing the hallmarks of slavery was widespread and probably growing.

Slavery

The UDHR was not the first time that slavery was condemned by the international community. Slavery and the slave trade were among the first human rights issues to receive attention after the establishment of the League of Nations. The League adopted the Slavery Convention of 1926, defining slavery as, "the status or condition of a person over whom any or all of the powers attaching to the right of ownership are exercised". Article 2 of the Convention required States Parties to prevent and suppress the slave trade and to bring about, progressively and as soon as possible, the complete abolition of slavery in all its forms. Article 5 distinguished slavery from forced labour, stating that "forced labour may only be exacted for public purposes" and requiring States Parties "to prevent compulsory or forced labour from developing into conditions analogous to slavery".

However, while the Slavery Convention required abolition of slavery "progressively and as soon as possible", the Universal Declaration adopted 22 years later made clear that states could not tolerate slavery or servitude in any form. The International Court of Justice has identified protection from slavery as an obligation owed by a state to the international community as a whole,[1] while an International Labour Organization (ILO) Commission of Inquiry noted in 1998 that, "[T]here exists now in international law a peremptory norm prohibiting any recourse to forced labour and that the right not to be compelled to perform forced or compulsory labour is one of the basic human rights".[2]

Forced labour

In 1930 the ILO adopted Convention No. 29 on Forced Labour, seeking to regulate the use of forced labour by government officials, rather than to abolish it. The term "forced or compulsory labour" was defined (in Article 2.1 of this convention) as "all work or service which is exacted from any person under the menace of any penalty and for which the said person has not offered himself voluntarily". From the 1920s until the 1970s, there was a clear demarcation between slavery (involving exploitation by private individuals, whether or not slavery and the slave trade were condoned or supported by the authorities of the state concerned) and forced labour, which involved government authorities requiring private individuals to work. First the League of Nations and later the United Nations responded to issues related to slavery, while the ILO focused on forced labour.

The Universal Declaration did not include an explicit reference to forced labour. However, the first regional human rights convention, the Council of Europe's Convention for the Protection of Human Rights and Fundamental Freedoms (1950), repeated the Universal Declaration's prohibition of slavery and servitude and also prohibited forced labour, specifying four restricted circumstances in which states were entitled to force people to work.[3] Later, the International Covenant on Civil and Political Rights (1966) also stipulated that, "No one shall be required to perform forced or compulsory labour" and referred to the same four sets of circumstances in which government officials were justified in forcing people to work.

The ILO adopted a second convention in 1957 that focuses on forced labour imposed by state officials, prohibiting the use of forced labour for public works (ILO Convention No. 105 on the Abolition of Forced Labour). However, in the 1980s its treaty-monitoring body, the Committee of Experts on the Application of Conventions and Recommendations, started interpreting cases in which workers were forced to remain in their jobs by private employers, rather than by government officials, as forced labour. This started the process of redefining how terms were used in relation to economic exploitation in general.

Servitude

In the wake of World War II and atrocities committed against forced labourers in Germany, Japan and elsewhere, the Universal Declaration gave priority attention to unacceptable forms of exploitation. When drafting the Declaration, the second session of the UN Commission on Human Rights included an article saying that, "Slavery, in all its forms, being inconsistent with the dignity of man, shall be prohibited by law".[4] Members of the drafting group intended the article "to cover traffic in women, involuntary servitude and forced labour".[5] The term 'involuntary servitude' had its origins in the Thirteenth Amendment to the United States' Constitution (1865), abolishing slavery in the wake of the American Civil War.

This draft was referred to the UN General Assembly's Third Committee, where the Australian representative registered his objection, noting that, "After consulting the Oxford Dictionary, he had come to the conclusion that it would be wiser to omit the word 'involuntary' before 'servitude' in the English text".[6] Shortly afterwards, he was joined by a more influential voice, that of René Cassin, the representative of France and one of the initial drafters of the Universal Declaration. He commented on the reasons for adding a reference to servitude, but noted his reservation to the word 'involuntary' that qualified it:

> The Commission on Human Rights had thought it necessary to include some wording which would cover indirect and concealed forms of slavery. The word "servitude" had been used to cover such aspects as the way in which the Nazis had treated their prisoners of war and the traffic in women and children. In French the term "servitude volontaire" did not have any meaning.[7]

The question of whether to maintain the word 'involuntary' with respect to servitude was put to the vote, and the word 'involuntary' was deleted. This severed the clear link with jurisprudence in the US on involuntary servitude and contributed to the term 'servitude' and the practices it covered seeming vague.

To assess whether further action was required by the international community to repress slavery and the slave trade, and to fill the gap in international law about what constituted servitude, the UN established an *ad hoc* Committee on Slavery in 1949. A few years later, a committee was set up specifically to draft a 'Supplementary Convention on Slavery and Servitude'. The United Kingdom proposed a draft for this new convention in 1954, referring explicitly to 'servitude'. However, the following year the same country said it wanted to delete the reference to servitude and replace it with the phrase 'institutions and practices similar to slavery' and 'servile status', terms which obfuscated and cause confusion to this day.[8] Imperial civil servants in the United Kingdom had realised that the wording of the Universal Declaration ("No one shall be held in slavery or servitude") required action to be taken straight away to stop any cases of servitude. They regarded this as inopportune, for several Emirates in the Gulf where slavery or servitude persisted were still under British rule. Consequently, in 1956 the UN adopted the Supplementary Convention on the Abolition of Slavery, the Slave Trade and Institutions and Practices Similar to Slavery. Instead of introducing an immediate ban on the institutions and practices concerned, the Supplementary Convention required States Parties to, "take all practicable and necessary legislative and other measures to bring about progressively and as soon as possible the[ir] complete abolition or abandonment" (Article 1).

The four institutions and practices which were defined in the Supplementary Convention are debt bondage, serfdom, three categories of forced marriage and a way of exploiting children that has become known subsequently as 'the sale of children'. Debt bondage was common in South Asia (where it is known as 'bonded labour' and is still common today). It is also common among migrants around the world. It was defined as:

> the status or condition arising from a pledge by a debtor of his personal services or of those of a person under his control as security for a debt, if the value of those services as reasonably assessed is not applied towards the liquidation of the debt or the length and nature of those services are not respectively limited and defined.

Serfdom was defined as the status of a person who "is by law, custom or agreement bound to live and labour on land belonging to another person and to render some determinate service to such other person, whether for reward or not, and is not free to change his status". In comparison to debt bondage, far fewer cases have been identified.

The category of child exploitation prohibited by the Supplementary Convention concerned children who were handed over by a child's parents to be exploited by someone else (a cultural practice known as 'false adoption' was behind this concept, concerning cases in which young children were nominally adopted by a family, but in practice exploited as servants). This category was reviewed and developed 40 years later in the Optional Protocol to the Convention on the Rights of the Child on the Sale of Children, Child Prostitution and Child Pornography (2000).

The provisions relating to marriage were the most controversial ones in the Supplementary Convention, which required the eradication of three practices:

(1) A woman, without the right to refuse, is promised or given in marriage on payment of a consideration in money or in kind to her parents, guardian, family or any person or group; or
(2) The husband of a woman, his family, or his clan, has the right to transfer her to another person for value received or otherwise; or
(3) A woman on the death of her husband is liable to be inherited by another person.

The first of these provisions provoked dissent among social anthropologists, who feared that payments of so-called bridewealth by bridegrooms in sub-Saharan Africa to their bride's family were being interpreted as the purchase of a bride, and they disputed this interpretation in a series of publications in the 1950s and 1960s.[9] The provisions of the Supplementary Convention on marriage and those on the three other institutions and practices similar to slavery did not result in new laws being drafted or implemented in many countries. However, as a complementary measure to banning some practices, Article 2 required states:

> to prescribe, where appropriate, suitable minimum ages of marriage, to encourage the use of facilities whereby the consent of both parties to a marriage may be freely expressed in the presence of a competent civil or religious authority, and to encourage the registration of marriages

(and was intended to contribute to the implementation of the Universal Declaration's provision in Article 16, that "[m]arriage shall be entered into only with the free and full consent of the intending spouse").[10]

Regional conventions

The European Convention for the Protection of Human Rights and Fundamental Freedoms (1950) echoed the Universal Declaration's prohibition of slavery and servitude and also prohibited forced labour. The American Convention on Human Rights (1969) contained explicit references to involuntary servitude, traffic in women and forced labour (Article 6). The Organization of African Unity's African Charter on Human and Peoples' Rights (1981) included a wide-ranging provision covering slavery and "all forms of exploitation and degradation", but did not include explicit references to servitude, forced labour or trafficking in persons. The Association of Southeast Asian Nations (ASEAN) Human Rights Declaration (2012) states that, "No-one shall be held in servitude or slavery in any of its forms, or be subject to human smuggling or trafficking in persons, including for the purpose of trafficking in human organs".

Trafficking in persons

In addition to the Supplementary Convention, one other convention was adopted in the decade after the Universal Declaration focusing on another form of exploitation. This was the UN Convention for the Suppression of the Traffic in Persons and of the Exploitation of the Prostitution of Others (1949), the last of a series of international instruments intended to discourage what had been called 'the white slave trade' – recruitment into prostitution – making it a crime to earn a living from the earnings of a prostitute (i.e., as a pimp or by renting out accommodation used to entertain clients paying for sex). However, half a century later, a new international instrument was adopted containing a significantly different (and broader) definition of trafficking in persons. This followed numerous discussions in the UN General Assembly and its Commission on Human Rights (as well as the Sub-Commission on Human Rights and its Working Group on Contemporary Forms of Slavery, which was established in the 1970s) about the nature of human trafficking in the 1990s. In the end, the new definition came in an instrument devoted to stopping crime, the UN Protocol to Prevent, Suppress and Punish Trafficking in Persons, Especially Women and Children (2000), supplementing the UN Convention against Transnational Organized Crime (2000). It paid little attention to issues such as protection (of trafficked persons) and prevention. The definition was complex, containing at least two elements (an action committed with an exploitative purpose) and, in the cases involving trafficked adults, a third (an abusive means used to commit the action of trafficking).[11]

A similar definition was adopted in Europe to refer to 'trafficking in human beings' in the Council of Europe Convention on Action against Trafficking in Human Beings (2005). Most other recent regional conventions have applied the same definition.

Changing interpretations of what constitutes slavery

During the 1950s, two armed conflicts (France's colonial war against independence in Algeria and a conflict in Yemen, pitting Egypt against Saudi Arabia) were marked by accusations of slavery being levelled by one party to the conflict against another, with accusers claiming the moral high ground. After Saudi Arabia abolished slavery as a lawful practice in 1962, slavery disappeared as a bone of contention until the 1990s, and there was a pause in the efforts of the UN and ILO to address slavery and forced labour. The ILO developed a convention on child labour in 1973, but this was essentially a consolidation of a series of separate ILO conventions seeking to prohibit children in industrialised countries from engaging in particular jobs, rather than a new initiative to reduce the exploitation of children in developing countries.

In the 1970s, the UN set up a Working Group on Slavery to review reports about slavery. Most of the reports initially submitted to the five members of the Sub-Commission on the Promotion and Protection of Human Rights who comprised the Working Group concerned historical cases of slavery, so its title was revised to 'Working Group on Contemporary Forms of Slavery'.[12] The UN Sub-Commission also appointed a Special Rapporteur, Benjamin Whitaker, to investigate whether slavery was still a live issue, who reported in 1982 that, "[A]lthough chattel-slavery in the former traditional sense no longer persists in any significant degree, the prevalence of several forms of slavery-like practice continues unabated".[13] During the 1960s and 1970s, the use of forced labour "for the benefit of private individuals" was still not the object of substantial attention by the ILO.[14] However, in the 1980s the ILO's treaty-monitoring body started calling for action to end a wider range of exploitation related to forced labour than before, condemning cases involving exploitation by private employers, as well as governments or government officials.

In an attempt to reconcile the terminology about forced labour used by the ILO with twenty-first-century worries about human trafficking, in 2014 the International Labour Conference adopted a Protocol to the Forced Labour

Convention of 1930. This reaffirms the definition of forced labour in the ILO's 1930 Convention, while recognising that,

> the context and forms of forced or compulsory labour have changed and trafficking in persons for the purposes of forced or compulsory labour, which may involve sexual exploitation, is the subject of growing international concern and requires urgent action for its effective elimination.

Unlike previous international instruments about slavery, servitude, forced labour and human trafficking, which contained few or weak provisions on assistance to people leaving exploitative situations, only imposing an explicit obligation in the case of child victims,[15] Article 9 of the ILO Forced Labour Protocol is much less ambiguous: "Members should take the most effective protective measures to meet the needs of all victims for both immediate assistance and long-term recovery and rehabilitation".[16]

In the 1990s, any continuing assumptions in the Western world that slavery or practices similar to slavery were a relic of the past disappeared as crimes which bore the hallmarks of slavery were revealed during the war in the former Yugoslavia. This ensured that offences related to slavery were listed in the Rome Statute of the International Criminal Court (1998), confirming the 1926 definition as far as the terms 'slavery' and 'enslavement' were concerned, while adding that the term 'enslavement' could also refer to situations of human trafficking.[17]

After half a century during which Western human right lawyers devoted little attention to slavery or servitude, and few cases came to court, there has been a spate of such cases in the twenty-first century, confirming the continuing relevance of the Universal Declaration's Article 4. Outside the West, however, public interest litigation had already achieved important results in South Asia, first in India, in response to a Writ Petition in 1982, and later in Pakistan, in response to a similar petition in 1988. The Government of India adopted legislation banning bonded labour in the 1970s, but the Supreme Court's 1984 judgement (*Bandhua Mukti Morcha v Union of India*) was not only critical in determining how government officials were to respond to reports of bonded labour, but also in asserting the rights of bonded labourers.[18] In Pakistan, a petition from a group of brick-kiln workers led to a ruling by the Supreme Court that bonded labour was unconstitutional. This obliged the government to pass a law prohibiting it in 1992.[19]

Most key cases in the twenty-first century have been in international or regional courts. In 2001, the International Criminal Tribunal for the Former Yugoslavia issued its decision in the Kunarac case, where the charges included 'enslavement'.[20] Women held in private accommodation had been forced to cook, clean and provide sexual services to Serb soldiers. In 2005, the European Court of Human Rights issued a judgement about quite different circumstances involving a young migrant live-in domestic worker from Togo, Henriette Siwa-Akofa Siliadin, who had been held in servitude in France during the 1990s. The court concluded that France's laws on servitude were too vague and the penalties imposed on the couple who had exploited her were too lenient, especially as she had been aged under 18 for her first two years that she was exploited.[21]

Some of the trials that have followed were also a response to armed conflicts marked by extreme acts of cruelty. The Special Court for Sierra Leone convicted three men in 2009 for crimes against humanity involving sexual slavery and forced marriage (as an inhumane act).[22] Other cases have addressed long-established forms of exploitation or recent patterns involving migrants. In a case before an Economic Community of West African States (ECOWAS) court in 2008, the court ruled that the Republic of Niger had taken inadequate measures to secure the release of a woman held in servitude – a case linked to traditional slavery.[23] In 2010 the European Court of Human Rights condemned both Cyprus and the Russian Federation in a case involving a woman recruited in Russia for the purpose of prostitution in Cyprus, who had been killed while in Cyprus.[24] In this case of human trafficking, the European Court noted that states have an obligation to investigate, whether or not a victim (or the victim's relative or representative) makes a formal complaint. It noted that the Russian authorities had conducted no investigation at all and consequently condemned them for a violation of their procedural obligation under Article 4 of the European Convention on Human Rights to investigate alleged trafficking.[25]

Nevertheless, reporting to the UN Human Rights Council in 2017, the Special Rapporteur on contemporary forms of slavery described a series of obstacles which continued to impede access to justice for victims of slavery, practices similar to slavery, servitude and forced labour. She said these included discrimination (particularly against people of "low" caste status, indigenous people and other minority groups, and also against migrants) and lack of trust in criminal justice systems.[26]

After a series of judgements that emphasised states' obligations to strengthen legal responses to offences related to slavery, servitude, forced labour or human trafficking, a judgement by the Inter-American Court of Human Rights in 2016, on a Brazilian case involving workers exploited on an isolated ranch in Amazonia, emphasised what preventive measures states are required to take (in this case to implement Article 6 of the American Convention on Human Rights):

> [T]o act with due diligence, States must take comprehensive measures in cases of servitude, slavery, trafficking in persons and forced labour. In particular, States must have an adequate legal framework for protection, with effective enforcement and prevention policies and practices to enable them to respond effectively to complaints. The prevention strategy must be comprehensive, that is, it must prevent risk factors and at the same time strengthen institutions so that they can provide an effective response to the phenomenon of contemporary slavery. In addition, States should take preventive measures in specific cases where it is clear that certain groups of persons may be victims of trafficking or slavery.[27]

In the same year, a UN Special Rapporteur also drew attention to the range of measures that states have an obligation to take to prevent debt bondage, noting that, alongside obligations to enact legislation on this particular practice similar to slavery and form of forced labour, to identify anyone subjected to it, to provide them with short-term protection and long-term rehabilitation and to ensure that victims have access to justice and remedies,

> States have an obligation to prevent debt bondage through prevention of discrimination, regulation of wages, enforcement of labour law and regulation of recruitment practices, and by protecting persons in debt bondage against violations in the context of business activities.[28]

After decades of being interpreted narrowly by jurists – to require little more than formal abolition of slavery – by the 70th anniversary of the Universal Declaration, its Article 4 is reckoned to impose far wider obligations on states to prevent slavery, practices similar to slavery, servitude, forced labour and human trafficking, as well as to protect everyone from all these forms of abuse, notably by adopting and implementing an appropriate legal framework. Far from being redundant, it seems that many states still have a great deal to do to bring legislation and policy into line with the requirements of Article 4. It is an irony, therefore, that since the UN Trafficking Protocol was adopted in 2000, most of the emphasis on the need for more pro-active measures by states has been on the need to prosecute individual traffickers and to amend the law to bring this about, rather than to give greater priority to prevention and to protecting the human rights of the adults and children who have been subjected to any of these forms of extreme exploitation. Fortunately, this anomaly is being addressed by regional human rights courts and individual experts mandated by the Human Rights Council.

Notes

1 Barcelona Traction, Light and Power Co, Ltd. (*Belgium v Spain*) (1971).
2 ILO, Forced Labour in Myanmar (Burma), Report of the Commission of Inquiry appointed under article 26 of the Constitution of the ILO to examine the observance by Myanmar of the Forced Labour Convention, 1930 (No. 29).
3 After stating "No one shall be required to perform forced or compulsory labour", article 4(3) of the European Convention specifies that, "For the purpose of this article the term "forced or compulsory labour" shall not include:

   a any work required to be done in the ordinary course of detention imposed according to the provisions of Article 5 of this Convention or during conditional release from such detention;
   b any service of a military character or, in case of conscientious objectors in countries where they are recognised, service exacted instead of compulsory military service;
   c any service exacted in case of an emergency or calamity threatening the life or well-being of the community;
   d any work or service which forms part of normal civic obligations".

4 Article 11, UN Doc. E/CN.V57, 10 December 1947.
5 Ibid.
6 Records of the 110th meeting (of the Third Committee of the United Nations General Assembly), 22 October 1948 (UN General Assembly, 1948).

7 Ibid.
8 Allain, 2008.
9 Mair, 1969.
10 The UN followed this up in 1962 by adopting the Convention on Consent to Marriage, Minimum Age for Marriage and Registration of Marriages. The Convention on the Elimination of All Forms of Discrimination against Women (1979) stipulates in Article 16(2) that "[t]he betrothal and the marriage of a child shall have no legal effect, and all necessary action, including legislation, shall be taken to specify a minimum age for marriage and to make the registration of marriages in an official registry compulsory".
11 The text of the Protocol was accessed at (United Nations, 2000).
12 This held its final session in 2006, when it was dissolved at the time that the UN Human Rights Council replaced the Commission on Human Rights.
13 Whitaker, 1982.
14 See ILO Committee of Experts on the Application of Conventions and Recommendations, 1979.
15 Article 39 of the Convention on the Rights of the Child (1989) requires states to "take all appropriate measures to promote physical and psychological recovery and social reintegration of a child victim of . . . any form of neglect, exploitation, or abuse". Article 6 of the UN Trafficking Protocol, concerning the protection of victims of trafficking in persons, stipulates only that "Each State Party *shall consider* implementing measures to provide for the physical, psychological and social recovery of victims of trafficking in persons" (emphasis added), and does not make assistance measures mandatory.
16 The Forced Labour Protocol still notes that a state's "national circumstances" may be taken into account in meeting its obligations under Article 9. By February 2017 the Protocol was in force in four countries and was scheduled to come into force in seven others later in 2017.
17 Article 7(2) of the Rome Statute defined 'enslavement' as "the exercise of any or all of the powers attaching to the right of ownership over a person and includes the exercise of such power in the course of trafficking in persons, in particular women and children."
18 Writ Petition No. 2135 of 1982 (Indiankanoon.org, 2017). 'Bandhua Mukti Morcha' means 'Bonded Liberation Front'.
19 *Darshan Masih alias Rehmatay and others v The State* (1989).
20 International Criminal Tribunal for the Former Yugoslavia, 2001; International Criminal Tribunal for the Former Yugoslavia, 2002.
21 *Siliadin v France* (2005).
22 *Prosecutor v Sesay, Kallon and Gbao* (2009).
23 *Hadijatou Mani Koraou v Niger* (2008).
24 *Rantsev v Cyprus and Russia* (2009).
25 Like Article 4 of the Universal Declaration, Article 4 of the European Convention does not include an explicit reference to human trafficking.
26 Bhoola (2017).
27 *Workers of the Green Brazil Ranch v Brazil* (*Caso Trabajadores de la Hacienda Brasil Verde Vs. Brasil*) (2016).
28 Bhoola (2016).

References

Allain, J. (2008). *The Slavery Conventions: The Travaux Préparatoires of the 1926 League of Nations Convention and the 1956 United Nations Convention*. The Hague: Martinus Nijhoff.

Bandhua Mukti Morcha vs Union of India & Others [1984] SCR (2) 67 (India Supreme Court). [online] Available at: http://indiankanoon.org/doc/595099/ [Accessed 22 Dec. 2015].

Barcelona Traction, Light and Power Co, Ltd. (Belgium v. Spain) [1971] (International Court of Justice).

Bhoola, U. (2016). *Report of the Special Rapporteur on contemporary forms of slavery, including its causes and consequences.* UN document A/HRC/33/46 of 4 July 2016. Geneva: United Nations.

Bhoola, U. (2017). *Report of the Special Rapporteur on Contemporary Forms of Slavery, Including Its Causes and Consequences.* UN document A/HRC/36/43 of 2 August 2017. Geneva: United Nations.

Darshan Masih alias Rehmatay and others v. The State [1989] PLD 1990 SC 513 (Pakistan Supreme Court).Global Alliance Against Traffic in Women. (2016). *Brazil Responsible for Contemporary Slavery and Trafficking of Workers on Haciendas.* [online] Available at: http://gaatw.org/e-bulletin/attachments/Brazil%20responsible%20for%20contemporary%20slavery%20and%20trafficking.pdf [Accessed 12 Feb. 2017].

Hadijatou Mani Koraou v. la République du Niger [2008]. Economic Community of West African States (ECOWAS) Court of Justice. Arrêt No. ECW/CCJ/JUD/06/08 du 27 octobre 2008 (Judgment No. ECW/CCJ/JUD/06/08 of 27 October 2008). [online] Available at: www.juricaf.org/arret/CEDEAO-COURDEJUSTICE-20081027-ECWCCJJUD0608 [Accessed 8 Feb. 2016]; unofficial English translation at www.unodc.org/res/cld/case-law-doc/traffickingpersonscrimetype/ner/2008/h_m__v__republic_of_niger_html/Hadijatou_Mani_v._Republic_of_Niger_Community_Court_of_Justice_Unofficial_English_translation.pdf

International Criminal Tribunal for the Former Yugoslavia. (2001). *Prosecutor v. Dragoljub Kunarac, Radomir Kovac and Zoran Vukovic, IT-96–23 and IT-96–23/1, Judgement of 22 February 2001.* [online] Available at: www.icty.org/x/cases/kunarac/tjug/en/kun-tj010222e.pdf [Accessed 5 Jan. 2016].

International Criminal Tribunal for the Former Yugoslavia. (2002). *Prosecutor v. Dragoljub Kunarac, Radomir Kovac and Zoran Vukovic, IT-96–23 and IT-96–23/1, Judgement of 12 June 2002.* [online] Available at: www.icty.org/x/cases/kunarac/acjug/en/kun-aj020612e.pdf [Accessed 5 Jan. 2016].

International Labour Organization (ILO). (1998). *Report of the Commission of Inquiry Appointed Under Article 26 of the Constitution of the ILO to Examine the Observance by Myanmar of the Forced Labour Convention, 1930 (No. 29).* Geneva: International Labour Organization.

International Labour Organization (ILO) Committee of Experts on the Application of Conventions and Recommendations. (1979). *General Survey of the Reports relating to the Forced Labour Convention, 1930 (No. 29), and the Abolition of Forced Labour Convention, 1957 (No. 105).* Geneva: International Labour Organization.

Mair, L. (1969). *African Marriage and Social Change.* London: Frank Cass.

Rantsev v. Cyprus and Russia [2009]25965/04 (European Court of Human Rights).

Siliadin v. France [2005]73316/01 545 (European Court of Human Rights).

United Nations. (2000). *The Optional Protocol to the Convention on the Rights of the Child on Sale of Children, Child Prostitution and Child Pornography.* G.A. res. A/RES/54/263. Geneva: United Nations.

United Nations General Assembly. (1948). *Records of the 110th Meeting of the Third Committee of the United Nations General Assembly, 22 October 1948.* United Nations Official Document. [online] Available at: www.un.org/en/ga/search/view_doc.asp?symbol=A/C.3/SR.110 [Accessed 31 Dec. 2016].

United Nations General Assembly. (2000). *Protocol to Prevent, Suppress and Punish Trafficking in Persons, Especially Women and Children, Supplementing the UN Convention Against Transnational Organized Crime.* UN Doc A/55/383 of 2 November 2000. [online] Available at: https://treaties.un.org/doc/source/docs/A_55_383-E.pdf [Accessed 6 Sep. 2017].

Whitaker, B. (1982). *Updating of the Report on Slavery Submitted to the Sub-Commission in 1966: Report.* UN document E/CN.4/Sub.2/1982/20/Rev.1 of 7 July 1982. Geneva: United Nations.

Workers of the Green Brazil Ranch v Brazil (Caso Trabajadores de la Hacienda Brasil Verde Vs. Brasil) [2016] (Inter-American Court of Human Rights).

7 Article 5

No one shall be subjected to torture or to cruel, inhuman or degrading treatment or punishment

Carla Ferstman

Torture is the calculated infliction of severe pain or suffering for a specific purpose such as coercion, punishment, intimidation or discrimination. What makes torture so horrible is the intentional infliction of cruelty by the powerful – those with the power and responsibility to protect – against the powerless. Torture can forever change its victims; it causes shame and stigma and affects belief systems. In addition to the physical impacts, the practice typically results in long-term and often lifelong psychological consequences.

The right to be free from torture and other forms of cruel, inhuman or degrading treatment or punishment is reflected in Article 5 of the UDHR. It wasn't a particularly controversial article of the Declaration and was included in the earliest draft text, which set out that "No one shall be subjected to torture, or to any unusual punishment or indignity".[1] While the formulation evolved slightly during the drafting process,[2] the emphasis of the article remains unchanged from its initial conception. Charles Malik, the representative from Lebanon, underscored that it was felt that the

> attention of the world should be called to these inhuman acts. . . . [T]he time had come to explain to the world what we mean by torture, inhuman punishment and inhuman indignity. The basic idea was to explain in an international instrument that the conscience of mankind had been shocked by inhuman acts in Nazi Germany, and therefore a positive condemnatory article was needed.[3]

In the drafters' minds were the Nazi medical experiments in concentration camps.[4]

The Article 5 prohibition recognises the inherent and fundamental dignity of all persons, regardless of who they are, what they may be accused of and irrespective of the operating context. But the articles of the UDHR, including Article 5, are formulated vaguely. Indeed, the Declaration provides no definition of torture or of other forms of cruel, inhuman or degrading treatment or punishment, nor does it distinguish clearly between the rights and obligations which stem from such conduct, different from the later UN Convention Against Torture and Other Cruel, Inhuman or Degrading Treatment or Punishment.[5] Yet, the Convention Against Torture's later demarcations between torture and cruel, inhuman and degrading treatment or punishment (demarcations which themselves are still vague) have perhaps done a disservice to the progressive evolution of standards in this domain. A number of standards which apply to torture do not apply clearly in the Convention to other forms of prohibited ill-treatment,[6] and as will be described, some states have used those distinctions to carve out questionable areas of 'permissible' conduct. For instance, the Convention does not prohibit explicitly the refoulement of persons who face a real risk of cruel, inhuman or degrading treatment or punishment (as opposed to torture), nor does it contain an explicit requirement for states to criminalise cruel, inhuman or degrading treatment or punishment, to afford reparation or to outlaw confession evidence procured by such treatment (as opposed to torture). Nonetheless, for the most part the jurisprudence as well as the Committee Against Torture – the Convention's official interpretive body – have interpreted progressively states' obligations and have recognised that both torture and other forms of prohibited ill-treatment form part of a continuum of ill-treatment that states are obligated to prevent, prohibit and repair.[7]

The UDHR was clear in iterating the international community's abhorrence of torture and other forms of prohibited ill-treatment, though it did little to define those terms. To an extent this was a case of delegates operating under the assumption that all 'know what they meant', but also there was pressure not to over-complicate the Declaration with lengthy definitions that might impede consensus. The definition of torture had to wait for later standard-setting texts, though there continues to be wide debate about the precise contours of what distinguishes torture from other forms of cruel, inhuman or degrading treatment or punishment.

Defining torture post-UDHR

Following on from the Article 5 UDHR prohibition, the ban on torture and other prohibited ill-treatment has been incorporated into an array of human rights treaties and standard-setting texts, including Article 7 of the International Covenant on Civil and Political Rights,[8] Article 3 of the European Convention on Human Rights,[9] Article 5 of the American Convention on Human Rights,[10] Article 5 of the African Charter on Human and Peoples' Rights[11] and Article 8 of the Arab Charter on Human Rights.[12] It has also featured in specialist conventions and standard-setting texts dealing with children,[13] women,[14] persons with disabilities[15] and migrant workers.[16] The prohibition of torture and other ill-treatment has also been included in various international humanitarian law treaties, both for crimes occurring in international and non-international armed conflicts, as well as in international criminal law statutes. It is outlawed in the 1907 Hague Regulations respecting the Laws and Customs of War on Land.[17] Common Article 3 of the four Geneva Conventions of 1949 and various other provisions in those conventions prohibit cruel treatment and torture and outrages upon personal dignity, in particular humiliating and degrading treatment of civilians and persons *hors de combat*.[18] Torture is also outlawed in the two Additional Protocols.[19] In addition, torture or inhuman treatment and wilfully causing great suffering or serious injury to body or health constitute grave breaches of the Geneva Conventions.[20] Torture is also reflected as an underlying offence in the statutes of international and *ad hoc* or specialised criminal tribunals and the International Criminal Court.[21]

While the definition of torture had been considered in jurisprudence, in 1975, the UN General Assembly adopted the Declaration on the Protection of All Persons from Being Subjected to Torture and Other Cruel, Inhuman or Degrading Treatment or Punishment,[22] which was the first standard-setting text to set out in clear terms what torture means. It defined torture as,

> any act by which severe pain or suffering, whether physical or mental, is intentionally inflicted by or at the instigation of a public official on a person for such purposes as obtaining from him or a third person information or confession, punishing him for an act he has committed or is suspected of having committed, or intimidating him or other persons. It does not include pain or suffering arising only from, inherent in or incidental to, lawful sanctions to the extent consistent with the Standard Minimum Rules for the Treatment of Prisoners. Torture constitutes an aggravated and deliberate form of cruel, inhuman or degrading treatment or punishment.[23]

This was followed nine years later with the adoption of the UN Convention Against Torture and Other Cruel, Inhuman or Degrading Treatment or Punishment,[24] which has been ratified widely by states in all parts of the world. The Convention put in place a comprehensive framework to outlaw torture, including positive obligations on states parties to "take effective legislative, administrative, judicial and other measures to prevent acts of torture in any territory under its jurisdiction" (Article 2), an absolute prohibition on refoulement to torture (Article 3), detailed rules on investigations and prosecutions (Articles 4–9) and a clear requirement for states to afford a remedy, including compensation and rehabilitation (Article 14).

The Convention definition, set out in its Article 1,[25] differs from the earlier 1975 Declaration, in a number of important respects. First, the Convention definition is silent on the distinction between acts amounting to torture and acts which amount to other forms of prohibited ill-treatment, unlike the Declaration, which characterised torture as "an aggravated and deliberate form of cruel, inhuman or degrading treatment or punishment". There is debate about whether the differences between the different forms of ill-treatment stem from the threshold severity of pain and suffering, the requirement of a specific purpose for acts amounting to torture or some combination of the two.[26] Second, the Convention definition broadens the purposes of torture to include "any reason based on discrimination of any kind". Third, the Declaration clarifies that the exception for lawful sanctions must be limited to those sanctions that are consistent with the

Standard Minimum Rules for the Treatment of Prisoners, a clarification which is absent from the Convention definition. The definition of the Inter-American Convention to Prevent and Punish Torture[27] contains slight differences from the Declaration and UN Convention.

The definitions of torture appearing in the human rights treaties referred to earlier recognise that torture can be a discrete crime or one-off act causing severe pain or suffering. Those treaties do not enumerate a finite list of acts which may fall within the definition, owing perhaps to the truism that new and innovative forms of cruelty could always be dreamt up to avoid falling foul of an enumerated list of prohibited acts. Instead, the definitions set out the prohibition in broad terms, relying on the nature, purpose and severity of the treatment applied, which "will depend on the circumstances of the case, such as the duration of the treatment, its physical or mental effects and, in some cases, the sex, age and state of health of the victim, etc."[28] It has also been recognised that the classification of a particular act as ill-treatment (as opposed to torture) might change with the times, owing to "the increasingly high standard being required in the area of the protection of human rights and fundamental liberties correspondingly and inevitably requires greater firmness in assessing breaches of the fundamental values of democratic societies".[29]

Under human rights law, torture must take place by or at the instigation of or consent or acquiescence of public officials. This differs from how torture is understood when it constitutes one of the underlying offences for a war crime, a crime against humanity and/or genocide. Torture can constitute a crime against humanity if it is perpetrated as part of a widespread or systematic practice or attack on a population, which is a requirement for all crimes against humanity. It can constitute a war crime in both international and non-international armed conflicts when it is perpetrated on persons protected under one or more of the Geneva Conventions. Torture can also constitute genocide in certain circumstances. The ICC Statute provides that causing serious bodily or mental harm to members of an ethnical, racial or religious group as such, committed with intent to destroy, in whole or in part, that group, satisfies the definition of the crime of genocide.[30] This draws from the International Criminal Tribunal for Rwanda's *Akayesu* judgement, in which the Trial Chamber noted, in respect of the sexual violence perpetrated by the accused, that "[s]exual violence was a step in the process of destruction of the Tutsi group – destruction of the spirit, of the will to live, and of life itself".[31] When torture operates as one of those underlying offences, the definition diverges from the one applicable to a discrete crime of torture, in that there is no need for the involvement of a public official.[32] What is important is the nature of the act committed rather than the status of the person who committed it. This difference has been justified on the basis of the need to take 'into account the specificities of international humanitarian law'.[33] Another divergence applies specifically to the ICC Statute where the underlying offence of torture as a crime against humanity does not require a specific purpose.[34]

The international criminal law understanding that acts of torture could be perpetrated by persons other than state actors was an important broadening of the circumstances in which torture could take place and coincided with a widening of the understanding of where torture could take place (not only in a centre of detention), who could be the victims (not only male crime suspects). But there were additional factors at play which contributed to this wider understanding. Increasingly, human rights jurisprudence began to take cognisance of the horrific impacts of crimes perpetrated in the private sphere, and articulated with increased clarity the principle of due diligence – that states were not only obligated to prohibit their own officials from perpetrating acts which violated individuals' rights, but they were obliged equally to take positive steps, to exercise due diligence – to prevent violence and other abuses perpetrated by other actors. Where they failed to do so, they would bear state responsibility for this failure and the resulting harm caused to the victims. Thus in the *El Masri* case, which concerned Macedonia's failure to protect El Masri from extraordinary rendition and torture carried out mainly by American CIA agents, the European Court Grand Chamber determined that a state is obliged to take measures to ensure that individuals within its jurisdiction are not tortured, and must take measures to prevent a risk of ill-treatment about which it knew or should have known.[35]

The absolute nature of the prohibition of torture and state obfuscations

Torture has a non-derogable status under human rights law, which means that there can be no circumstances in which states may torture or cause torture to happen. Even during times of war or civil unrest, or in the context of a terrorist threat or other recognised threats to a nation, which may in certain circumstances justify the suspension or limitation of other human rights, the prohibition of torture cannot be suspended.[36] It is immaterial if the person is a non-citizen, illegal migrant, terror suspect, convicted criminal or person suspected to have vital information about planned crimes. No person can be tortured, nor can the prohibition of torture be balanced against other state interests, such as the need to protect national security or to locate evidence that may help protect others.

But there is a conundrum with this absolute prohibition. Just about all states reject torture, yet the practice continues. This incongruity is able to persist because of a series of justifications used by several states and the liberal notion of the need to 'balance' competing interests which has fed into those justifications. When one of the interests to be balanced – protection against terrorism – is explained as the absolute priority, the other interests sought to be protected – human rights and the inherent dignity of the individual – pale by comparison, certainly in the eyes of the public, even though the phrases 'absolute prohibition' and 'non-derogable rights' are ill-suited to such balancing. As Senator Dick Marty has said in the context of his review of the practice of extraordinary rendition,

> [b]y characterising the people held in secret detention as "different" from us – not as humans, but as ghosts, aliens or terrorists – the US Government tries to lead us into the trap of thinking they are not like us, they are not subjects of the law, therefore their human rights do not deserve protection.[37]

Torture has been re-defined by some states to cover only a narrow subset of the behaviour that the accepted definitions of torture cover, or has been re-cast with other less offensive words – 'enhanced interrogation techniques', 'moderate physical pressure', 'water-boarding'. For instance, in a memo issued on 1 August 2002,[38] the US Office of Legal Counsel interpreted "severe physical or mental pain" to encompass only "extreme acts . . . akin to that which accompanies serious physical injury, such as death or organ failure".[39] The memorandum further provided that "even if an interrogation method might violate Section 2340A . . ., necessity or self-defence could provide justifications that would eliminate any criminal liability".[40] The memorandum was eventually withdrawn.

Some states have sought to argue before courts that exceptions should be introduced in cases involving terror suspects to balance the risk of ill-treatment such persons could face with the need to ensure the safety and security of innocent civilians, sometimes using illusory 'ticking bomb' scenarios.[41] Some have argued that the status of the individuals put them outside the purview of the law,[42] whereas others have sought to introduce exceptions to certain aspects of the torture prohibition such as the non-refoulement prohibition when national security considerations are at issue.[43] In the face of such arguments, most courts have remained resolute: as the European Court of Human Rights has noted,

> The Court is well aware of the immense difficulties faced by States in modern times in protecting their communities from terrorist violence. However, even in these circumstances, the Convention prohibits in absolute terms torture or inhuman or degrading treatment or punishment, irrespective of the victim's conduct.[44]

In other circumstances, courts have been more malleable. Certain states have sought to agree memorandums of understanding with states known to regularly resort to torture – that they will not resort to torturing particular individuals, in order to reduce or minimise what would otherwise be an unacceptably high risk that persons transferred to such countries would be subjected to torture in contravention of the principle of non-refoulement. For the most part, courts have been prepared to assess the merits of such memorandums on a case-by-case basis.[45] This in and of itself provides some cover and justification for this questionable practice.

The obligation to investigate and prosecute torture

States are required to investigate all acts of torture. Investigations must be prompt and carried out impartially by competent authorities. The obligation to investigate torture is not displaced when the acts took place outside of the state's territorial jurisdiction in a difficult security environment. Amnesties and certain other procedural bars are inconsistent with the obligation to investigate torture. In *Barrios Altos*, the Inter-American Court of Human Rights determined that the Peruvian amnesty law violated the right to judicial protection and was manifestly incompatible with the American Convention.[46] Similarly, the UN Human Rights

Committee determined that Uruguay's amnesty law violated the International Covenant on Civil and Political Rights because it prevented "the possibility of investigation into past human rights abuses and thus preventing the state from discharging its responsibility to provide effective remedies".[47]

Because of the international character of the prohibition of torture, it has been recognised in Article 5(2) of the UN Convention Against Torture that states are obligated to "take such measures as may be necessary to establish its jurisdiction over such offences in cases where the alleged offender is present in any territory under its jurisdiction and it does not extradite him". This article of the convention is designed to outlaw safe havens for alleged torturers. Extraterritorial torture convictions have been entered, for instance, in France,[48] Germany,[49] the Netherlands,[50] the US[51] and the UK.[52] In the application of Article 5(2), the UK Law Lords determined that a former head of state has no immunity for torture.[53] The International Court of Justice applied Article 5(2) in a case relating to former President of Chad, Hissène Habré. It held that Senegal must immediately take the necessary measures to submit the case "to its competent authorities for the purpose of prosecution, if it does not extradite him".[54] The UN Committee Against Torture had previously determined that Senegal violated Article 5(2) UNCAT because a reasonable time frame had been considerably exceeded.[55] Following these and other efforts, Senegal has embarked on a process to try Habré and has established Extraordinary African Chambers for that purpose.[56] In 2014, the South African Constitutional Court recognised that police were obligated to investigate torture allegedly carried out in Zimbabwe, even if the suspects were outside the country during the investigation stage.[57] The Constitutional Court considered that South Africa should only investigate international crimes committed abroad if the state with jurisdiction is unwilling or unable to prosecute.

The inadmissibility of evidence obtained by torture

Article 15 of the UN Convention Against Torture provides that statements extracted by torture cannot be used in any proceedings against the torture victim or anyone else except a person accused of torture as evidence the statement was made. The rationale for this prohibition is to dis-incentivise law enforcement officials from resorting to torture to secure confessions. Also, the prohibition recognises that the introduction of torture evidence into legal proceedings would taint those proceedings: "Any other conclusion would only serve to legitimate indirectly the sort of morally reprehensible conduct which the authors of Article 3 of the Convention sought to proscribe".[58]

Reparations for torture survivors

Article 14 of the UN Convention Against Torture recognises that survivors of torture are entitled to an "enforceable right to fair and adequate compensation, including the means for as full rehabilitation as possible". The Committee

Against Torture has recently issued a General Comment on Article 14, which underscores the importance of reparations and clarifies the nature and extent of states' obligations, in line with the Committee's own jurisprudence and other relevant standards which had been adopted since the coming into force of the Convention. The state is also required to take measures to prevent recurrence.

The force of the torture prohibition 70 years after the UDHR was adopted

Already in 1948, the prohibition against torture was an important principle upon which there was wide agreement amongst states. Article 5 was an important articulation of this resolve, and can be seen as the first in a series of important steps that have been taken to clarify the content of the prohibition and to develop the tools to see it implemented across the globe. The fact that torture and other cruel, inhuman and degrading treatment and punishment continue to be used to this day underscores the challenges we continue to face to ensure respect for fundamental rights and the need to continually affirm these basic but crucial principles.

Notes

1 Commission on Human Rights, 1947.
2 See, e.g., Commission on Human Rights, 1948i, draft Article 7: 'No one shall be subjected to torture or to cruel or inhuman punishment or to cruel or inhuman indignity'; Commission on Human Rights, 1948ii, draft Article 8(3): 'No one shall be subjected to torture, or to cruel or inhuman punishment or indignity'; Commission on Human Rights, 1948iii, Draft International Declaration of Human Rights, draft Article 4(2): 'No one shall be subjected to torture or to cruel, inhuman or degrading treatment or punishment.'
3 Commission on Human Rights, 1948iv, 3, 10 May 1948.
4 Morsink, 1997: 42–43.
5 Adopted 10 December 1984, entered into force 26 June 1987.
6 This is a problem that is particular to the UN Convention Against Torture. Most other international and regional treaties which prohibit torture, such as the International Covenant on Civil and Political Rights Article 7 (adopted 16 December 1966, entered into force 23 March 1976) and the European Convention on Human Rights Article 3 (adopted 4 November 1950, entered into force 3 September 1953), address simultaneously torture and other forms of prohibited ill-treatment.
7 See, e.g., UN Committee against Torture, 2012, para 1.
8 Adopted 16 December 1966, entered into force 23 March 1976.
9 Council of Europe, Convention for the Protection of Human Rights and Fundamental Freedoms (adopted 4 November 1950, entered into force 3 September 1953), article 3.
10 Adopted 22 November 1969, entered into force 18 July 1978, article 5.
11 Adopted 27 June 1981, entered into force 21 October 1986, article 5.
12 Adopted 22 May 2004, entered into force 15 March 2008.
13 Article 37(a) Convention on the Rights of the Child (adopted 20 November 1989, entered into force 2 September 1990).

14 Article 3(h) Declaration on the Elimination of Violence against Women, Proclaimed by General Assembly resolution 48/104 of 20 December 1993.
15 Article 15, Convention on the Rights of Persons with Disabilities (adopted on 13 December 2006, entered into force on 3 May 2008).
16 Article 10, International Convention on the Protection of the Rights of All Migrant Workers and Members of Their Families (adopted 18 December 1990, entered into force 1 July 2003).
17 Convention (IV) respecting the Laws and Customs of War on Land and its annex: Regulations concerning the Laws and Customs of War on Land (adopted 18 October 1907, entered into force 26 January 1910), 36 Stat.2207, Regulations Article 4.
18 Convention (I) for the Amelioration of the Condition of the Wounded and Sick in Armed Forces in the Field (adopted 12 August 1949, entered into force 21 October 1950) (GC1) Art. 12(2); Convention (II) for the Amelioration of the Condition of Wounded, Sick and Shipwrecked Members of Armed Forces at Sea (adopted 12 August 1949, entered into force 21 October 1950) (GC2) Art. 12(2); Convention (III) relative to the Treatment of Prisoners of War (adopted 12 August 1949, entered into force 21 October 1950) (GC3) Arts. 13, 17(4), 87(3), 89; Convention (IV) relative to the Protection of Civilian Persons in Time of War (adopted 12 August 1949, entered into force 21 October 1950) (GC4) Arts. 27, 32.
19 Protocol Additional to the Geneva Conventions of 12 August 1949, and relating to the Protection of Victims of International Armed Conflicts (adopted 8 June 1977, entered into force 7 December 1978) (Protocol I) Art. 75(2); Protocol Additional to the Geneva Conventions of 12 August 1949, and relating to the Protection of Victims of Non-International Armed Conflicts (adopted 8 June 1977, entered into force 7 December 1978) (Protocol II) Art. 4(2).
20 GCl Art. 50; GC2 Art. 51; GC3 Art. 130; GC4 Art. 147; Protocol I Art. 11.
21 E.g., Rome Statute of the International Criminal Court (adopted 17 July 1998, entered into force 1 July 2002) Arts. 7(1)(f); 8(2)(a)(ii) and 8(2)(c)(i).
22 Adopted by General Assembly resolution 3452 (XXX) of 9 December 1975.
23 Article 1(1), (2).
24 (adopted 10 December 1984, entered into force 26 June 1987).
25 Article 1(1) provides: "For the purposes of this Convention, the term 'torture' means any act by which severe pain or suffering, whether physical or mental, is intentionally inflicted on a person for such purposes as obtaining from him or a third person information or a confession, punishing him for an act he or a third person has committed or is suspected of having committed, or intimidating or coercing him or a third person, or for any reason based on discrimination of any kind, when such pain or suffering is inflicted by or at the instigation of or with the consent or acquiescence of a public official or other person acting in an official capacity. It does not include pain or suffering arising only from, inherent in or incidental to lawful sanctions."
26 Considered in Rodley and Pollard, 2011, 98–100, 143–144.
27 (Adopted 9 December 1985, entered into force 28 February 1987). Article 2 provides: "For the purposes of this Convention, torture shall be understood to be any act intentionally performed whereby physical or mental pain or suffering is inflicted on a person for purposes of criminal investigation, as a means of intimidation, as personal punishment, as a preventive measure, as a penalty, or for any other purpose. Torture shall also be understood to be the use of methods upon a person intended to obliterate the personality of the victim or to diminish his physical or mental capacities, even if they do not cause physical pain or mental anguish.

The concept of torture shall not include physical or mental pain or suffering that is inherent in or solely the consequence of lawful measures, provided that they do not include the performance of the acts or use of the methods referred to in this article."

28 Selmouni v France (1999), para. 100.
29 Ibid, para 101.
30 Article 6(b) ICC Statute.
31 Prosecutor v Akayesu (1998), para. 732.
32 Prosecutor v Kunarac et al. (2001), paras. 495–496; Prosecutor v Kunarac et al. (2002), para.148; Prosecutor v Semanza (2003), paras. 342–343.
33 Prosecutor v Kunarac et al. (2001), para. 459.
34 Article 7(1)(f) ICC Statute.
35 El-Masri v The Former Yugoslav Republic Of Macedonia (2012), paras. 218–221.
36 Art. 4 ICCPR; Art. 15 ECHR; Art. 27 ACHR.
37 Committee on Legal Affairs and Human Rights, 2007, 36 at para. 234.
38 Memorandum from J. S. Bybee, Asst. Attorney-General, Office of Legal Counsel, to A. R. Gonzales, Counsel to the President, Re: Standards of Conduct for Interrogation under 18 U.S.C. $$ 2340–2340A (1 Aug. 2002), 46.
39 Ibid.
40 Ibid, 46.
41 Felner, 2005: 28–43.
42 *Hamdan v Rumsfeld* (2006).
43 *Chahal v United Kingdom* (1996); *Saadi v Italy* (2008).
44 *Chahal v United Kingdom* (1996).
45 *Othman (Abu Qatada) v the United Kingdom* (2012).
46 *Chumbipuma Aguirre et al. v Peru* (The Barrios Altos Case) (2001), paras. 41–44.
47 Human Rights Council, 1994, para 12.
48 *Prosecutor v Ely Ould Dah* (2002).
49 *Prosecutor v Maksim Sokolovic* (2001).
50 *Prosecutor-General of the Supreme Court v Désiré Bouterse* (2001); *Public Prosecutor v Joseph Mpambara* (2011); *Public Prosecutor v Sebastien Nzapali* (2004).
51 *United States v Roy Belfast* a.k.a. Charles 'Chuckie' Taylor, Jr. (2010).
52 *Regina v Faryadi Sarwar Zardad* (2005).
53 UK Parliament. House of Lords, 1999.
54 International Court of Justice, 2017, paras. 118–119.
55 Human Rights Council, 2006, para 9.5.
56 See Chambresafricaines.org, 2017.
57 *National Commissioner of the South African Police Service v Southern African Human Rights Litigation Centre and Another* (2014).
58 *Jalloh v Germany* (2006), para. 105. See also *Gäfgen v Germany* (2010), paras. 103–109.

References

Chahal v United Kingdom [1996] Application no. 22414/93 (European Court of Human Rights).

Chambresafricaines.org. (2017). *Chambres Africaines Extraordinaires.* [online] Available at: www.chambresafricaines.org/ [Accessed 14 Dec. 2017].

Chumbipuma Aguirre et al. v Peru (The Barrios Altos Case) [2001] Series C No. 75 (IACtHR).

Commission on Human Rights. (1947). *Draft Outline of International Bill of Rights.* UN Doc E/CN.4/AC.1/3. Geneva: United Nations.

Commission on Human Rights. (1948i). *Drafting Committee, Second Session.* UN Doc E/CN.4/AC.1/19. Geneva: United Nations.
Commission on Human Rights. (1948ii). *Drafting Committee, Second Session.* UN Doc E/CN.4/95. Geneva: United Nations.
Commission on Human Rights. (1948iii). *Drafting Committee, Second Session.* UN Doc E/CN.4/AC.1/SR.23. Geneva: United Nations.
Commission on Human Rights. (1948iv). *Report of the Third Session, 28 May–18 June 1948.* UN Doc E/800, 28 June 1948. Geneva: United Nations.
Committee on Legal Affairs and Human Rights. (2007). *Secret Detentions and Illegal Transfers of Detainees Involving Council of Europe Member States: Second Report, Explanatory Memorandum.* Strasbourg: Council of Europe.
El-Masri v The Former Yugoslav Republic Of Macedonia [2012] Application no. 39630/09 (European Court Grand Chamber).
Felner, E. (2005). Torture and Terrorism: Painful Lessons from Israel. In: K. Roth, M. Worden and A. Bernstein, eds., *Torture Does It Make Us Safer? Is It Ever OK? A Human Rights Perspective.* New York: The New York Press.
Gäfgen v Germany [2010] App. No. 22978/05 (European Court of Human Rights, Grand Chamber).
Hamdan v Rumsfeld [2006] 548 U.S. 557 (US Supreme Court).
Human Rights Council. (1994). *Rodríguez v Uruguay, Communication No. 322/1988.* UN Doc CCPR/C/51/D/322/1988. Geneva: United Nations.
Human Rights Council. (2006). *Suleymane Guengueng et al. v Senegal, Communication No. 181/2001.* UN Doc CAT/C/36/D/181/2001. Geneva: United Nations.
International Court of Justice. (2017). *Questions Relating to the Obligation to Prosecute or Extradite (Belgium v Senegal).* Judgment, 20 July 2012, ICJ Reports 2012. The Hague: International Court of Justice.
Jalloh v Germany [2006] App. No. 54810/00 (European Court of Human Rights, Grand Chamber).
Morsink, J. (1997). *The Universal Declaration of Human Rights: Origins, Drafting, and Intent.* Philadelphia: University of Pennsylvania Press.
National Commissioner of the South African Police Service v Southern African Human Rights Litigation Centre and Another [2014] No. CCT 02/14 [2014] ZACC 30 (South African Constitutional Court).
Othman (Abu Qatada) v the United Kingdom [2012] Application no. 8139/09 (European Court of Human Rights).
Prosecutor v Akayesu [1998] ICTR-96-94-T (ICTR).
Prosecutor v Kunarac et al. [2001] IT-96-23-T & IT-96-23/I-T (ICTY, Trial Chamber).
Prosecutor v Ely Ould Dah [2002] No. 02-85379 (French Cour de cassation, chambre criminelle).
Prosecutor v Kunarac et al. [2002] IT-96-23&23/1 (ICTY, Appeals Chamber).
Prosecutor v Maksim Sokolovic [2001] 3 StR 372/00, 3 StR 244/00 (Germany Federal Supreme Court).
Prosecutor v Semanza [2003] ICTR-97-20 (ICTR, Trial Chamber).
Prosecutor-General of the Supreme Court v Désiré Bouterse [2001] No. LJN: AB1471 (Netherlands Supreme Court).
Public Prosecutor v Joseph Mpambara [2011] No. 22-002613-09 (ECLI:NL:GHSGR:2011:BR0686) (Court of Appeal of The Hague).

Public Prosecutor v Sebastien Nzapali [2004] LJN: AO7178 (Rotterdam District Court).

Regina v Faryadi Sarwar Zardad [2005] No. T2203 7676 (UK Central Criminal Court).

Rodley, N. and Pollard, M. (2011). *The Treatment of Prisoners under International Law*. 3rd ed. Oxford: Oxford University Press.

Saadi v Italy [2008] Application no. 37201/06 (European Court of Human Rights).

Selmouni v France [1999] Application no. 25803/94 (European Court of Human Rights, Grand Chamber).

UK Parliament. House of Lords (1999) *Commissioner of Police for the Metropolis and Others, Ex Parte Pinochet*. (HL 1998–1999 (17)). London: The Stationary Office.

UN Committee Against Torture (2012). *General Comment No. 3 (2012): Implementation of Article 14 by States Parties.* UN Doc CAT/C/GC/3. Geneva: United Nations.

United States v Roy Belfast a.k.a. Charles 'Chuckie' Taylor, Jr. [2010]11th Cir. No. 09–10461 (US Court of Appeals).

8 Holocaust property theft and restitution

The right to an effective remedy under Article 8 of the Universal Declaration of Human Rights

Michael J. Bazyler and Kristen L. Nelson

Introduction

Article 8 of the UDHR provides that "Everyone has the right to an effective remedy by competent national tribunals for acts violating the fundamental rights granted him by the constitution or by law". The rationale behind introducing a general procedural protection for remedies was to protect "against abuses by the authorities".[1] Johannes Morsink links this need for protection back to the legal barbarism of Nazi Germany:

> The Reichstag Fire Decree, which Hitler announced after the Reichstag went up in flames, "annulled almost all the basic rights guaranteed by the [Weimar] constitution." Ernest Huber, the Nazi theoretician, concluded from this that "the constitution of the Nationalistic Reich is therefore not based on a system of inborn and inalienable rights of the individual [that might] . . . limit and hamper the leadership of the Reich". Since there no longer were any standards that fell "outside the realm of the state and which must be respected by the state", officials could not [be] and were not held accountable, he said [ ]. The result was a totalitarian police state.[2]

This chapter explores how the UDHR's 'effective remedy' norm was partially inspired by the mass theft of World War II and how a panoply of remedies came into being in the immediate post-war era, often independent of Article 8 of the UDHR, but not necessarily in contradiction to it. It also examines other so-called soft-law remedies dealing with property restitution that developed in the last quarter-century to better explain what an effective remedy means in the context of human rights law, and in particular, Holocaust-era immovable property restitution, including land, houses, apartments, commercial buildings and businesses. Last, it analyses how in practice the principle of an effective remedy, with the goal of full reparation,[3] has often been displaced by what other scholars have coined 'remedial shortfall'. Less than full reparative measures are meant to provide a measure of justice in lieu of none at all, and often take the form of mass claim or bulk settlement agreements and *ex gratia* payment schemes.

Early remedies and the drafting of the UDHR

Pre–World War II notions of remedy and restitution

Remedies for property-related violations date back to Roman law and so were not new legal concepts in the post–World War II period.[4] Particularised references to reparation by a government to its own citizens have also been traced to treaties as far back as the 1648 Treaty of Westphalia.[5]

If the principle of reparation was an understood and agreed-upon concept before World War II, then the prevailing understanding as to the scope of reparations is chiefly where principle and practice have diverged. The Permanent Court of International Justice articulated the scope of restitution in the Chorzów Factory case in 1928. It held that the appropriate remedy was return to the *status quo ante*, that "reparation must, as far as possible, wipe out all consequences of the illegal act and reestablish the situation which would, in all probability, have existed if that act had not been committed".[6] Thus, what was taken must be returned and if it cannot be returned, full compensation must be paid.[7] As we will see, this notion of full restitution of stolen property was also the aspiration guiding early post–World War II property restitution, though it never came close to being fulfilled.

World War II statements on remedy and reparation

Historian Peter Hayes describes plunder of property during World War II as:

> robbery on a scale scarcely seen in European history, the more so because the plunder of the Jews outside of Germany during World War II took place alongside the looting of even greater quantities of precious metals, stocks and bonds, cash, art works, enterprises, real estate, and labor from non-Jewish sources in the occupied countries.[8]

With regard to theft of Jewish property, the process was often quite orderly and covered by a legal veneer. Adolf Eichmann's thievery operation was described by Franz Meyer during the Eichmann trial in 1961:

> It was like a flour mill connected to some bakery. You put in at the one end a Jew who still has capital and has, let us say, a factory or a shop or an account in a bank, and he passes through the entire building from counter to counter, from office to office – he comes out at the other end, he has no money, he has no rights, only a passport in which is written: You must leave this country within two weeks: if you fail to do so, you will go to a concentration camp.[9]

European and other Allied governments did not stand idly by during this grand theft. Even as the war raged on, they created a framework for property restitution in anticipation of German defeat. In 1943, 17 governments endorsed the London Declaration,[10] whereby each reserved the right to declare invalid property transfers made during the war. Governments-in-exile in London during the war, including Belgium, Luxembourg, the Netherlands, Norway and Poland, also issued decrees and other legal pronouncements annulling German laws that confiscated property.

Armistice agreements signed between the Allied powers and defeated Axis states such as Romania included requirements that the country would "repeal all discriminatory legislation and restrictions imposed thereunder".[11] This provision was particularly relevant for post-war restitution in Romania because Romania's war-time Antonescu regime had confiscated Jewish urban and rural property through a series of racially discriminatory laws.[12]

The Paris Peace Treaties between the Allied powers and the other defeated Axis states – including Bulgaria, Finland, Hungary and Italy – were also specific in terms of reparations requirements. The Treaty of Peace with Hungary required property taken from the United Nations[13] either to be returned to the owner or, if it could not be returned, then the Hungarian government would be obliged to pay the owner two-thirds compensation. In addition, property confiscated "on account of the racial origin or religion of such persons" was to be restored or, when that was not possible, "fair compensation" was required.[14]

Jewish leaders in the US and Mandate Palestine were also concerned with the issue, and "[i]n 1944, the World Jewish Congress called for 'uniform laws' [on restitution] to be enacted 'in all territories formerly occupied, annexed, dominated, or influenced by Axis powers'."[15]

In sum, the right to property restitution as a remedy for looting and confiscation was repeatedly recognised and confirmed both during the waning years of World War II and thereafter.

Laws and remedies in the immediate post-war period

The first period of property restitution took place in the immediate post-war years. This period was driven by the Allied efforts to recover and return assets stolen by the Nazis.[16] Throughout formerly occupied Europe, restitution measures were broadly enacted. Yet, the amount compensated or returned was rarely of equivalent value to what had been taken.[17]

The chief focus of the Allies was what to do with the vast amounts of stolen property located within defeated Germany. The Allied powers divided the country into four zones of occupation. Efforts to enact a restitution law that applied to all four zones of occupation failed. The result was that in 1947 Military Government Law No. 59 on Restitution of Identifiable Property was enacted in the US zone of occupation.[18] It permitted restitution claims from any person, regardless of citizenship, whose identifiable, movable and immovable, private and communal property was confiscated between 30 January 1933 and 8 May 1945 for reasons of race, religion, nationality, ideology or political opposition to National Socialism.[19] The law required restitution of property irrespective of whether it was in the hands of the state or third parties.

Other liberated countries in Western Europe enacted legislation that nullified property transfers prescribed by German law or the laws of occupying authorities. However, in these early post-war years, there were large carve-outs in the legislation. Some laws only applied to citizens of the respective countries, capped recovery amounts or came with onerous requirements to get the property back.[20] Halik Kochanski describes the uncertain situation facing Jews returning to Poland:

> There were numerous instances of anti-semitism among the Polish population directed towards survivors, which stemmed from a number of factors. There was a severe shortage of housing because of the damage caused by war, and some of the reluctance of the Gentile Poles to vacate Jewish homes had its roots not in anti-Semitism but in a simple fear of homelessness. Indeed, the state passed a series of decrees during 1945, which placed 'abandoned and formerly German properties' under state administration, but many of these 'abandoned' properties had been owned by Jews, who faced the prospect of court action against the state to reclaim them.[21]

For many survivors, especially Jewish survivors returning from camps, the hurdles attendant to recovering property compounded tragedy with tragedy, and ultimately the law failed them.

Administrative and judicial processes set up for the return of property were often complex and created without any acknowledgement of the country's own participation in the confiscation in the first place.

In France, it was not until 1995 when French President Jacque Chirac declared "the criminal folly of the occupiers was seconded by the French, by the French state", that a real reckoning with the past began to occur in France.[22] The process of national reflection has continued across Europe, and in July 2017, French President Emmanuel Macron commemorated the 75th anniversary of the roundup of 13,000 Jews at the Paris stadium *Vélodrome d'Hiver* by stating "It was indeed France that organized" the roundup. "[N]ot a single German" was directly involved.[23]

Between 1997 and 2000, a French government-sponsored fact-finding commission was established to examine the various forms of robbery committed on its Jewish populace 60 years prior. The investigation was informally known as the 'Mátteoli Commission' after the chairperson, the former cabinet minister and Resistance fighter Jean Mátteoli. The commission found that every segment of the French economy, except for agriculture, fishing, mining and forestry, in which few Jews were involved, had engaged in thievery.[24] The commission also examined the extent of immediate post-war restitution, and Mátteoli, in his foreword to the final commission report, noted that "the victims did not always receive all of their property nor enjoy all the compensation to which they were entitled".[25]

The liberated countries of Eastern Europe also enacted restitution legislation. In fact, many were compelled to do so by the terms of their respective armistice agreements or treaties of peace.[26] However, the restitution process in Eastern Europe came to a halt with the onset of Soviet-style Communism. The new Soviet-dominated people's republics nationalised property, this time targeting private property of *all* persons and not just particular groups. With few exceptions, private property owners were not compensated for property nationalised by the Communist authorities. With the fall of the Berlin Wall, the new post-Communist regimes of Eastern Europe resumed the process that had begun more than 50 years earlier. But the half-century delay meant that these countries were playing catch-up to their European Union sister states that for the most part had completed restitution of immovable Nazi-confiscated property by the 1950s.

Understanding the right to an effective remedy for Holocaust-era immovable property reparations through recent soft-law measures

Since World War II, the vehicles for immovable property restitution have taken the form of remedies not only before Article 8's plainly prescribed "competent national tribunals", but also before administrative bodies and through compensation treaties, bulk settlements and *ad hoc* schemes with *ex gratia* payments. This begs the question: for individuals whose property was confiscated during the Holocaust (or for that matter any atrocity with attendant property theft), can the remedy still be considered effective even if it is not issued by a "competent national tribunal"? And if the property is not returned *in rem*, or if compensation is not made in full, can this remedy be considered effective under Article 8? To answer these questions, recent 'soft law' roadmaps are an illuminating place to begin.

The UN basic principles and guidelines

More than half a century after Article 8 of the UDHR was agreed, renewed interest appeared in defining standards for an effective remedy. Sonja Starr describes the 1980s and 1990s as a period where there was, "a shift of focus of the human rights movement towards enforcement, driven by the ever-starker disparity between the ambitious rhetoric of human rights instruments and the reality of the widespread violation".[27] Article 8 of the UDHR had given persons the right to an effective remedy, but 50 years later that remedy had yet to be articulated and violations of the right frequently went unchecked.

Beginning in the late 1980s, an initial study concerning the right to restitution, compensation and rehabilitation for victims of gross violations of human rights and fundamental freedoms was commissioned. It was authored by UN Special Rapporteur Theo van Boven and submitted to the UN Sub-Commission on the Prevention of Discrimination and Protection of Minorities in 1993.[28] Contained in the study were illustrative examples of national reparations practices following gross violations of human rights, including that of post-war Germany, which the study described as "[t]he most comprehensive and systematic precedent of reparation by a Government to groups of victims for the redress of wrongs suffered".[29] While discussing the triumphs of the German reparations laws, the study also highlighted shortcomings, such as the principle of territoriality, which caused disadvantage to those who were not residents of Germany, or who were stateless or refugees.[30]

Following the presentation of the study and another 12 years of further research and negotiation, the UN General Assembly finally adopted a set of Basic Principles on the Right to an Effective Remedy. The Basic Principles sought to address in part "the questions of remedies and reparation for victims of gross violations of international human rights law".[31]

As Antoine Buyse points out, the US and other countries "insisted [that] the [Basic] [P]rinciples were aspirational and certainly not a statement of existing law".[32] However, the Preamble of the Basic Principles stands for the contrary view when it states that the Basic Principles "do not entail new international or domestic legal obligations ***but identify mechanisms, modalities, procedures and methods for the implementation of existing legal obligations under international human rights law and international humanitarian law***" (emphasis added). Van Boven also suggests that the lengthy consultative process between state and non-state actors in the development of the Basic Principles is evidence that they set forth the legal standard in the field and are not merely aspirational.[33]

The Basic Principles require that countries adopt measures that provide fair, effective and prompt access to justice[34] and make statutes of limitations inapplicable to gross violations of international human rights law and international humanitarian law.[35] States are encouraged to disseminate to their citizens information about available remedies,[36] and provide privacy protection and safety for victims and their representatives.[37] Measures should be developed for groups of victims to present claims for reparation and receive such reparations.[38] National programmes should be developed for reparation and other assistance to victims in the event that parties liable for the harm are unable or unwilling to meet obligations.[39]

Returning to the principles enunciated in 1928 in the Chorzów Factory case, the Basic Principles proclaim the return to the *status quo ante* as the ultimate goal. They also provide that compensation should be paid for any economically assessable damage,[40] and satisfaction should include instituting measures that will curtail continuing violations,[41] arrange for public apologies[42] and so on.

While the Basic Principles are comparatively more descriptive than the language of Article 8, they still lack detail. In 2009, in the context of Holocaust-era property confiscations, an even more precise standard came into being.

The Terezin Declaration and the guidelines and best principles

With the fall of the Iron Curtain, the 1990s and early 2000s became a period of renewed vigour for World War II property restitution efforts. This came in the form of large-scale restitution programmes in Eastern Europe (often, but not always, addressing Holocaust- and Communist-era takings together). Western European countries reflected on the achievements and failures of earlier restitution efforts in the immediate post-war era. Conference after conference took place where lingering issues of unrestituted Nazi-looted gold and art, unpaid insurance policies, uncompensated slave labour and other looted property issues were discussed. However, these international conclaves led to few enforceable and effective legal standards and even fewer tools for victims and heirs to use to pursue their effective remedy. For example, when litigants in American courts seeking the return of Nazi-looted art sought to rely on guidelines created to be consistent with the Washington Principles, American judges rejected the move on the ground that the Washington Principles did not create a legally binding norm that museums throughout the world must follow.[43]

While Nazi-looted art became the best-known object of German thievery (depicted in the Hollywood feature films *Woman In Gold* and *Monuments Men*), the much larger theft of Jewish private (and communal) immovable property – land, businesses, synagogues, schools – remained largely forgotten. Eventually the topic of unrestituted immovable property was addressed in June 2009, when 46 countries[44] met at a conference in Prague hosted by the Czech Republic. At the site of the Terezin (Theresienstadt) concentration camp, the delegates issued the so-called Terezin Declaration,[45] by which these countries agreed to continue and enhance their efforts to right the economic wrongs that accompanied the genocide of European Jews and other targeted groups during the Holocaust. The Terezin Declaration articulated that endorsing nations,

> consider it important, where it has not yet been effectively achieved, to address the private property claims of Holocaust (Shoah) victims concerning immovable (real) property of former owners, heirs or successors, by either *in rem* restitution or compensation, as may be appropriate, in a fair, comprehensive and nondiscriminatory manner consistent with relevant national law and regulations, as well as international agreements. The process of such restitution or compensation should be expeditious, simple, accessible, transparent, and neither burdensome nor costly to the individual claimant.

A year later, 43 of the Terezin Declaration–endorsing states endorsed a companion document, the 2010 Guidelines and Best Practices for the Restitution and Compensation of Immovable (Real) Property, which *exclusively* addressed the restitution and compensation of private, communal and heirless immovable property.[46]

The Guidelines and Best Practices do not specifically mention the right to an effective remedy; instead, they describe their aim as bringing "a measure of justice" to victims of Nazi persecution.[47] The Guidelines and Best Practices reaffirm the principles from the Terezin Declaration and articulate additional criteria for private property restitution, including: the development of solutions to overcome citizenship and residency requirements;[48] free access to archives;[49] and that restitution *in rem* is preferred, and when not possible, substitute property of equal value must be given or payment made of "genuinely fair and adequate compensation".[50]

The result is that for Holocaust-era property confiscations, there now exist clearly defined goals for what it means to provide an effective remedy. Nevertheless, the Achilles heel remains: both the Terezin Declaration and the Guidelines and Best Practices remain non-binding documents.[51]

Effective remedies in practice – settling for less

Whether it is because of the problem that judicial proceedings often outlive the life of the claimant (especially those of octogenarian and nonagenarian Holocaust survivors), the belief that something is better than nothing, or purely for political reasons, the reality is that victims typically settle for less than full restitution. In describing *ex gratia* payment schemes – where generally no acknowledgement of wrongdoing is offered but some payment is made – Ágnes Peresztegi tellingly describes the paradox: "No facts are found, no conclusions of law are drawn, no judgment is entered, and no opinion is written. . . . In other words[,] we sacrifice justice for efficiency and peace".[52]

The current situation is that victims may be forced to settle for less because of the still-wide gap between entitlements and realities.[53]

If Article 8 of the UDHR, the UN Basic Principles and the Terezin Guidelines and Best Practices articulate the gold standard for effective remedies relating to Nazi-confiscated property, then the mass claim and bulk settlement agreements and *ex gratia* payment schemes that have defined the last 20 years of restitution almost always fall short of these standards. Yet, confidence in the full measure of the restitution remedy is not lost. Domestic legislators in some countries are taking an interest in incorporating the soft-law components of the right to an effective remedy into national legislation, thereby transforming soft law at the international level to hard law at the national level.

'Effective' judicial remedies

Promisingly, the European Court of Human Rights in Strasbourg (ECtHR) has also stepped into the debate on effective remedies.

In 2010 in *Atanasiu and Others v Romania*,[54] the ECtHR issued a pilot judgement addressing the widespread issue of the ineffectiveness of Romania's property restitution and compensation scheme for claimants whose property had been stolen from 1945 onwards.[55] The Court observed, "that it is clear from the present case that the ineffectiveness of the compensation and restitution mechanism continues to pose a recurrent and large-scale problem in Romania".[56] The Court gave Romania 18 months to secure effective protection of the right to restitution.[57]

In response to the Court's decision, the Romanian government passed a law in 2013 revising the property compensation mechanism.[58] And in 2016, the government enacted further legislation giving priority to restitution claims filed by Holocaust survivors.[59]

Less than full restitution

Partial reparations and bulk settlements

Many Holocaust-era restitution programmes fall short of the return to the *status quo ante*. The programmes or settlements are meant to facilitate some type of restitution on behalf of a specific group of individuals, but in negotiating mass relief the right to a full remedy is bartered away in the name of providing *some* restitution or compensation for a large group of individuals.

An early instance occurred shortly after the conclusion of the war. Many governments entered into dozens of bilateral claim settlement agreements which espoused claims for compensation for property of their own nationals that was either confiscated during the war, nationalised after the war or both. As an example, a 1963 Agreement between the US and the People's Republic of Bulgaria for payment by Bulgaria of a US $3,543,398 lump sum operated as a full and final settlement and discharge of claims of nationals of the US for losses arising out of war damages, nationalisation, compulsory liquidation, or other taking of property by Bulgaria prior to 9 August 1955.[60] In the end, successful US nationals of the Bulgarian settlement programme each received US $1,000 plus approximately 70 percent of the principal amount of their awards.[61] Many other US bilateral settlement award programmes had even lower rates of restitution; American claimants under the US-Poland and US-Hungary claims agreements received only about 37 percent of the principal of the awards granted to them.[62]

Other instances of partial reparations include a 2005 Polish restitution scheme whereby successful Polish claimants who lost property in the borderlands of Poland east of the Bug River – when the post-war border of the USSR and Poland shifted in 1945 – received just 20 percent of the value of the property that was taken from them.[63] The ECtHR in 2005 approved in principle the 20 percent payout.[64]

Hungary's denationalisation laws from 1991 to 1992 are other examples of partial reparations. In drafting these laws, the Hungarian legislature determined that due to the number of potential claims, the large amount of property in issue, and the impact of the cost of compensation and the country's economic situation, full compensation was impossible. The Constitutional Court of Hungary examined the laws and determined that Article 1(1) of the 1947 Treaty of Peace with Hungary permitted 'fair compensation' when restitution *in rem* was impossible and that taking all of the aforementioned factors into account, the partial compensation provided for in the laws was 'fair' within the meaning of the treaty.[65] Yet, notwithstanding these findings, compensation under the Hungarian laws was a maximum of US $21,000 paid in not easily transferrable vouchers to individual claimants. Thus, the payments cannot be viewed as even partial compensation and are only *symbolic* measures.

Ex gratia *payment programmes*

Even further afield from the list of procedural benchmarks from the UN Basic Principles and the Terezin Guidelines and Best Practices are property-related remedies in the form of *ex gratia* payments. This is where a government denies it is obliged to provide compensation for complicity in the wrongdoing that led to the loss or confiscation of property, but still provides some type of reparation on a moral or voluntary basis.

In the case of Austria in the early 2000s, the filing of class action lawsuits against Austrian companies in the US and on-going reflection by other European countries on the issue of restitution "led Austria to search for adequate measures both to provide compensation for assets plundered from Nazi victims and to make up for gaps and deficiencies in the previous restitution and compensation measures".[66] This resulted in the establishment of a General Settlement Fund tasked with resolving open questions of compensation for victims of National Socialism and recognising via *ex gratia* payments for property losses suffered between 1938 and 1945.[67] Austria has been praised for this and other programmes established in the early 2000s, though successful property claimants receive on average only between 10 and 18 percent of the value of their accepted claim.[68]

Thus, when looking at reparations from a victim-centred perspective, the effective remedy has to be about more than the amount written on a cheque – because the amount is more often than not symbolic. Perhaps therefore, the focus should be on securing the integrity of the process and ensuring that victims meaningfully participate.[69]

Conclusion

The indignities to person and property that occurred during World War II prompted swift denunciations and commitments to return what was taken, and to endeavour to prevent future recurrence. Armistice agreements, treaties of peace and domestic legislation in the immediate post-war years set out regimes – though far from perfect – that provided property reparations to those victimised by domestic and foreign governments. In addition to national legislation, nations also made a commitment to fundamental values at the international level – through Article 8 of the UDHR – that everyone has a right to an effective remedy.

That basic tenet of Article 8 has been further crystallised through soft-law documents. Although they are non-binding, the UN Basic Principles and the Terezin Declaration and its Guidelines and Best Practices set out a road map to ensuring the achievement of a measure of justice. Countries' willingness to endorse concrete principles on restitution demonstrates a willingness to engage in efforts to provide an effective remedy.

The reality may be that while *full* restitution and compensation is the international standard, a *fraction* of restitution is often what is ultimately offered and accepted. Many recent restitution programmes meant to redress World War II–era takings have provided partial restitution, bulk settlements or *ex gratia* restitution in lieu of no remedy at all.

That is not to say that Article 8 has failed – quite the contrary. International and regional bodies now monitor domestic effective remedies; countries endorse principles such as the Terezin Best Practices, which challenge them to become better protectors of the rights of their citizens; and the conversation continues to evolve.

It is not just Holocaust-era property restitution that is informed by the UDHR and its progeny of soft law. There are numerous other instances of restitution schemes that have been established in the aftermath of modern conflict. Examples include the Commission for Real Property Claims of Displaced Persons and Refugees set up in Bosnia-Herzegovina by the Dayton Accords after the conflicts in the Balkans. According to Article XI of Annex 7 of the Accords, the Commission was competent to determine property ownership where the property had not voluntarily been sold or otherwise transferred since April 1, 1992.[70] In Rwanda, following the genocide in 1994, more than 9,000 informal community courts, known as *gacaca* courts, were tasked with trying approximately 300,000 persons accused of property-related crimes, and restitution (not compensation) to the victim could be ordered.[71] A final example is the Commission for the Resolution of Real Property Disputes in Iraq, formed to address property expropriation during the Baathist era, between 1968 and 2003.[72]

In addition to discrete examples of restitution schemes, in the aftermath of post-Communist property restitution and property issues arising from the late-1990s conflicts in the Balkans, the United Nations developed principles meant to provide a uniform approach for effectively dealing with property restitution claims for refugees and displaced persons.[73] And so as of 2005, we now have the UN Principles on Housing and Property Restitution for Refugees and Displaced Persons (Pinheiro Principles). With the Pinheiro Principles, the international community has shifted the conversation from reactive to proactive. Article 8 of the UDHR and its effective remedy was reactive to the horrors of war. The Pinheiro Principles pragmatically acknowledge that it is better to have a universal rubric for navigating a way to a remedy in hand as we face future injustices. And for the next challenge, we must ensure that the mechanisms and processes established in the vision of all of these international principles and declarations and guidelines actually provide the effective remedies and redress for which they were established.

Notes

1 Morsink, 1999: 48.
2 Morsink, 1999: 48–49.
3 Reparation is a broad concept which encompasses restitution, compensation, rehabilitation, satisfaction and guarantees of non-repetition. This essay focuses on the narrow subset of restitution and compensation of immovable property.
4 Peresztegi, 2017: 136.
5 Peresztegi, 2017: 137.
6 Chorzów Factory (*Germany v Poland*) (1928). (For a more detailed discussion of the Chorzów Factory case and the notion of *status quo ante*, see Starr, 2008.)
7 See also International Law Commission, 2001. Article 34 on Forms of Reparation states "Full reparation for the injury caused by the internationally wrongful act shall take the form of restitution, compensation and satisfaction, either singly or in combination".

8 Hayes, 2010: 541.
9 Eichmann Trial, Session No. 17, 1961.
10 Inter-Allied Declaration against Acts of Dispossession committed in Territories under Enemy Occupation and Control, 5 Jan 1943.
11 Article 6, Agreement Between the Governments of the United States of America, the United Kingdom, and the Union of the Soviet Socialist Republics, on the One Hand, and the Government of Rumania, on the Other Hand, Concerning an Armistice, 12 September 1944.
12 See Ionescu, 2015.
13 Not the United Nations international organisation as we know it today, but the nearly two dozen countries that banded together to form the Allied forces.
14 Treaty of Peace with Hungary, 10 February 1947, 61 Stat. 2065.
15 Meng, 2011.
16 See Bazyler, 2016: 155–159.
17 Friedländer, 2007: 541.
18 Shortly thereafter, on 10 November 1947, Decree No. 120 of the French Commander in Chief for the Restitution of Stolen Assets was passed in the French Occupation Zone, and on 12 May 1949, British Military Law No. 59 on Restitution of Identifiable Property to Victims of Nazi Oppression was passed in the British Occupation Zone. Prior to the unification of Germany in 1990, no restitution regime was established in the Soviet Occupation Zone, which later became the German Democratic Republic (or East Germany).
19 See US Military Government Law No. 59.
20 For example, in Italy persecuted property owners were required to pay the government all of the administrative expenses that were associated with managing their confiscated property during the war.
21 Kochanski, 2012: 549.
22 Goldman, 2017.
23 Ibid.
24 Mátteoli Commission, 2000; 4; see also Bazyler, 2016: 179.
25 Bazyler, 2016: 179 (quoting Mátteoli Commission, 2000: 5).
26 See. e.g., Armistice Agreement with Bulgaria, 28 October 1944, which required Bulgaria to cancel all discriminatory legislation.
27 Starr, 2013: 479–480.
28 UNCHR, 1993.
29 UNCHR, 1993, chapter VI, National Law and Practice, para. 107.
30 UNCHR, 1993, chapter VI, National Law and Practice, para. 111.
31 UN General Assembly, 2005.
32 Buyse, 2008: 139.
33 van Boven, 2009: 33.
34 UN General Assembly, 2005, Section I.2.b.
35 UN General Assembly, 2005, Section IV.
36 UN General Assembly, 2005, Section VIII.12.a.
37 UN General Assembly, 2005, Section VIII.12.b.
38 UN General Assembly, 2005, Section VIII.13.
39 UN General Assembly, 2005, Section IX.16.
40 UN General Assembly, 2005, Section IX.20.
41 UN General Assembly, 2005, Section IX.22(a).
42 UN General Assembly, 2005, Section IX.22(e).
43 See, e.g., Toledo Museum of Art v Ullin (2006), holding that the 1999 American Association of Museums' Guidelines Concerning the Unlawful Appropriation of Objects During the Nazi Era, which are consistent with the Washington Principles, "were not intended to create legal obligations or mandatory rules but rather were intended to 'facilitate the ability of museums to act ethically and legally as stewards' through 'serious efforts' on a 'case by case basis'" (internal citations omitted).

44 Serbia attended the 2009 Prague Conference on Holocaust Era Assets as an observer, and later became the 47th country to endorse the Terezin Declaration.
45 For the full text of the Terezin Declaration, see shoahlegacy.org.
46 See Guidelines and Best Practices for the Restitution and Compensation of Immovable (Real) Property Confiscated or Otherwise Wrongfully Seized by the Nazis, Fascists and Their Collaborators during the Holocaust (Shoah) Era between 1933–1945, n.d. (Guidelines)
47 Guidelines, Criteria for Guidelines and Best Practices.
48 Guidelines, para. d.
49 Guidelines, para. e.
50 Guidelines, para. h.
51 See, e.g., Preamble of Terezin Declaration ("Keeping in mind the legally non-binding nature of this Declaration and moral responsibilities thereof, and without prejudice to applicable international law and obligations . . .").
52 Peresztegi, 2017: 140 (quoting Coleman and Silver, 1986).
53 See van Boven, 2009, 20.
54 Atanasiu and Others v Romania (2010).
55 While Romania's property restitution scheme provides for restitution of property seized from 1945 onwards, the issue continues to have an acute effect on those whose property was initially confiscated by the Nazis during the war. A number of laws were enacted between 1944 and 1945, whose stated aim was to unwind the war-time confiscations either *de jure* or via claims filed with local courts (see, e.g., Decree Law No. 607/1945 (regarding the annulment of certain contracts that transferred [property] during exceptional circumstances)). These restitution measures, however, were short-lived, with Romania becoming a People's Republic from 1947–1965, and the Socialist Republic of Romania from 1965–1989. Under Communist rule, extensive portions of the economy, including most land and buildings, were nationalised. The result was that Nazi-confiscated property that had been returned was taken for a second time as part of nationalisation process.
56 *Atanasiu and Others v Romania* (2010): 216.
57 *Atanasiu and Others v Romania* (2010): 241.
58 *Preda and Others v Romania* (2014).
59 Gillet, 2016.
60 Agreement Between the United States of America and the Government of the People's Republic of Bulgaria Regarding Claims of United States Nationals and Related Financial Matters, 2 July 1963.
61 United States Department of Justice, Foreign Claims Settlement Commission of the US, n.d.i.
62 United States Department of Justice, Foreign Claims Settlement Commission of the US, n.d.ii.
63 See *Wolkenberg and Others v Poland* (2007).
64 *Wolkenberg and Others v Poland* (2007): para. 64.
65 See Hungarian Constitution (1993)
66 Lessing and Azizi, 2006, 230.
67 National Fund of the Republic of Austria for Victims of National Socialism, "Media Information" (September 2016).
68 Idem, 20.
69 See, e.g., Ferstman and Goetz, 2009: 341.
70 For further discussion of challenges of the Commission, see generally Ferstman and Rosenberg, 2009.
71 For further discussion of effectiveness of more informal dispute resolution mechanisms in connection with achieving an effective remedy, see generally Waldorf, 2009.

72 For further discussion of the Iraq property restitution scheme, see generally van der Auweraert, 2009.
73 Centre on Housing Rights and Evictions, 2005: 4.

References

Agreement Between the Governments of the United States of America, the United Kingdom, and the Union of the Soviet Socialist Republics, on the One Hand, and the Government of Rumania, on the Other Hand, Concerning an Armistice, 12 September 1944.

Aly, G. (2005). *Hitler's Beneficiaries: Plunder, Racial War, and the Nazi Welfare State.* New York: Metropolitan Books.

Armistice Agreement with Bulgaria, 28 October 1944.Article 5.

Atanasiu and Others v Romania [2010] Application Nos. 30767/05 and 33800/06 (European Court of Human Rights).

Bazyler, M. (2016). *Holocaust, Genocide, and the Law: A Quest for Justice in a Post-Holocaust World.* Oxford: Oxford University Press.

Broniowski v Poland [2005] Application No. 31443/96 (European Court of Human Rights).

Buyse, A. (2008). Lost and Regained? Restitution as a Remedy for Human Rights Violations in the Context of International Law. *Heidelberg Journal of International Law*, 68.

Centre on Housing Rights and Evictions (COHRE). (2005). *The Pinheiro Principles: United Nations Principles on Housing and Property Restitution for Refugees and Displaced Persons.* Geneva: Centre on Housing Rights and Evictions.

Chorzów Factory (Germany v Poland) [1928] 17 (Permanent Court of International Justice).

Coleman, J. and Silver, C. (1986). Justice in Settlements. *Social Philosophy and Policy*, 4.

Eichmann Trial, Session No. 17. (1961). [video] Available at: www.youtube.com/watch?v=wukqci59zRA [Accessed 11 Dec. 2017].

European Shoah Legacy Institute. (2017). *Home – European Shoah Legacy Institute.* [online] Available at: http://shoahlegacy.org [Accessed 22 Aug. 2017].

Ferstman, C. and Goetz, M. (2009). Reparations before the International Criminal Court: The Early Jurisprudence on Victim Participation and its Impact on Future Reparations Proceedings. In: C. Ferstman, M. Goetz and A. Stephens, eds., *Reparations: For Victims of Genocide, War Crimes and Crimes Against Humanity.* Leiden: Martinus Nijhoff.

Ferstman, C. and Rosenberg, S. (2009). Reparations in Dayton's Bosnia and Herzegovina. In: C. Ferstman, M. Goetz and A. Stephens, eds., *Reparations: for Victims of Genocide, War Crimes and Crimes against Humanity.* Leiden: Martinus Nijhoff, pp. 515–539.

Friedländer, S. (2007). *Nazi Germany and the Jews. 1939–1945: The Years of Extermination.* New York: Harper Collins.

Gillet, K. (2016). Romania Takes Step Toward Restitution to Holocaust Survivors. *New York Times.* [online] Available at: www.nytimes.com/2016/05/11/world/europe/romania-holocaust-survivors-jews-restitution-claims.html?_r=1 [Accessed 6 Dec. 2017].

Goldman, R. (2017). Macron Denounces Anti-Zionism as 'Reinvented Form of Anti-Semitism. *New York Times.* [online] Available at: www.nytimes.com/2017/07/17/world/europe/macron-israel-holocaust-antisemitism.html [Accessed 6 Dec. 2017].

Guidelines and Best Practices for the Restitution and Compensation of Immovable (Real) Property Confiscated or Otherwise Wrongfully Seized by the Nazis, Fascists and Their Collaborators During the Holocaust (Shoah) Era Between 1933–1945, (n.d.). European Shoah Legacy Institute.

Hayes, P. (2010). Plunder and Restitution. In: P. Hayes and J. Roth, eds., *The Oxford Handbook of Holocaust Studies*. Oxford: Oxford University Press.

Hungarian Constitution [1993]15/1993 (III.12) and 16/1993 (III.12) (Constitutional Court of Hungary).

Inter-Allied Declaration Against Acts of Dispossession Committed in Territories Under Enemy Occupation and Control, 5 January 1943.

International Law Commission. (2001). *Articles on Responsibility of States for Internationally Wrongful Acts, Adopted by the Commission at Its Fifty-Third Session in 2001 (Final Outcome)*. UN Doc A/56/10. Geneva: United Nations.

Ionescu, S. (2015). *Jewish resistance to "romanianization"*. Basingstoke: Palgrave Macmillan, pp. 34–65.

Kochanski, H. (2012). *The Eagle Unbowed: Poland and the Poles in the Second World War*. Cambridge, MA: Harvard University Press.

Lessing, H. and Azizi, F. (2006). Austria Confronts Her Past. In: M. Bazyler and R. Alford, eds., *Holocaust Restitution: Perspectives on the Litigation and Its Legacy*. New York: NYU Press.

Mátteoli Commission. (2000). *Summary of the Work by the Study Mission on the Spoliation of Jews in France*. [online] Mátteoli Commission. Available at: https://clinton.presidentiallibraries.us/items/show/29352 [Accessed 6 Dec. 2017].

Meng, M. (2011). *Shattered spaces*. Cambridge, MA: Harvard University Press.

Morsink, J. (1999). *The Universal Declaration of Human Rights: Origins, Drafting and Intent*. Philadelphia: University of Philadelphia Press.

Peresztegi, Á. (2017). Reparation for Holocaust-Era Human Rights Violations. In: A. Kovács and E. Andor, eds., *CEU Jewish Studies Yearbook 2002–2003*. Budapest: CEU.

Pinheiro, P. and Leckie, S. (2005). *The Pinheiro Principles: United Nations Principles on Housing and Property Restitution for Refugees and Displaced Persons*. Geneva: Centre on Housing Rights and Evictions.

Preda and Others v Romania [2014] Application Nos. 9584/02, 33514/02, 38052/02, 25821/03, 29652/03, 3736/03, 17750/03, 28688/04.

Starr, S. (2008). Rethinking 'Effective Remedies': Remedial Deterrence in International Courts. *New York University Law Review*, 83.

Starr, S. (2013). The Right to an Effective Remedy: Balancing Realism and Aspiration. In: M. Ssenyonjo, ed., *International Human Rights Law: Six Decades After the UHDR and Beyond*. Oxford: Ashgate.

Toledo Museum of Art v Ullin [2006]477 F.Supp.2d 802, 808 (Ohio).

Treaty of Peace with Hungary, 10 February 1947, 61 Stat. 2065. Articles 26–27.

UN General Assembly. (2005). *Basic Principles and Guidelines on the Right to a Remedy and Reparation for Victims of Gross Violations of International Human Rights Law and Serious Violations of International Humanitarian Law by the Commission on Human Rights*. UN Doc A/RES/60/147 (Annex). Geneva: United Nations.

UNCHR. (1993). *Study Concerning the Right to Restitution, Compensation and Ehabilitation for Victims of Gross Violations of Human Rights and Fundamental Freedoms*. UN Doc E/CN.4/Sub.2/1993/8. Geneva: United Nations.

United States Department of Justice, Foreign Claims Settlement Commission of the US. (n.di.). *Completed Programs – Bulgaria*. Washington, DC: US Department of Justice.

United States Department of Justice, Foreign Claims Settlement Commission of the US. (n.dii.). *Completed Programs – Hungary*. [online] Washington, DC: US Department of Justice. Available at: www.justice.gov/fcsc/completed-programs-hungary [Accessed 11 Dec. 2017].

US Military Government Law No. 59.Article 1.

van Boven, T. (2009). Victims' Rights to a Remedy and Reparation: The New United Nations Principles and Guidelines. In: C. Ferstman, M. Goetz and A. Stephens, eds., *Reparations: for Victims of Genocide, War Crimes and Crimes Against Humanity*. Leiden: Martinus Nijhoff.

van der Auweraert, P. (2009). Policy Challenges for Property Restitution in Transition – the Example of Iraq. In: C. Ferstman, M. Goetz and A. Stephens, eds., *Reparations: for Victims of Genocide, War Crimes and Crimes Against Humanity*. Leiden: Martinus Nijhoff, pp. 459–481.

Waldorf, L. (2009). Goats & Graves: Reparations in Rwanda's Community Courts. In: C. Ferstman, M. Goetz and A. Stephens, eds., *Reparations: for Victims of Genocide, War Crimes and Crimes Against Humanity*. Leiden: Martinus Nijhoff, pp. 515–539.

Wolkenberg and Others v Poland [2007] 50003/99 (ECHR).

Section III

The rights of the individual in civil and political society

(Articles 12–17)

Introduction to Section III

Carla Ferstman

This section of the book focuses on the second column of the Declaration – individuals' rights and freedoms as they live and interact in civil and political society. These rights, including freedom of movement, the right to privacy, family, honour and reputation, the right to a nationality and the right to own personal property are concerned with how individuals perceive their identity and engage with others in their societies and communities.

Some of the rights differ from those in the first column in that it is recognised that such rights cannot be applied in a vacuum; the realisation of one person's rights should not be to the detriment of another person's rights. As Woods explains in her chapter in relation to the right to privacy, "[c]ertainly, it cannot be understood independently from individuals and their interrelationships." Therefore, the bulk of second column rights are framed in less than absolute terms: individuals are protected from any *arbitrary* interference of the enjoyment of privacy; freedom of movement and residence is a right *within the borders of each state*; no one shall be *arbitrarily* deprived of his nationality. Later human rights treaties and their interpretive texts which have considered these rights have underscored that any restriction to the exercise of these rights cannot be arbitrary; it must be provided by law, proportionate and limited to what is strictly necessary.[1] For instance, in regards to freedom of movement, the UN Human Rights Committee has explained that "[t]he permissible limitations which may be imposed . . . must not nullify the principle of liberty of movement, and are governed by the requirement of necessity . . ., and by the need for consistency with the other rights recognized in the Covenant."[2] A constant theme is therefore how to achieve the appropriate balance.

Developments in modern society such as advancements in information and cyber technology and communications, as well as the use of big data analytics, have given rise to new challenges with respect to the protection of second column rights, particularly the right to privacy. However, as Woods explains, "as technology has the capacity to intrude further and more easily into our private life, so the greater the need for privacy." Furthermore, new technologies underscore the need to protect against potential infringements by non-state as well as state actors. Similar to other areas of rights protection, it has been recognised progressively that states are obligated to exercise due diligence to prevent non-state actors from infringing individuals' rights to privacy and other second column rights.

Yet in other contexts, the realisation of second column rights is made difficult by states' reluctance to acknowledge and enforce practically any limitation on their discretion to regulate what they perceive to be within their *domaine reserve*. This is the case with respect to the right to nationality (discussed by van Waas). As she notes, despite the crystallisation of norms in this area, states' resolve to address statelessness has focused mainly on ensuring that stateless persons could enjoy a minimum set of rights; efforts to reduce the incidence of statelessness, while also reflected in the UDHR and other texts, were less successful. She explains that, "All the while, the failure to deal with conflicts of nationality laws and the restrictive nature of some nationality rules was also continuing to generate new instances of statelessness." A similar reluctance to fully enforce individuals' rights can be observed with respect to the right to seek and to enjoy in other countries asylum from persecution, set out in Article 14(1) of the Declaration. Here, the UDHR watershed formulation was not replicated or expanded upon in the later 1951 Convention on the Status of Refugees nor in later universal human rights treaties.

Notes

1 See, e.g., Articles 12 and 17 of the ICCPR; Articles 15, 21 and 32 of the International Convention on the Protection of the Rights of All Migrant Workers and Members of Their Families.
2 UN Human Rights Committee, 'General Comment No. 27: Article 12 (Freedom of Movement)', UN Doc CCPR/C/21/Rev.1/Add.9 (2 November 1999) para 2.

9 Article 12

The right to privacy

Lorna Woods

Introduction

Although privacy is widely recognised as a right, its precise content is open to debate. Certainly, it cannot be understood independently from individuals and their interrelationships.[1] One of the important drivers of change, at least over the last few decades, has been the development in the fields of digital technologies and electronic communications. We are moving to a world of near-ubiquitous communicating devices: the Internet, smart devices (Internet of Things, IoT), and wearable and mobile technologies. As technology has the capacity to intrude further and more easily into our private life, so the greater the need for privacy protection.[2] This chapter will consider the development of the right to privacy, before discussing the challenges posed by the use of new technologies.

Given the similarity between Article 12 UDHR and Article 17 International Covenant on Civil and Political Rights (ICCPR), materials on Article 17 are relevant for understanding Article 12. Further insight could be found in the jurisprudence on the regional instruments: Article 8 European Convention on Human Rights (ECHR) and Article 11 American Convention on Human Rights (ACHR). Their respective jurisprudence and commentary thereon, where relevant, will also be used here, reflecting the approach taken by various UN bodies.[3]

The text of Article 12: starting points

While many state constitutions recognise some aspects of privacy, such as protection against search and seizure, the recognition of a broad notion of privacy was new with the UDHR.[4] It is notable that despite the difficulties in definition, there was no dispute that such a right should be included.[5] The right to privacy is amorphous,[6] but at a basic level constitutes acceptance of a private sphere into which interference is not permitted without good reason.[7] It is linked to autonomy[8] and human dignity, and has been described as "the core concept of freedom".[9] It is not just a right to be left alone; rather, it provides a regime for protecting a range of privacy interests from unjustified intrusion.[10] Feldman argued that the rights relating to honour and to reputation, which may seem a little disconnected from the rest of the listed elements,[11] fit well in this framing because of their importance to dignity both in relation to the views others hold about us and our own self-view,[12] a perspective which may become increasingly important in the digital environment. Academic commentary on privacy has suggested it encompasses different spheres, for example: physical integrity, mental integrity and the sphere of intimate relationships, none of which are location specific or limited to secret information.[13]

The text of Article 12 stipulates a number of elements: privacy, family, home or correspondence, honour and reputation. This is a disparate group, and the relationship of the several elements one to another is not clear; indeed, some of the terms are vague, perhaps seeking to allow agreement on a text when there was no positive agreement on principle. It is tempting to suggest that privacy, which is listed first, is an umbrella term[14] within which the other aspects sit, but it is unclear that this was the intended interpretation. In the initial draft of the Declaration, the term 'privacy' did not come first, and in some drafts was excluded altogether, with no explanation as to why.[15] 'Privacy' nonetheless remains a term of particularly wide ambit, which may overlap with other interests identified by Article 12. It does not protect one uniform right, but protects a range of overlapping and interconnecting interests[16] operating in different contexts,[17] which may be harmed in different ways.[18]

The UN Human Rights Committee (HRC) has defined some of the elements in Article 17, such as 'family' and 'home', and done so broadly.[19] Significantly, the HRC takes a technology-neutral approach to forms of communication, listing letters, telephone,[20] telegraph or other forms of communication.[21] 'Privacy', however, is not specifically defined. The HRC has recognised that Article 17 encompasses rights beyond those listed in the text of the provision, often linking the interests protected to a general notion of privacy, sometimes in conjunction with another listed element (such as family). Reflecting theoretical perspectives, a right to intimacy can be inferred from General Comment 16,[22] as well as from HRC decisions. In *Coerial and Aurik*, "the notion of privacy refers to the sphere of a person's life in which he or she can freely address his or her identity".[23] It also encompasses the right to be different. While the text of both articles identifies some areas – such as family and correspondence – which have a clear importance in terms of the interests protected, the articles are not closed but seemingly can be applied in other contexts. They are in this sense open-ended.

Notably, Article 12 is not expressed to be subject to a limitation clause, although Article 12 protects only against "arbitrary interference". That guarantee nonetheless applies to all of the aspects identified in Article 12. Article 17, however, distinguishes between honour and reputation, on the one hand, which are protected from "unlawful attacks" and the other elements listed in Article 17, on the other hand, which receive protection from "arbitrary or unlawful interference". The significance of the difference is unclear, though it seems that reputation receives lower protection under Article 17.[24] *Arbitrary* has been suggested as meaning "without justification in valid motives and contrary to established legal principles".[25] In *Toonen v Australia*, the HRC clarified that the concept of reasonableness required that, "any interference with privacy must be proportional to the end sought and be necessary in the circumstances of any given case",[26] a point it has re-iterated.[27] Furthermore, according to General Comment 16, arbitrariness can catch even lawful interference.[28] Despite the absence of an express limitation clause, from the HRC's consistent practice state action is subject to the overarching principles of legality, necessity and proportionality – as seen in respect of other rights.[29] Specifically, it must not render the essence of the right meaningless and must be consistent with other human rights,[30] including the prohibition of discrimination. It seems reasonable that this interpretation of arbitrary could be read back to Article 12, despite the slight difference in wording between Article 12 UDHR and Article 17 ICCPR.

Digital technologies

Material scope of protection

Applying Articles 12 and 17 to the digital environment in some contexts is straightforward. Word-processed documents are functionally the same as handwritten or typed documents;[31] they are our 'papers'. Similarly, some new means of communication, such as text messages and email, fall clearly within the ambit of correspondence,[32] especially given the technology-neutral approach to interpretation. Respect for correspondence suggests the right to uninterrupted and uncensored communications with others in confidence.[33] Interception of communications has long been recognised as a serious infringement of the right to protection of correspondence and to privacy.[34]

This element of confidentiality, however, may cause us to think before we view other forms of distance communications as also falling with 'correspondence'. What of, for example, communications on social networking sites, especially where settings allow public access?[35] Even in the era of hard copies, postcards, which lack confidentiality, would still be seen as correspondence. Even assuming that social media are not correspondence, they may nonetheless be protected by Article 12. Given the breadth of privacy interests and the role that some of these platforms can play in individuals' lives, these online spaces could be considered to be functionally equivalent to 'home'. In *Bernh Larsen*, the ECtHR found that the seizure of the applicant companies' documents held on servers constituted an interference with the applicants' privacy rights as regards their homes,[36] illustrating the acceptance of the need to protect virtual space as well as space in physical reality.[37] The online environment might also be seen as part of individuals' identity, in that it is a place where an individual can freely express his or her identity, or a different aspect of that identity, thus falling within the protected scope of Article 12 noted prior. An emerging question is the extent to which the right to privacy should recognise the right to a digital identity, as well as other forms of identity, and what any such right should look like.

One particular issue in relation to our ability to portray ourselves online is the extent to which that gives us the right to control how others perceive us and whether we have the right to change our identity. Both questions lead to the further question of whether there is a right to erase data, more generally referred to as the right to be forgotten. As yet, this has not been directly addressed in human rights decisions. The EU data protection regime does give rise to a 'right to be forgotten'.[38] Even though this right is not absolute, it is controversial, and concerns have been expressed that, at least in the political context, it may be open to abuse.

A further question is how the principle of confidentiality – expressed in the context of the human interaction and intentional communication – applies in the IoT, where devices are interconnected with one another, collecting data and communicating autonomously. Of course, this communication is not the sharing of ideas between individuals, but the content of these communications will reveal information about individuals whether those devices are communicating sensitive information (such as fitness trackers in relation to health data) or not (smart fridges and metres). On this basis, IoT communications should fall within our understanding of privacy, even if not the concept of correspondence.

The ECtHR has also recognised that communications 'metadata' – that is, information about the communications – also falls within Article 8 ECHR, as matters protected by private life and correspondence, although there was some uncertainty as to the level of protection it required.[39] Subsequent case law clarified that the concern about metadata was not limited to telephone conversations but could extend to other forms of electronic communication, for example, internet use.[40] UN bodies also accepted that metadata can produce a revealing picture of an individual's networks and interests.[41]

The issue of metadata links to the more general matter of 'informational privacy', which is central to concerns about privacy at a time when many human interactions, specifically those mediated by electronic communications networks, leave a data trail which can be collected and analysed by a range of actors, often unbeknownst to the individual. Informational privacy can be understood to refer to the ability to control the collection, use and disclosure of one's personal information. According to Nowak, the right to privacy has evolved to include specific rights to access and control of one's personal data.[42] While communications metadata can be used to draw inferences about the person, other data can also be used this way. The entire range of information recorded, often automatically, as a consequence of our interaction with a range of technological devices, can be analysed. The combination of these groups of data allows more detailed profiles still, with the result that individuals are categorised, their behaviour predicted; the combination of data can reveal information more sensitive than the content of a communication.[43] In the context of the IoT, not only is there more data collected and analysed, but this collection and analysis is also virtually invisible: devices are built into the architecture of our everyday lives and the sensors operate automatically, not requiring on-going human intervention to trigger the recording process.[44] A car's satnav,[45] or items with radio-frequency identification (RFID) chips embedded in them, for example, can be used to track a person's movements. Indeed, there have been instances where RFID chips have been implanted in individuals.[46] As well as concerns about 'dataveillance' and constant oversight on autonomy, freedom and dignity, there are risks that individuals' options will be restricted by the operation of a 'personalised' digital environment. This is almost the reverse of a space protective of digital identity and human dignity.

Existence of interference

It has been suggested by some states that privacy is not engaged because, for an interference to occur, data in relation to the applicant must be examined by a human. This argument is particularly important in the context of the mass acquisition and retention of data, where only a small proportion of the data collected is in this sense 'used'. The ECtHR has rejected this position. It held that the existence of a law which allows secret surveillance can constitute an interference with Article 8 ECHR without an individual having to prove that he or she was actually targeted.[47] In *Zakharov*, the ECtHR reviewed its jurisprudence to emphasise that secret surveillance measures should not be effectively unchallengeable.[48] A similar point has been made within the context of the UN; Emmerson suggested that the existence of a system of mass surveillance is itself an intrusion into privacy.[49] Moreover, within the ECtHR there is a consistent line of case law holding that the storage of communications data itself constitutes interference with privacy, whether or not there is any use made or disclosure of that data.[50] This point was re-iterated in the OHCHR Report.[51]

Is the interference arbitrary?

It is an open question whether the mass collection of data can ever be justified by reference to the criteria of lawful, necessary and proportionate, no matter how weighty the public interest objective that that surveillance seeks to protect. The fight against terrorism, for example, is not a trump card in this respect,[52] though the weightier the public interest objective, the easier it would be to satisfy a proportionality assessment. Some difficulties can be seen by comparing mass surveillance with (traditional) targeted surveillance. Targeted, individual surveillance, while clearly an intrusion into the privacy (as well as potentially of the home and correspondence) of the individuals concerned, can be justified in a legitimate public interest where safeguards are in place. Independent oversight is normally required, to check whether the measures are necessary and appropriate and that there is "some factual basis, related to the behaviour of an individual, which justifies the suspicion".[53] The surveillance of an individual, such as entailed by what is essentially population-level surveillance, does not relate to an activity or a person that is 'of interest' to law enforcement. This disconnects the surveillance from suspicious activity, although that link has traditionally been seen both as a limiting factor for state intrusion and a justifying factor for that intrusion. Independent oversight becomes difficult, if not impossible. While there are issues about the oversight bodies' understanding of technological advances, as well as the far-from-transparent relationship between telecommunications and technology companies and governments, there is an underlying structural issue. With a scheme in which data is gathered massively, review of the process at that stage can turn into a review of the scheme, but only at that general level. Given the secrecy that surrounds mass surveillance and the intelligence services, it is hard to know if the evidence is there to justify its use. That is, whether the acquisition, retention and analysis of the data is necessary or rather just (possibly) useful (in some cases).[54] The case has not been made that the use of mass surveillance is "the least intrusive instrument among those which might achieve the desired result".[55] The necessity and proportionality of untargeted surveillance is thus questionable.

The development of new analytical techniques, in conjunction with the use of big data, compounds problems. Big data analytics looks for patterns; correlations are flagged, rather than looking for causal links or the original cause.[56] It depends on having large amounts of data to work with, rather than pre-selected, 'relevant' data. In this situation, everyone is part of the analysis, whether an individual has done something to warrant surveillance or not. Furthermore, individuals will be attributed to categories on the basis of correlation between factors in a way that cannot be predicted, rather than the consequence of intentional actions by the individual. This hardly respects a right to choose how to view yourself and to project yourself to others. Even more problematic is the process of profiling when carried out in a predictive manner on the basis of broad characteristics, such as age, sex or membership in a racial or religious group. In some instances, as well as being both over- and under-inclusive, the use of such profiles risks being discriminatory. Caution must be used to ensure that the datasets are representative of the relevant population groups, as otherwise there is a risk of a distortion in the analysis. Even when evidence of past cases might suggest that specific characteristics constitute valid risk factors, caution should be exercised as this may be the outcome of bias in the training data used. In any event, use of very general characteristics runs the risk of stereotyping – itself undermining of human dignity that Articles 12 and 17 seeks to protect – and imposes a significant emotional toll on those groups so profiled.[57]

The traditional criterion of lawfulness requires not only that surveillance be based on domestic law, but also that the applicability of the law to given individuals is predictable.[58] In the context of bulk access or acquisition of data, there are no limits to the categories of persons who may be subject to surveillance and no limits on the duration of the surveillance, which is problematic not just in terms of proportionality but also in this requirement of lawfulness. It is also difficult, if not impossible, to rely on *ex ante* independent review of intrusion in relation to mass surveillance;[59] insofar as review takes place, it relates to use of data in relation to a person, rather than bulk acquisition or automated mass processing. National legislative frameworks, which might seek to limit surveillance and provide oversight as to how agencies operate, are weak and outdated, some have said intentionally so.[60] In terms of impact on the privacy of a person who is not under suspicion, the impact is disproportionate no matter how the data is used, if used at all, and no matter how strong the safeguards.[61] Attempts to suggest that the acquisition, retention and analysis of data are proportionate become harder to justify the more datasets are included.

The current concerns have focussed mainly on communications (content and metadata); they have not considered particular issues pertaining to biometric data (e.g., fingerprint-based technologies, facial recognition software). With the development of ubiquitous computing and the IoT, there will be more data, providing a richer picture of individuals' lives. Insofar as proportionality can currently be secured by oversight mechanisms, these will be increasingly challenged when analytical techniques involve machine learning, a process which tends to lack transparency, and near population-level datasets. We are left with the question of whether this means that mass surveillance is unjustifiable or whether the privacy framework itself needs to be revised. It is submitted that the former is more in keeping with the objectives of the UDHR, with its concerns about the abuse of state power, than the latter.

Role of private companies

The increase in data and the ability to analyse them is possible because of increased computing power, decreased storage costs as well as the Internet (and now the IoT). Much of the infrastructure and services are provided by private actors. The possibilities exist that these data constitute a threat to privacy in private hands just as in the hands of the state. A corresponding risk of discrimination exists, too. The scale of the issue is large: in 2012 it was reported that one data broker in the US had about 500 million active consumers worldwide, with about 1,500 data points per person.[62] While private actors are not generally bound by international law, Article 2 ICCPR requires states to respect the Covenant rights and to ensure them to all individuals in their territory and subject to their jurisdiction.[63] The text of Article 12 UDHR specifically enjoins states to legislate to protect privacy and, in General Comment 16, the HRC stated that "[t]he gathering and holding of personal information on computers, data banks and other devices, whether by public authorities or private individuals or bodies, must be regulated by law".[64] Many states have responded by enacting data protection laws, but whether they are sufficient is open to question. There are issues, in the light of global flows of information, regarding the extent of states' obligations in the context of the import/export of data; this makes the existence of a global privacy standard even more important. There are further issues regarding the interpretation of national laws and their application to new technologies and techniques. In this context, the existence of a technology-neutral guarantee provides a benchmark against which the adequacy of national measures may be assessed. Nonetheless, the new environment poses challenges for privacy, especially where it has been safeguarded via the mechanisms of data protection and the possibility of individuals to consent to data processing. It is questionable whether consent can be said to occur when individuals have no choice (i.e., 'consent' to data processing is a precondition for access to services), especially when those individuals may not be aware of the fact that they are so consenting. Big data processing makes the situation more problematic: it is impossible to foresee the uses and consequences of that processing, especially where machine learning makes the process even less transparent. This then may result in the need to re-think the basis on which the issues of informational privacy and data protection are approached.[65]

Conclusions

The right to privacy as contained in Article 12 covers similar ground to the guarantees contained notably in Article 17 ICCPR, but also the regional human rights instruments. The right is notoriously difficult to define, but it is also open-ended and capable of being applied in new contexts where individuals' integrity, autonomy and dignity are under threat. Thus, there is both a need for protection for privacy and the applicability of Article 12 in the context of the digital environment. While it is possible to understand the material scope of Article 12 by analogy to the existing terms listed in that provision, developments in technology, especially in the context of mass surveillance, raise new questions about when intrusion occurs and how to assess whether that intrusion is arbitrary. Potentially there is new power given to state bodies to have constant and detailed oversight over individuals. Similar concerns arise in relation to private actors, which seem to have unprecedented access to data about virtually all aspects of individuals' lives. While the UN bodies have recognised this challenge, to date an adequate solution has not yet been found. The danger of a data-driven approach in attempting to predict and prevent is that it is too easy to focus on the data, forget that human beings are behind the data and thereby minimise or underplay the degree and extent of intrusion.

Notes

1 Solove, 2006: 484; see similarly Nowak, 2005: 378; HRC General Comment 16, para 7.
2 Rengel, 2013: 108.
3 See, e.g., OHCHR, 2014ii, para 13.
4 Diggelmann and Cleis, 2014: 441–442.
5 Diggelmann and Cleis, 2014: 443.
6 Lillich, 1984.
7 Rehof, 1999: 256–257.
8 See definition proposed in Joseph, Schultz and Castan, 2005, that privacy encompasses 'freedom from unwarranted and unreasonable intrusion into activities [. . .] belonging to the realm of individual autonomy'.
9 Nowak, 2005: 377.
10 Feldman, 1994: 41, 42.
11 Rehof notes free speech concerns about their inclusion in Article 12, Rehof, 1999: 255.
12 Feldman, 1994: 56, citing Nowak in support.
13 Rehof, 1999: 258; contrast typology given in Feldman, 1994: 52; Gavison, 1980: 428 suggests: secrecy, anonymity and solitude; A Westin proposed four "basic states of individual privacy": (1) solitude; (2) intimacy; (3) anonymity; and (4) reserve ("the creation of a psychological barrier against unwanted intrusion"), Westin, 1967: 31–32; and as regards Article 17, see Nowak, 2005: 385–392.

14 Rehof questions whether this is the case: Rehof, 1999: 251.
15 Diggelmann and Cleis, 2014: 447–448.
16 In the case of the *Ituango Massacres v Colombia*, the Inter-American Court noted that "an individual's home and private life are intrinsically connected, because the home is the space in which private life can evolve freely".
17 Solove, 2006: 481; Feldman, 1994: 57.
18 Solove classifies activities which may harm privacy: information collection; information processing; information dissemination; and invasion, in Solove, 2006: 489.
19 HRC General Comment 16.
20 See the tapping of telephones in Comm. 903/1999 in Van Hulst v NL (2004).
21 HRC, General Comment 16, para 8.
22 See General Comment, para 8.
23 Communication 453/1991, Coerial and Aurik v NL (1991).
24 Nowak, 2005: 381; Rehof, 1999: 255.
25 Rehof, 1999: 253.
26 Toonen v Australia, 1992, Communication No. 488/1992, para 8.3.
27 See, e.g., Communications Nos. 903/1999, para 7.3, and 1482/2006, paras. 10.1 and 10.2.
28 General Comment 16, para 4.
29 OHCHR, 1999, para 16–18.
30 Canepa v Canada, 1997, para 11.4 (1997).
31 Wieser and Bicos Beteiligungen GmbH v Austria (2007), para 45.
32 Copland v UK (2007), para 42l; the ECtHR has not discussed whether seizure of business papers and correspondence also involves 'private life' as well as correspondence and home.
33 Emmerson, 2014: para 58.
34 *Van Hulst v NL*, 2004, Communication No. 903/1999 UNDoc. CCPR/C/82/D/903/1999 (2004).
35 Emmerson, 2014: para 17.
36 *Bernh Larsen Holdings AS v Norway* (2013).
37 In general terms, UN General Assembly resolution 68/187 recognises the relevance of privacy to digital communications.
38 Articles 12(b) and 14(a) of Data protection Directive (95/46/EC) 24 October 1995, Case C-131/12 Google Spain, Google Inc v AEPD and Mario Costeja González, EU:C:2014:317; Article 17 General Data Protection Regulation April 27th, 2016.
39 *Malone v UK* (1984).
40 *Copland v UK* (2007).
41 OHCHR, 2014i, para 19.
42 Nowak, 2005: 388.
43 DRI etc., cited approvingly by the OHCHR Report.
44 For development, see Gow, 2005.
45 TomTom navigation devices collect user data that includes point of origin, point of destination, journey times, speeds and routes taken. This data has been shared with law enforcement authorities.
46 See, e.g., Wahlqvist, 2017.
47 *Weber and Saravia v Germany* (2006), para 78.
48 *Zakharov v Russia*, 2015, GC, para 171.
49 Emmerson, 2014.
50 *Rotaru v Romania* (2000), para 43.
51 Human Rights Council, 2017, para 20.
52 OHCHR, 2009, para 13.

53 OHCHR, 2009, para 21, in relation to terrorism.
54 See, e.g., Independent Reviewer of Terrorism Legislation, 2016, which specifically excluded a proportionality analysis and the Comments of the Special Rapporteur on the right to Privacy (A/HRC?34/60), paras 16–18.
55 OHCHR, 1999.
56 See Boyd and Crawford, 2012: 662.
57 OHCHR, 2009: para 56.
58 See, e.g., Human Rights Committee, 2004, para 19.
59 See, e.g., CCPR, 2009, para 18.
60 OHCHR, 2009, para 57.
61 OHCHR, 2009, para 52.
62 Singer, 2012.
63 See further General Comment 31; Shelton and Gould, 2013.
64 General Comment 16, para 10.
65 See, e.g., Solove, 2013: 1880; Mai, 2016: 192.

References

Bernh Larsen Holdings AS v Norway [2013] App no. 24117/08 (European Court of Human Rights).

Boyd, D. and Crawford, K. (2012). Critical Questions for Big Data – Provocations for a Cultural, Technological and Scholarly Phenomenon. *Information, Communication & Society*, 15(5), pp. 662–679.

Canepa v Canada [1997] UNDoc. CCPR/C/59/D/558/1993 Communication No. 558/1993 (Human Rights Committee).

CCPR. (2009). *Consideration of Reports Submitted by States Parties under Article 40 of the Covenant: Concluding Observations, The Netherlands.* UN Doc CCPR/C/NLD/CO/4. [online] Geneva: United Nations. Available at: www.refworld.org/docid/4aa7aa642.html [Accessed 22 Dec. 2017].

Coerial and Aurik v NL [1991] (Human Rights Committee).

Copland v UK [2007] App no. 62617/00 ECHR 2007 (European Court of Human Rights).

Diggelmann, O. and Cleis, M. (2014). How the Right to Privacy Became a Human Right. *Human Rights Law Review*, 14(3), pp. 441–458.

Emmerson, B. (2014). *Report on Mass Digital Surveillance and Article 17.* New York: United Nations.

Feldman, D. (1994). Secrecy, Dignity, or Autonomy? Views of Privacy as a Civil Liberty. *Current Legal Problems*, 47(Part 2), pp. 41–71.

Gavison, R. (1980). Privacy and the Limits of Law. *The Yale Law Journal*, 89(3), p. 421.

Gow, G. (2005). Privacy and Ubiquitous Network Societies – Background Paper. *International Communication Union – Workshop on Ubiquituous Network Societies.* Available at: www.itu.int.osg/spu/ni/ubiquitous/Papers/Privacy%20background%20paper.pdf

Human Rights Committee. (2004). *Consideration of Reports Submitted by States Parties Under Article 40 of the Covenant, Concluding Observations Russia.* Geneva: United Nations.

Human Rights Council. (2017). *HRC report on Recent Developments and Thematic Updates.* A/HRC/34/61. Geneva: United Nations.

Independent Reviewer of Terrorism Legislation. (2016). *Report of the Bulk Powers Review*. London: Independent Reviewer of Terrorism Legislation.

Joseph, S., Schultz, J. and Castan, M. (2005). *The International Covenant on Civil and Political Rights: Cases, Materials, and Commentary*. Oxford: Oxford University Press.

Lillich, R. (1984). Civil Rights. In: T. Meron, ed., *Human Rights in International Law: Legal and Policy Issues*. Oxford: Clarendon Press.

Mai, J. (2016). Big Data Privacy: The Datafication of Personal Information. *The Information Society*, 32(3), pp. 192–199.

Malone v UK [1984] App. No. 8691/79 (European Court of Human Rights).

Nowak, M. (2005). *UN Covenant on Civil and Political Rights: CCPR Commentary*. 2nd ed. Arlington: NP Engel.

OHCHR. (1999). *CCPR General Comment No. 27: Article 12 (Freedom of Movement)*. CCPR/C/21/Rev.1/Add.9. [online] Geneva: United Nations. Available at: www.refworld.org/docid/45139c394.html [Accessed 22 Dec. 2017].

OHCHR. (2009). *Report of the Special Rapporteur on the Promotion and Protection of Human Rights and Fundamental Freedoms while Countering Terrorism*. Geneva: United Nations.

OHCHR. (2014i). *HRC, Concluding Observations on the Fourth Periodic Report of the United States of America*. CCPR/C/USA/CO/4. Geneva: United Nations.

OHCHR. (2014ii). *The Right to Privacy in the Digital Age*. A/HRC/27/37. Geneva: United Nations.

Rehof, L. (1999). Article 12. In: G. Alfredsson and A. Eide, eds., *The Universal Declaration of Human Rights*. The Hague: Martinus Nijhoff.

Rengel, A. (2013). *Privacy in the 21st Century*. The Hague: Martinus Nijhoff.

Rotaru v Romania [2000] App No. 28341/95 (European Court of Human Rights).

Shelton, D. and Gould, A. (2013). Positive and Negative Obligations. In: D. Shelton, ed., *The Oxford Handbook of International Human Rights Law*. Oxford: Oxford University Press.

Singer, N. (2012). Mapping, and Sharing, the Consumer Genome. *The New York Times*. [online] 16 June 2012. Available at: www.nytimes.com/2012/06/17/technology/acxiom-the-quiet-giant-of-consumer-database-marketing.html?pagewanted=all&_r=1 [Accessed 27 Apr. 2017].

Solove, D. (2006). A Taxonomy of Privacy. *University of Pennsylvania Law Review*, 154(3), p. 477.

Solove, D. (2013). Privacy Self-Management and the Consent Dilemma. *Harvard Law Review*, 126.

Toonen v Australia [1992] (Human Rights Committee).

Van Hulst v NL [2004] Doc. A/60/40, Vol. II (Human Rights Committee), p. 29.

Wahlqvist, C. (2017). Under the Skin. *The Guardian*. [online] Available at: www.theguardian.com/technology/2017/nov/01/under-the-skin-how-insertable-microchips-could-unlock-the-future [Accessed 6 Nov. 2017].

Weber and Saravia v Germany [2006] App. No. 54934/00 (European Court of Human Rights).

Westin, A. (1967). *Privacy and Freedom*. New York: Atheneum.

Wieser and Bicos Beteiligungen GmbH v Austria [2007] App no 74336/01 ECHR 2007-IV (European Court of Human Rights).

Zakharov v Russia [2015] (European Court of Human Rights).

10 Article 15

The right to a nationality

Laura van Waas

A student examining the UDHR for the first time may pick out Article 15 as something of a curiosity, given the philosophy that lies at the heart of the Declaration. If "all human beings are born free and equal in dignity and rights", then what purpose does (the right to a) nationality serve? Yet, even as the UDHR enshrined a philosophy of denationalisation of rights, the centrality of the state system and of the role that nationality plays in positioning human beings within that system could not be ignored. Nationality was still understood to be of fundamental importance: securing for people a place to call home, a community to participate in and a status which empowers the exercise of other rights.

In fact, nationality has been described as the "right to have rights" – a phrase most famously employed by Hannah Arendt in her 1951 work *The Origins of Totalitarianism*,[1] but one which recurs with regularity in human rights scholarship to this day. Even if on paper human rights law promises protection (largely) regardless of nationality, in reality, nationality indeed acts as an enabler right. The vulnerable position and daily struggle of so many of the world's stateless people provides stark evidence of that.[2]

In this light, this chapter discusses the content and significance of Article 15 of the UDHR. It traces the evolution of the international community's approach to nationality 'problems', with a particular focus on its response to statelessness. The first section explains how nationality emerged from the reserved domain of states to become an individual human right, with the adoption of the UDHR as a key – although not the only – watershed in this process. The essay then looks at what realising the right to a nationality demands of states: concrete examples from around the world are used to illustrate some of the contexts in which statelessness can arise, and an examination is made of the progressive development of norms that give further content to the right to a nationality. Finally, the chapter closes by commenting on emerging developments in respect of the right to a nationality and the international community's response to statelessness.

Nationality: from state prerogative to individual right

As with many of the rights contained within the UDHR, the story of the right to a nationality begins some time before 1948. In the mid-1920s, the Assembly of the League of Nations tasked a Committee of Experts with preparing a "list of the subjects of International Law the regulation of which by international agreement would seem to be most desirable and realisable at the present moment".[3] Nationality found its way to the top of their provisional shortlist. At the time, regulating acquisition and loss of nationality was the sole prerogative of states – it fell within their *domaine reservé*.[4] This led to conflicts of nationality laws that bestowed some people with multiple nationalities and left others without any, two scenarios identified as problematic by states.

At the 1930 Hague Codification Conference, a Convention on certain questions relating to the conflict of nationality laws and three Protocols were adopted. According to the preambles, these embodied the "first attempt at progressive codification" on nationality matters, with the aim of realising the "abolition of all cases of statelessness and of double nationality". They laid down a number of rules for states to adhere to in their domestic law in order to resolve these two nationality anomalies that were considered undesirable. For the first time, governments accepted the notion of international law constraints on their freedom to regulate nationality.

Although an element of their stated ambition was to ensure that everyone could enjoy a nationality, the instruments drawn up in 1930 treated nationality as a technical issue and were designed to deal with situations that were considered a problem from the perspective of inter-state relations. As such, while the reserved domain was being eroded, people remained the object rather than the subject of these international norms. It was not until the adoption of the UDHR that the position and interests of individuals were given real credence and the language in which nationality was discussed was infused with the vocabulary of 'rights'. The first paragraph of Article 15 of the UDHR proclaims that "everyone has the right to a nationality", a norm that can be understood as a rights-based re-statement of the ambition that statelessness should be avoided. Then, "reflecting the international community's condemnation of the mass expulsions and manipulative denationalization of Russians, Jews and other racial and ethnic minorities in Europe that had occurred in the 1920s, 1930s, and 1940s",[5] the second paragraph adds that, "no one shall be arbitrarily deprived of his nationality nor denied the right to change his nationality".

Less than a year after the affirmation of nationality as an individual right in the UDHR, the UN released a 'Study of Statelessness'. Undertaken to help inform "the adoption of interim measures to afford protection to stateless persons and action to ensure that everyone shall have an effective right to a nationality",[6] the report comments on why statelessness presents a problem for states, but also goes into some detail on the impact of statelessness on those affected. In this way, it helps to further inform an understanding of the statelessness that places the individual at the centre of interest. For instance, it explains that:

> Normally every individual belongs to a national community and feels himself a part of it. He enjoys the protection and assistance of the national authorities. When he is abroad, his own national authorities look after him and

> provide him with certain advantages. The organization of the entire legal and economic life of the individual residing in a foreign country depends upon his possession of a nationality. The fact that the stateless person has no nationality places him in an abnormal and inferior position which reduces his social value and destroys his own self-confidence.[7]

The study laid the groundwork for the eventual adoption of the 1954 Convention relating to the Status of Stateless Persons and the 1961 Convention on the Reduction of Statelessness (UN Statelessness Conventions).[8] The former is designed to ensure that anyone who finds him or herself without a nationality[9] could still enjoy a minimum set of rights while the latter contains rules designed to reduce the incidence of statelessness and counter arbitrary deprivation of nationality more generally. With the adoption of these two dedicated conventions on statelessness, a multilateral framework was put in place to give further content to Article 15 of the UDHR and promote its realisation.

Statelessness: putting the right to nationality into practice

After the two UN Statelessness Conventions were adopted, statelessness seemingly disappeared as a topic of interest to the international community. The conventions themselves "drew very little interest . . . state parties were unforthcoming and the instruments were relatively slow to enter into force".[10] States continued to be fierce guardians of their sovereignty to regulate the conditions for access to nationality, and the 1961 Convention on the Reduction of Statelessness was distinctly unpopular, attracting just 15 states' parties over the course of its first 30 years of existence. Meanwhile, although the Office of the United Nations High Commissioner for Refugees "was originally mandated in its 1950 Statute to address the situation of stateless persons . . . this was limited to stateless persons who were refugees",[11] and the agency's activities on statelessness remained very restricted until the end of the century.[12]

In short, there was a dearth of statelessness-specific engagement by the international community, even as people around the world continued to face severe obstacles to enjoying a nationality. Indeed, in countries as diverse as Kuwait, Bangladesh, Syria, Myanmar and Kenya, processes of decolonisation, population registration and the construction of new national identities left situations of large-scale statelessness in their wake throughout the 1960s, 70s and 80s. All the while, the failure to deal with conflicts of nationality laws and the restrictive nature of some nationality rules was also continuing to generate new instances of statelessness.

For some time then, there appeared to be a significant mismatch between the scale of the statelessness challenge and the level of attention paid to the phenomenon. Yet, as the field of human rights developed, nationality as an individual right stayed in view and evolved in content. As set out in the following sections, the progressive crystallisation of the right to a nationality has helped to lay a solid normative basis – complementary to the framework created through the UN Statelessness Conventions – for addressing a variety of the contexts in which statelessness arises across the globe.

The exclusion of minorities from nationality

In 1962, the Syrian government carried out a one-day census in al-Hasakah, re-registering all inhabitants of this Kurd-dominated province. The stated purpose of the exercise was to root out 'infiltrators' (Kurds who had illegally crossed into the country from Turkey and elsewhere), but the census is widely understood to have been an instrument used to strengthen Syria's Arab national identity.[13] As people registered in the census, they were categorised as foreigners (*Ajanib*) if they were unable to furnish sufficient documentation to prove their ties by birth or ancestry to Syria, which many Kurds could not. Those who, for whatever reason, did not participate in the census at all were left unregistered (*Maktooumeen*) and were also no longer deemed to be Syrian. The census resulted in large-scale deprivation of nationality from members of Syria's Kurdish community: an estimated 120,000 people became stateless overnight.[14]

The Syrian census is just one example of nationality policy targeting a minority group for exclusion. In fact, across the globe, ethnic and religious minorities have commonly been vulnerable to the denial or deprivation of nationality and to statelessness:[15] the Rohingya community in Myanmar and Nubians in Kenya; the Lhotshampas in Bhutan and Faili Kurds in Iraq; the Urdu-speakers in Bangladesh and persons of Haitian descent in the Dominican Republic, as well as other groups around the world.

All nationality laws, by virtue of their nature as instruments which define who belongs to a state and who does not, must *exclude* as well as *include*. Nevertheless, the use of nationality policy as a means to disenfranchise, marginalise and even expel minority populations is manifestly at odds with human rights law as it has developed with and since the adoption of the UDHR. Indeed, the prohibition of arbitrary deprivation of nationality, contained in paragraph 2 of Article 15 of the UDHR, aims to prevent precisely this. The Convention on the Elimination of All Forms of Racial Discrimination, adopted in 1965, includes the right to a nationality in its Article 5, and the Committee which supervises this instrument has explained that, "deprivation of citizenship on the basis of race, colour, descent, or national or ethnic origin is a breach of states parties' obligations to ensure non-discriminatory enjoyment of the right to nationality".[16] This Committee and other human rights bodies have expressed concern over racially, ethnically or religiously biased nationality laws and practices around the globe. From the mid-1990s onwards, the UN Human Rights Council (previously the Commission) has also regularly adopted resolutions on 'Human rights and arbitrary deprivation of nationality', helping to secure greater visibility for the issue in the human rights domain, including by prompting a number of UN studies on the topic.[17]

Perhaps most notable of all developments in respect of minorities' enjoyment of the right to a nationality, however, is their successful appeal to (quasi-)

judicial bodies to assert their claim to citizenship. In the cases of *Yean and Bosico v Dominican Republic* and *Minors of Nubian descent v Kenya*, the Inter-American Court of Human Rights and the African Committee of Experts on the Rights and Welfare of the Child, respectively, ruled in favour of the complainants, whose access to nationality was being obstructed because of their specific racial or ethnic origins.[18] In both instances, the defendant states were instructed to amend their procedures and fulfil the right to nationality without discrimination. These decisions, dating from 2005 to 2011, demonstrate how far human rights law has progressed the influence of international law on nationality matters since the early 1900s when it was part of the *domaine reservé* of states. There remains a long way to go to achieve, in practice, the inclusion of all stateless minorities within their national communities and the non-discriminatory enjoyment of the right to a nationality, but it is an area in which human rights law provides a strong foundation for action.

Women's (equal) nationality rights

Another form of discrimination which has contributed to nationality problems, including statelessness, is that of targeting women. In the early- and mid-twentieth century, it was widespread practice for the nationality of women and children to be dictated by that of the male head of household: a woman who married a man holding another nationality would have her nationality converted to align with this new connection, and children would acquire nationality through their father (not their mother). Such "gender-based discrimination in nationality matters stemmed from the 'principle of unity of nationality of the family' according to which every member of the family should have the same nationality – that of the husband or father".[19] This system of dependant nationality can cause statelessness, for instance, where a woman loses her original nationality upon marriage, without securing access to a new nationality through her husband, or a child is born to an unknown, deceased or stateless father. These problems were among the scenarios dealt with by early international instruments relating to the conflict of nationality laws – offering a technical solution to something that was considered to be an unfortunate by-product of the way the predominant rules operated.[20]

The emergence of nationality as a human right altered the perspective on this issue too, and when the Convention on the Elimination of All Forms of Discrimination Against Women (CEDAW) was adopted in 1979, it enshrined the protection of women's equal and independent nationality rights in its Article 9. Since then, one country after another has completed the transition to gender-neutral nationality rules. At the time of writing of this essay, there were just 26 states remaining where women do not have the same right as men to transmit nationality to their children (although over 50 still disadvantage women in the ability to pass nationality to a foreign spouse).[21] The social and political dynamics around nationality rules make this an uphill struggle in several places where women are still awaiting equal rights. In June 2016, for example, the population of the

Bahamas voted 'no' (for the second time) in a referendum which would have amended the constitution to – among others – ensure that Bahamian women can transmit their nationality to their children on the same terms as men. Nevertheless, those countries in which the nationality law continues to treat women differently from men are under growing pressure from the global human rights system to enact reform, with this issue drawing attention from not only the CEDAW Committee but also other UN treaty bodies and within the Universal Periodic Review.[22]

The right of every child to acquire a nationality

Where nationality problems arise, they have a tendency to spread: citizenship by descent (*jus sanguinis*) is the most common rule for the conferral of nationality at birth,[23] and a stateless parent has no nationality to give. If the country of birth does not offer a safety net, statelessness is passed from one generation to the next. It is estimated that a child is born stateless, for precisely this reason, every ten minutes.[24] Outside of these contexts, children also sometimes fail to acquire a nationality for other reasons. These can include the lack of provision for the nationality of, for instance, abandoned children ('foundlings'), children who fall victim to a conflict of nationality laws and now, as a result of new technologies, also children born in the context of international commercial surrogacy – not to mention the risk of statelessness that arises from bureaucratic problems such as lack of access to birth registration for marginalised groups.[25] As a result, childhood statelessness is a challenge faced the world over.

In the further codification of the right to a nationality after the adoption of the UDHR, children have been a central focus. The International Covenant on Civil and Political Rights explicitly protects the right of every *child* to acquire a nationality (in Article 24), and the Human Rights Committee has held that, "States are required to adopt every appropriate measure, both internally and in cooperation with other States, to ensure that every child has a nationality when he is born".[26] Numerous other international and regional instruments promulgate similar standards, including the Convention on the Rights of All Migrant Workers and Members of their Families, the Convention on the Rights of Persons with Disabilities, the African Charter on the Rights and Welfare of the Child and the Covenant on the Rights of the Child in Islam. The *Yean and Bosico* and *Nubian Minors* cases mentioned earlier were also both decisions relating to the nationality rights of children.[27]

The Convention on the Rights of the Child (CRC) though is the most influential instrument when it comes to children's rights, and it too provides for the right of every child to acquire a nationality. The second paragraph of Article 7 CRC goes on to specify that, "States parties shall ensure the implementation of these rights in accordance with their national law and their obligations under the relevant international instruments in this field, *in particular where the child would otherwise be stateless*" (emphasis added). Although the CRC Committee has yet to issue dedicated guidance relating to the interpretation and implementation of this norm, through its regular dialogue with states' parties it has addressed a wide array of problems that conspire to create cases of childhood statelessness. It has clarified that states have an obligation to put in place safeguards to ensure that a stateless child born on their territory can acquire a nationality, to repeal gender discriminatory nationality laws, to provide a nationality to foundlings, to refrain from depriving children of their nationality and so on.[28] Again, human rights law has developed in such a way as to give the right to a nationality meaningful and relevant content in the fight against the root causes of statelessness.

Old problems, new ambitions: nationality and statelessness today

As this chapter discussed, 70 years ago nationality problems commanded considerable attention from the international community, prompting not just the inclusion of the right to a nationality in the UDHR, but also the development of dedicated conventions to deal with statelessness. After that, however, interest in statelessness waned – even though the problem itself did not diminish, as also highlighted in this essay. The period succeeding the adoption of the second UN Statelessness Convention in 1961 is widely perceived as a kind of dark age in respect of international engagement on this issue, and as late as 1999, a document published by UNHCR described the instruments themselves as "orphan conventions".[29]

Only in the past few years has a fresh flurry of activity projected statelessness back onto the international agenda, where it has gained traction once more. Most notably, in 2014, the Office of the United Nations High Commissioner for Refugees announced a campaign to end statelessness within a decade,[30] signalling a new level of ambition. What this chapter has shown is that even if there remains some way to go in fulfilling every human being's right to a nationality, and despite statelessness suffering an extended period of neglect, since the UDHR was adopted, nationality has consolidated its position as an individual right. Today, with clear signs of renewed interest in relegating statelessness to history, human rights law offers critical tools for the job.

It is, nevertheless, a job which should not be underestimated. On the one hand, the adoption of the UDHR marked an important milestone in the evolution of nationality from state prerogative to individual right. Significant progress has since been made in the further codification of the right to a nationality through the promulgation of detailed normative frameworks to address non-discriminatory access to nationality and protect the right of every child to acquire a nationality. In the twenty-first century, rulings by (quasi-) judicial bodies have even demonstrated the justiciability of this right. On the other hand, the right to a nationality retains a somewhat peculiar nature. Statelessness can only be solved through state action: the authority to grant nationality rests with states alone. And nationality policy is fiercely guarded, still commonly viewed as a matter of state sovereignty, given the role that it plays in constructing the nation itself. The underlying inclusion-exclusion dilemma is also one which rings eternal. Perhaps statelessness is just an inevitable manifestation of the fact that humankind has always organised itself into 'in-groups' and 'out-groups'. There is evidently a tension between these two realities, which has contributed to the difficulty inherent in realising the right to a nationality for all and helps to contextualise where things stand.

The 1949 UN *Study of Statelessness* commented in passing that "statelessness is a phenomenon as old as the concept of nationality".[31] Seventy years on, in spite of the recognition of nationality as a human right, as many as 15 million people remain stateless globally.[32] There is much work still to be done before the UDHR and broader human rights system fully deliver on their promise to break the pattern of exclusion.

Notes

1 Arendt, 1979: 296.
2 See, for instance, UNHCR: A Special Report: Ending Statelessness Within 10 years, 2014.
3 United Nations: Documents on the Development and Codification of International Law, 1947.
4 Permanent Court of International Justice.
5 Adjami and Harrington, 2008: 100.
6 A Study of Statelessness, 1949.
7 Ibid.
8 The 1949 UN study adopted a broad definition of *statelessness*, which included both persons without nationality and persons displaced from their home countries. As such, it also formed the foundation for the 1951 Convention relating to the Status of Refugees.
9 A 'stateless person' is defined in article 1 of the 1954 Convention relating to the Status of Stateless Persons as "a person who is not considered as a national by any state under the operation of its law".
10 van Waas, 2014: 79.
11 Manly, 2014: 89.
12 See further, Seet, 2016.
13 For instance, Refugees, 1996.
14 See further, Albarazi, 2013.
15 UN Human Rights Council, 2008.
16 UN Committee on the Elimination of Racial Discrimination, 2004, para. 14.
17 For instance, UN Human Rights Council, 2011.
18 Yean and Bosico Children v the Dominican Republic (2005); African Committee of Experts on the Rights and Welfare of the Child, 2011.
19 Govil and Edwards, 2014: 172.
20 Not only the 1930 Hague Convention on Certain Questions Relating to the Conflict of Nationality laws, but also the 1957 United Nations Convention on the Nationality of Married Women.
21 See further, the work of the Global Campaign for Equal Nationality Rights (Rights, 2017).
22 Khanna and Brett, 2017.
23 With the exception of the Western hemisphere, where *jus soli* (i.e., citizenship by birth on the territory) is prevalent.
24 A calculation based on population size and birth rates of the five largest (non-refugee) stateless communities worldwide. UNHCR, Global Action Plan to

End Statelessness (2014), p. 9. Accessed 3 April 2017. www.refworld.org/docid/545b47d64.html.
25 See further, the 'Checklist of identifying issues relating to the child's right to a nationality' (Addressing the Right to a Nationality through the Convention on the Rights of the Child: A Toolkit for Civil Society, 2016).
26 Human Rights Committee, 1989, para. 12.
27 Above n14. For a discussion of other cases in this area, see Bingham and Gamboa, 2017.
28 Addressing the Right to a Nationality through the Convention on the Rights of the Child: A Toolkit for Civil Society, 2016.
29 UNHCR, 1999.
30 See further, the #ibelong campaign website (IBELONG, 2017).
31 A Study of Statelessness, 1949.
32 The World's Stateless, 2014.

References

Adjami, M. and Harrington, J. (2008). The Scope and Content of Article 15 of the Universal Declaration of Human Rights. *Refugee Survey Quarterly*, 27(3), pp. 93–109.

African Committee of Experts on the Rights and Welfare of the Child. (2011). *Institute for Human Rights and Development in Africa (IHRDA) and Open Society Justice Initiative on behalf of children of Nubian descent in Kenya vs. Kenya*. Communication No.002/2009. Addis Abada: African Union.

Albarazi, Z. (2013). The Stateless Syrians. *Tilburg Law School Legal Studies Research Paper Series*. [online], 11. Available at: https://papers.ssrn.com/sol3/papers.cfm?abstract_id=2269700 [Accessed 13 Apr. 2017].

Arendt, H. (1979). *The Origins of Totalitarianism*. 3rd ed. New York: Harcourt Brace & Company.

Bingham, L. and Gamboa, L. (2017). Litigating Against Statelessness. In: L. van Waas and M. Khanna, eds., *Solving Statelessness*. Oisterwijk: Wolf Legal Publishers.

Govil, R. and Edwards, A. (2014). Women, Nationality and Statelessness. In: A. Edwards and L. van Waas, eds., *Nationality and Statelessness Under International Law*. Cambridge: Cambridge University Press.

Human Rights Committee. (1989). *General Comment No. 17: Rights of the Child*. Art. 24. Geneva: United Nations.

IBELONG. (2017). *IBELONG – Join the Campaign to End Statelessness*. [online] Available at: www.unhcr.org/ibelong [Accessed 20 Apr. 2017].

Institute on Statelessness and Inclusion. (2016). *Addressing the Right to a Nationality Through the Convention on the Rights of the Child: A Toolkit for Civil Society*. Eindhoven: Institute on Statelessness and Inclusion.

Khanna, M. and Brett, P. (2017). Making Effective Use of the UN Human Rights Mechanisms to Solve Statelessness. In: L. van Waas and M. Khanna, eds., *Solving Statelessness*. Oisterwijk: Wolf Legal Publishers.

Manly, M. (2014). UNHCR's Mandate and Activities. In: A. Edwards and L. van Waas, eds., *Nationality and Statelessness under International Law*. Cambridge: Cambridge University Press.

Permanent Court of International Justice.Series B, No. 4 (1923).

Refugees, U. (1996). *Refworld | Syria: The Silenced Kurds.* [online] Refworld. Available at: www.unhcr.org/refworld/docid/3ae6a8260.html [Accessed 2 Apr. 2017].

Rights, G. (2017). *Home.* [online] Equalnationalityrights.org. Available at: www.equalnationalityrights.org [Accessed 13 Apr. 2017].

Seet, M. (2016). The Origins of UNHCR's Global Mandate on Statelessness. *International Journal of Refugee Law*, 28(1), pp. 7–24.

A Study of Statelessness. (1949). New York: United Nations.

UN Committee on the Elimination of Racial Discrimination. (2004). *General Recommendation 30: Discrimination Against Non-Citizens.* Geneva: United Nations.

UN Human Rights Council. (2008). *Promotion and Protection of all Human Rights, Civil, Political, Economic, Social and Cultural Rights, Including the Right to Development – Report of the Independent Expert on Minority Issues.* A/HRC/7/23. Geneva: United Nations.

UN Human Rights Council. (2011). *Human Rights and Arbitrary Deprivation of Nationality: Report of the Secretary General.* A/HRC/19/43. Geneva: United Nations.

UNHCR: A Special Report: Ending Statelessness Within 10 Years. (2014). Geneva: UNHCR.

UNHCR. (1999). *Information and Accession Package: The 1954 Convention Relating to the Status of Stateless Persons and the 1961 Convention on the Reduction of Statelessness.* Geneva: United Nations.

United Nations: Documents on the Development and Codification of International Law. (1947). *The American Journal of International Law.* [online], 41(4). Available at: http://legal.un.org/ilc/documentation/english/ASIL_1947_study.pdf.

van Waas, L. (2014). The UN Statelessness Conventions. In: A. Edwards and L. van Waas, eds., *Nationality and Statelessness Under International Law.* Cambridge: Cambridge University Press.

The World's Stateless. (2014). Eindhoven: Institute on Statelessness and Inclusion.

Yean and Bosico Children v the Dominican Republic [2005] Series C No. 130 (Inter-American Court of Human Rights).

Section IV

Spiritual, public and political freedoms

(Articles 18–21)

Introduction to Section IV

Alexander Goldberg

The collection of essays in this section explores the set of rights concerned with spiritual, public and political freedoms. Freedom of religion, expression, assembly and association relate to the ability to participate individually or collectively in the public and political sphere. These rights both protect the individual's right to participate in civil society – in religious life, in political associations, trade unions and government – as well as the right of individuals to act within such collectives.

In looking back over human rights in the last 70 years, the tension between collective and individual rights has been a challenge for inter-governmental bodies, governments, civil society organisations and individuals trying to uphold their own rights. What comes to the fore is this tension between the mainly individualist approach taken by the authors of the Declaration and the more collectivist approach taken by some of its early detractors.

Williams, in his essay on religious liberties and the need for moral universalism, unpacks this paradox: "So if the significance of the language of human rights is essentially about limiting the state, it is implicitly bound up with the recognition that individuals belong to communities and exercise identities other than those defined by the state." In his essay he calls for both an upholding of the moral universalism of human rights and further urges religious communities to do likewise, arguing that there is a need to respect difference. He contends that religious freedom can be upheld by allowing communities of faith to go about their business unfettered by state interference. He advocates that where there are strongly held religious convictions, the state should allow some flexibility: "Thus it seems entirely in accord with the basic principles of a publicly secular society to allow certain conscientious exemptions for religious believers in instances where the community teaching is clear."

In his essay on Articles 18 and 19, Wilkes claims that "few controversies over human rights draw more international attention than the clash setting a right of religious communities to defend their convictions against a right on the part of individuals to express criticism of those convictions." He analyses this conflict and calls in the end for a practical approach to resolving conflicting views, regarding these sets of rights, between secularists and the religious and between regional and other international blocs that dominate the political coalitions within the UN system.

Wilkes looks at perceived clashes of religious rights and freedom of expression from the Salman Rushdie Affair to the modern day. Helpfully, he dissects the intent of the drafters of the UDHR and the debate that ensued for decades over whether human rights per se could have what he describes as a 'Foundationalist Approach' – that some human rights should take pre-eminence over others.

Wilkes supports the approach that sees these rights, especially freedom of religion, as an individual's right to practice his or her own religion and to hold a set of beliefs. He challenges the foundationalist approach that "accords exceptional status to one right over others" as having "multiple problems." His view seems to both curtail optimism whilst refuting growing pessimism about how best to resolve this conflict of rights. His approach is one of realism that contextualises rights. In doing so, he holds these rights up as a gold standard. His advocacy for a pluralistic approach to rights maintains both the pre-eminence of the UDHR, whilst recognising that in a changing world there is a need to use these norms as tools for dissecting the issues of the age – security and terrorism, clashes between theocratic and democratic nation states and between the secularists and the religious wishing to express their own rights.

My own essay focuses on Article 20, freedom of peaceful assembly and association. Complementing Wilkes' essay, it looks at these rights in terms of their development since the UDHR, both within the ICCPR and regional mechanisms. Like Wilkes, I have explored other parts of the UN machinery and in particular the approach taken by the International Labour Organization (ILO) in developing these rights concurrent to the UDHR approach.

Freedom of peaceful assembly and association are enshrined not only within the UDHR and ensuing Covenants but also within the ILO's own instruments, namely the Declaration Concerning the Aims and Purposes of the International Labour Organisation (Declaration of Philadelphia) and the Convention concerning Freedom of Association and Protection of the Right to Organise. These have a more 'collectivist' feel and predate the UDHR approach by several months, and came into force decades before the two International Covenants. However, there is clearly an interplay between the ILO and UN human rights instruments with regional human rights bodies, national legislation and case law.

It seems that both the two sources for these rights and the different historical roots for both freedom of assembly and freedom of association have jolted a UN that is often reluctant to accept collective rights into doing precisely that.

All three essays consider in different ways how security has been a challenge and has been used to justify limiting or restricting these rights. Yet, the set of rights in this section are never far from the public eye and scrutiny, and remain as important today, if not more so, than they did in 1948. The challenge is how best to navigate the inevitable conflicts and to limit the restrictions on these rights and uphold the presumption in favour of their exercise.

In the words of Williams,

> the basic importance of all human rights discourse, I would argue, is its statement of the limits of executive power and state sovereignty. It declares that the state must recognise areas of human life where it has no authority to claim final control: it acknowledges that certain claims or liberties cannot be derogated, and so declares that it is answerable to more than its immediate self-interest.

Indeed, the way a state allows us the citizens to participate, individually or collectively, in the public and political sphere, is the litmus test of whether it is a democracy, and by extension its preparedness to uphold the human rights of all.

11 Religious liberties and the need for moral universalism

Rowan Williams

This collection of essays had its origins partly in an event commemorating the life and legacy of a remarkable Jewish human rights activist, Clemens Nathan. Among the many contributions he made to the advancement of legal and moral thoughtfulness was his involvement in the issue of post-Holocaust restitution, but his abiding passion in the whole area of human rights has been celebrated by many friends and associates, and is very appropriately continued through the work of the research centre which bears his name.

Clemens' witness in all this is a potent reminder of the world out of which the UDHR first emerged. It was a world that had seen the collapse in more than one nation of any pretence at maintaining the essentials of the rule of law – that is, the collapse of any ideal of a universal and non-negotiable claim by citizens on governments. It is more than the claim for protection, often treated as the basis of the legitimacy of government, and – importantly – still part of what the organs of the international community appeal to so as to support a 'duty to protect', a duty to provide citizens in extreme situations with the security their own governments have failed to provide. It is a somewhat more extensive ideal than protection alone, since it understands protection to involve *equal* security for all: a government's duty is to guarantee that every citizen has the same right of access to redress for injury – including injury inflicted *by* government or its agents.

The breakdown of the rule of law happens when certain classes of citizens cannot have the same expectation of redress as their neighbours or when the state asserts the right to override or ignore a citizen's claims against it. A 'lawful' state is one in which the agents of the state are subject to the law. There are conflicts and crises posed by states of emergency, in which government may claim the right to suspend certain liberties for the sake of security. But the declaration of such states of emergency has itself to be justified in terms of the long-term preservation of lawful universal redress; it cannot supersede this, and it is properly regarded as a measure that needs the most serious scrutiny. European jurists generally agree in postulating that there are liberties that cannot be 'derogated' from even in emergency (for example, the right not to be tortured), and the role of international law in this is affirmed by the UN provision that the Secretary-General should be notified if such a suspension occurs and that a full rationale should be provided.

Some jurisdictions are clear that lasting legal and constitutional changes cannot be made during a state of emergency.

The point is that even in extreme instances there is a widespread presumption that the rule of law implies the impossibility of simply taking the state's agents out of the reach of the law. In other words, this is a scheme in which the state is always answerable for its decisions and for its management of the equal claims of citizens as citizens. The totalitarian states of the twentieth century, in effect, claimed to be answerable not to the specified liberties of citizens but to one or another kind of ideological programme requiring the suspension or abolition of a fully independent legal system. And the effects of this have been invariably to take certain individuals and groups out of the law's protection – most horrifically and unequivocally in the policy of the Third Reich towards Jewish citizens, but also in the stripping of protection from other categories of German citizen – those classed as mentally 'deficient', sexual minorities, Roma and others. Other states show at least some parallels, as in the liquidation of parts of the rural Russian population by Stalin, and the state's general refusal to take responsibility for the families of executed criminals in China. It seems that it took these dreadful aberrations to awaken the nation states of the world to the fact that they were still taking for granted the existence of some areas of human life where mere political sovereignty did not confer absolute immunity; and that if they were taking this for granted, it might be a good idea to say so as clearly as possible. Hence the Declaration.

The 'Westphalian' era in European politics began at a time when new nation states wanted to curb the power of religious bodies precisely so as to create a system of law and equity open to all citizens; the state's sovereignty was in part what established the fact that no one community within the state could claim privilege over others (as in a confessional polity). The risk was of course that sovereignty could be understood simply as the state's monopoly on coercive force. Enlightenment universalism, the appeal to rational argument as the universally accessible vehicle for determining justice, proved a more slippery affair than some modern enthusiasts allow; it certainly did little or nothing to put an end to the original sin of the early modern world order, the expansion of national economies on the foundation of slavery. The great slogan of the English abolitionists, 'Am I not a man and a brother?', came not from secular universalism but from a robust and radical appropriation of explicitly Jewish-Christian themes. 'Fraternité' might have been an aspiration of the French Revolution, but its resonances were strongly theological for all that, grounded in the regular appeal in Jewish and Christian scripture to *kinship* as an ethical criterion – shared 'ancestry', shared relation to the same progenitor. In Jewish Torah, the primary community is the people who have been created by a common act of grace or liberation, whose simple ethnic unity is further grounded by a unity of calling and active relation with the one who calls. And this intra-community universalism, in which every member of the community lives under equal promise of justice and redress, is increasingly thought of as a focal point for judging the world's other societies, even for implying that they might share the benefit of this level of solidarity. It is a universalism of covenant – each person being seen as equally the object of a divine commitment. And in Christian scripture, the same basic pattern is developed in terms of a covenant community in which each is endowed by God – equally but not uniformly – with gifts for the life of the entire group. The covenant is lived out in the exchange of gifts; the life of each is seen as dependent on the life of all, and vice versa. There is no member of the community without an essential endowment for the common good, and so the well-being and flourishing of each is an essential concern. No-one is dispensable.

It is perhaps this principle that no-one is dispensable which marks out a religiously inflected approach to human rights from a purely forensic or claims-based one. If all we have is a conviction that each person is to be credited with a set of claims to equal redress, that is a positive step, but one that tells us nothing about why they are to be so credited. The emphasis in the Jewish-Christian framework on the imperative to allow each person to make the contribution they are capable of making, grounds the right to equal access to justice in the positive capacity to make a difference in the lives of others, simply by virtue of being a distinct human subject. This right is not therefore something that has to be earned or something that can be forfeited by inadequate performance. Nor is it a reward for behaviour conforming to certain kinds of religious teaching.

This point is worth underlining in the contemporary context, since it provides the basis on which a conservative Christian with reservations about the theological status of same-sex relationships should still want to affirm unconditionally the civic liberty and human dignity of sexual minorities; a point that currently bedevils much discussion of 'the human rights agenda' in the discourse of some conservative apologists, and which threatens at times to create a gulf between religious communities and the language of human rights. The acknowledgement of a certain moral and legal status in each person is the foundation on which the state may legitimately recognise the conscientious aspirations of a minority in respect of legal recognition and security for partnerships, even if these are not universally regarded as religiously acceptable.

It is a worrying fact that these issues contribute to the standoff that some see between religious faith and human rights. Some religious representatives dismiss the entire idea of 'rights' as an improper language for radically dependent and interdependent creatures, and associate such language with a simple idealisation of autonomy, the right of self-determination. On the other side, defenders of human rights see an intrinsic opposition between the affirming of human dignity in the ways usually associated with rights campaigns and the supposedly repressive influence of religious faith. It is disastrous for both human rights discourse and religious language if either is allowed to forget its historical implication with the other.

Another somewhat sensitive question is the hesitation in some Islamic quarters over the interpretation of religious freedom in terms of human rights. The Declaration recognises the right to change one's religion, a course of action that has almost universally been seen as punishable in the framework of Islamic law. Debates are developing as to what a contemporary Muslim jurist might say about this strongly rooted tradition, but a similar principle applies as in the case just discussed. A legal liberty granted in the framework of universal access to the same kinds of redress should be capable of recognition even by a community which would sanction the behaviour arising from that liberty; and the degree of sanction is therefore bound to be thought through in the context of that wider legal liberty. Any other option would be to create a theocratic ghetto where the law of the state does not run. Recognition of communal norms and minority conscience-driven practices is not the same as suspending the actual liberties of any individual.

This relates to the difficult question of whether our language about the rights of individuals should be balanced by attention to the rights of communities. I suspect that this is not quite the right question to be asking, to the extent that it implies a need to set these two things off against each other. The basic importance of all human rights discourse, I would argue, is its statement of the limits of executive power and state sovereignty. It declares that the state must recognise areas of human life where it has no authority to claim final control: it acknowledges that certain claims or liberties cannot be derogated, and so declares that it is answerable to more than its immediate self-interest. In a negative sense, it establishes the state as a *moral agent* to the extent that the state admits it is not the final arbiter of good and evil and commits itself to an absolute regard for every citizen, irrespective of the citizen's usefulness, conformity or whatever else. Its universalism is in recognising that all citizens are always more than *just* citizens: it treats them as moral agents, responsible to a variety of systems or convictions.

The paradox of human rights is that it is in one sense profoundly secular, in refusing to identify the state with any religious authority, while also being profoundly respectful of convictions derived from non-political, even non-'worldly' sources. When Lord Acton observed in the nineteenth century that religious freedom was the basis of all political freedoms, he was not claiming that religious freedom was more important than other kinds, but noting the fact that any kind of conviction not based on either political power or pragmatic calculation will imply a limit to the state's legitimate exercise of control. Religious conviction is the oldest and arguably strongest such phenomenon; accepting its role in the state and its security from the state's defining control is the beginning of an authentic political pluralism.

So if the significance of the language of human rights is essentially about limiting the state, it is implicitly bound up with the recognition that individuals belong to communities and exercise identities other than those defined by the state. The state itself cannot enforce the internal discipline of a religious body, but it can recognise both the way in which a communally held conviction or discipline shapes behaviour in the public square and the public and legal 'persona' of a religious community and its needs to be corporately secured against violence or threat. Thus it seems entirely in accord with the basic principles of a publicly secular society to allow certain conscientious exemptions for religious believers in instances where the community teaching is clear. This applies, to take one of the most immediate instances, in regard to wearing certain religious symbols or, as with the Sikh turban, accommodating conventional safety regulations to allow some flexibility. More seriously, the continuing legal exemptions relating to performing abortions or the redefinition of the historic legal rights of parishioners in respect of marriage so that churches will not be legally sanctioned for same-sex marriages reflect the same principle. There is discussion as to whether if some form of physician-assisted suicide were legalised, similar conscientious provision would be needed.

The point is, given that views on all these matters are disputed even among believers, that the law recognises a conscientious position based on what is still a quite strongly identifying communal position. It recognises that it must deal with convictions whose origins and legitimacy lie beyond its jurisdiction. And in prohibiting open incitement to violence or discrimination against any specific community, it recognises not only the rights of individual conscience but the rights of a community to be publicly visible and active within the law and to expect redress as a community. While the situation is often less clear in practice (how does the law determine whether something is a bona fide religious group? what counts as genuinely discriminatory behaviour by an employer?), there is an assumption that communities of conviction can expect to be guaranteed safety and protected from discrimination.

But at the present moment it seems as though the major priority in public ethics is the reaffirmation and reinforcement of the whole idea of universalism, in the sense that systematic thinking about the rule of law in contemporary democracies is not very much in evidence. The resurgence of populism in various Western societies, often accompanied by suspicion of human rights–based institutions or agencies (the European Court of Human Rights, the International Criminal Court and so on), suggests that there is a real risk of losing sight of some of the fundamental insights that fuelled the UDHR in the first place, a risk of reversion to an unexamined idea of national sovereignty unchastened by the challenges of universalist protocols about unrestricted and non-negotiable liberties.

The 'war on terror' has already raised questions about the limits of what can be derogated in terms of rights; torture or 'extreme interrogation' has been defended as a possibility in the international emergency believed to be confronting liberal democracies in an age of terrorism. The confusion and foot-dragging about the rights of refugees has been a symptom of a growing sense that the dignity and liberty of those who are not citizens of the same polity as ourselves is at best not a priority and at worst an embarrassing and debilitating drain on our communal self-interest. An uncomfortable number of jurisdictions, from Russia to Uganda, have discussed tightening the restrictions on the liberties of sexual minorities.

In this climate, we need – more than we have for some time – a clear set of statements about why the universalism of the UDHR matters and where it comes from. That's to say that we need two things. First, we need a simply pragmatic recognition that it is unrealistic in the extreme to think that problems can be held off at national borders any longer. Whether these are problems of environmental degradation, epidemic disease or the unprecedented displacement of populations as a result of war and social crisis, they cannot be contained. They will find their way back in a world more visibly and intractably interdependent than ever. Second, we need a way of talking about the philosophical foundations of universalism that keeps firmly at bay any suggestion that the state might after all seek to establish itself as arbiter of what is legitimate not only in the public square but in the realm of conscience and conviction.

The undermining of the credibility of an independent judiciary, press and intelligence service by certain agents in both the UK and the US augurs badly here. And to resist this, we have to articulate a strong doctrine not only of legal protection but of positive individual value. What we have noted earlier as the 'covenant'-based vision of Judaeo-Christian tradition deserves to be developed still further as a vehicle for defending universalist political ethics. In its fundamental and straightforwardly theological form, it affirms that every human subject is the object of a commitment by God, mediated in the community's life and history but still valid for the individual's sense of worth. Given that we cannot rely on theology as a natural idiom for public policy-making, we need therefore to translate this way of understanding human dignity in terms of the state affirming something like a covenant with its citizens – something very different from a 'contract'. The law of a state should communicate – as should the practices of social support and care – the proposition that the state is committed to the well-being of each citizen, and that it will not rest content with any practice which suggests that anyone is not needed. Historians and social analysts alike have underlined the effect of such a sense of being needed on vulnerable or disadvantaged elements in the population – and the ease with which the opposite message can be heard, with unequivocally destructive result.

The UDHR needs to be read and understood in this context, not as a potentially awkward and expensive statement of bald entitlements, but as crystallising positively the importance of educating a population in the security of being needed and negatively the importance of obliging the state to admit its limitations. Rather than allowing human rights and religious conviction to drift further apart, we should as a matter of urgency be seeking to clarify their significance for one another, so that religious faith does not slip into theocratic tyranny and human rights language does not become an abstract charter of claims. A better understanding of how the law as a matter of fact deals with religious diversity and conscientious reservation will help; so will the admission that moral universalism has a history, and one in which religious categories have played a decisive role. The vague belief that universal human rights is a self-evident good to be pursued will not long survive an honest historical study, and there are interested parties in all regions of the world today who would be more than content to bury any such motion of self-evidence for good and all in the name of various ideologies, nationalist or otherwise.

The UDHR stakes a claim that the most clearly legitimate society is one that builds in institutions and habits of self-criticism; without insisting on any one theological or philosophical justification, it simply announces that a state's legitimacy is always historically developed and refined in response to questions about its universal promise and universal assurance of redress. Those, including Christians and Jews, who drafted the UDHR in the wake of an unprecedented betrayal of the ideals of lawful government were not seeking to enforce an 'ideology' of rights, a new and sinister agenda; they were affirming that there will never be a time when states do not need challenge as to their behaviour. And the Declaration is there to guide and inform just such challenges.

12 Articles 18 and 19

When freedom of religion is pitted against freedom of expression

George R. Wilkes

Introduction

Seventy years after the UDHR, few controversies over human rights draw more international attention than the clash setting a right of religious communities to defend their convictions against a right on the part of individuals to express criticism of those convictions. Both religion and freedom of expression are seen by different communities as the most fundamental of rights, and the sense that they are engaged in a clash of civilisations is magnified by the record of violence and inter-state tensions associated with religious-secular antagonism over the last 40 years.

To place this in context, we begin with a brief history from the time of the UDHR itself. The Declaration continues to be recognised as a landmark document in international legal treatments of both of the rights we are concerned with here, but this brief history will highlight the reasons for which commentators commonly identify limits to its practical impact. We will examine in particular the marked contrast between the text itself and subsequent developments, notably due to the very political contest that strengthened some decades after 1948 over whether freedom of religion or freedom of expression should take priority when there is a perceived clash. Though some will fault the UDHR for not clarifying how to address potential conflicts between the rights set forth in Articles 18 and 19, and therefore enabling political antagonists to make use of such clashes for their own ends, others argue that conflicts over rights are so endemic that it would not be reasonable to expect such clarity in a declaration of rights – and the source of the politicisation of these clashes must be sought elsewhere.

What should we make of the fierce divisions over the relationship between these rights? In the second section, the chapter turns to the questions of principle that some perceive as fundamental to this conflict. We will see that for some commentators, the idea of a foundational clash of rights can appear overblown or even nonsensical, whether they argue this because of their concept of the nature of rights or because in practice they see the realities in which we negotiate claims about religion and freedom of expression resist a polarised simplification.

Will public debate nevertheless continue to burn as Western and non-Western protagonists advance their case on either pole of the moral or civilisational dispute?

The third and last section addresses this question, directing attention to what we can and what we cannot know, and assessing the kind of judgements that can reasonably be made about likely developments over the next 70 years.

As we address these questions, it is well to have in mind the connection between the different senses in which we can talk of these conflicts as 'political'. The highly political nature of these contests may not have been addressed in the UDHR, but these politicised conflicts might nevertheless be said to follow naturally from the place that Articles 18 and 19 share in the 'political' pillar of the UDHR. These rights are political in the sense that they reflect beliefs about the essential values on which our political systems are founded. They also generate political conflict because they concentrate attention on the divergent and complex political systems in which legal cases and public debates arise – 'Western' and 'Eastern', 'secular' and 'Islamic', 'democratic' and 'authoritarian'. In what follows, we trace the rise of international concern about these highly politicised conflicts not only to clashes between principles or types of state. These conflicts also reflect political 'settlements', engaging in some cases a wide range of actors, socially influential as well as politically dominant. Whereas the Rushdie Affair or the Danish Cartoons Affair witnessed antagonism between actors for whom human rights and religion are implacably opposed, we will see that there is no intellectual or political consensus behind this antagonistic representation of the state of our rights debate today. By contrast, the conceptual and practical political context for these conflicts remains one in which prominent actors view the topic in the light of a range of more or less cooperative relationships, ranging from common political action through institutional and social dialogues to an assumption of cross-civilisational consensus. The conclusion we advance towards is that the history and the future of those conflicts that do pit the freedom of religion against the freedom of expression will be understood better in light of these contextual political and social realities, rather than purely by reference to straightforward ideological oppositions.

A history, starting from the Universal Declaration of Human Rights

Where legal textbooks focus on this topic, the UDHR is generally granted recognition as a cornerstone or foundation for the development of international legal conventions treating religious freedom and freedom of expression. Its importance is commonly judged by the multitude of references to the UDHR in subsequent conventions, or by the fact that there are no subsequent conventions ratified by as many states as signed the UDHR. Nevertheless, from its inception, the UDHR has also been criticised, particularly in writing on Articles 18 and 19, for its lack of precision and the absence of concrete obligations or means of enforcement in courts of law.[1] In terms of purely international legal theory, this impression of abstraction may be deemed of little import: it is not the subject of as much academic attention as is, for instance, the question as to whether the UDHR has force as evidence of generally accepted customary law or as evidence that there is a core set of 'peremptory norms' (*jus cogens*) from which law-abiding actors cannot seek to deviate. This latter discussion has legal consequences wherever arguments for a state's restrictions on the exercise of rights are justified on the grounds of national security, and so the UDHR remains important in legal argument today for that reason.

The vagueness of the UDHR tends to be of more practical concern to campaigners for freedom of religion. These have commonly decried the absence of a follow-up convention concretising legal standards and commitments specifically focusing on religious freedom. The contrast is starkest when a comparison is made with some of the rights that have drawn inter-state coalitions to forge concrete agendas for treaty reform, notably through the conventions on the rights of the child, on the prohibition of torture and on the elimination of racial discrimination. Religious freedom is thus, it has been said, the 'orphaned' right.[2] Which might be said, too, of freedom of expression, also not the subject of a further convention promising increased institutional attention and mechanisms for legal enforceability.

This was far from the intention of the principal drafters of the UDHR, who viewed these rights to be of central importance. The preparations for the UDHR avoided the disputes of more recent decades over the apparent conflict between religious freedom and an individual's freedom of expression for at least two reasons. First, a number of the leading participants in the preparations of the UDHR advanced perspectives which rested on the centrality of religion to the full development of an individual's personal fulfilment.[3] That this was Eleanor Roosevelt's perspective might show the mark of distinctive American approaches to religion: her own debt to mainstream liberal American Protestantism, a long-term determination that American foreign policy should be anchored to the rejection of discrimination on religious grounds, and, in broader terms, the determination to promote religious liberty in other states. A range of other international perspectives also represented in the discussions laid equal weight on the importance of individual religious liberty. Proponents of a European Catholic personalism – a philosophy according to which a full and free personality is created through their most important subjective relationships – also had a weighty influence in the preparatory discussions. This was thanks in particular to the inspiration of Jacques Maritain, whose views were consistently represented in the discussions by the Lebanese delegate, Charles Malik.

Religious freedom, as these discussants conceived it, was an individual's freedom, including their freedom to choose a different religion and the freedom to do so in community with others. The freedom of members of a religious community remained, in their understanding, the freedom of the individual, not a right belonging separately to a community. As Malik expressed it, this freedom needed to be defended against intolerant sectarianism. Even the Soviet representative appeared to accept the personal framing advanced for religious freedom, and none of those active in the discussions were focused on liberty for an institutional or clerical religion rather than for individual humans. After the fact, the UDHR would be faulted by critics for excessive individualism, for uprooting the individual from the religious institutions that give meaning to their faith. Neither Roosevelt, Maritain, Malik or the others at the table raised this opposition. They did not see rights language focused on the individual as wrongfully divorcing individuals from their religious institutions or their religious personhood. They did not seek to identify areas of contention that followed from their divergent approaches to the rights of the individual in their religious community, nor from their differences over the status of religious communities vis-à-vis the state. As Linde Lindqvist points out, religious liberty was seen then as a first line of defence for religion against secularism – it came later to be seen instead as one of the 'defining features' of liberal secularism,[4] and therein lies a part of the background to the subsequent conflicts between defenders of religious liberty and the freedom of expression. Yet, if a fuller picture of the continuing significance of the UDHR is sought, it will be seen in a different light in the extent to which the focus on the freedom of the individual has been magnified in subsequent conventions: religious liberty soon became understood to encompass an individual's freedom *from* religion as part of the freedom of belief and conscience.

A second reason for this focus on the rights of the individual was the desire to avoid the conflicts surrounding minority rights that were associated with the rise of the National Socialist threat and the eclipse of the League of Nations in the 1930s.[5] Each of the great powers represented at the discussions in 1947 and 1948 continued to see minority rights being used against them by critics. Although the affirmation of religious freedom would inevitably generate public support for individuals from religious minorities, the members of the drafting committee preferred that a remedy be sought through the affirmation of religious liberty for all citizens. As a consequence of this focus on the rights of the individual – and not institutions representing minority groups – the individual's state-protected freedom of expression most naturally appeared to be in full harmony with their freedom of religion. Much of the subsequent contest between supporters of one of these rights over the other entails a dispute over the scope for a religious institution to be properly representing the claims of co-religionists to be protected from the free expression of their antagonists. Were this to have been acknowledged in the drafting of the UDHR, the young United Nations could have opened the door to the minority politics that the National Socialist government in Germany used to such disruptive effect, as it did, for instance, in the Sudetenland in the years preceding its invasion of Czechoslovakia in 1938.

The UDHR was not, then, framed in such a way that a clash between these rights could be addressed or limited, neither conceptually nor practically through precise legal definition. This vagueness in the framing of the UDHR[6] may be held to have been responsible – if only partially or indirectly – for the sometimes-violent international controversies characteristically pitting 'Western' approaches to free speech against 'Islamic' defences of religion. Subsequent international legal documents, while often affirming the significance of the UDHR in relation to these rights, have elaborated in greater detail on the nature of both freedoms. Gradually, some 'teeth' have been added as well: whereas the declaratory approach adopted in 1948 was deliberately not supplemented by the divisive creation of effective legal mechanisms to sanction obstructions of human rights,[7] a number of subsequent legal developments have meant cases could be presented in court, and this too may be one of the proximate causes of the developing perception that the two rights can and do clash in practice.

Further definition was given to the rights in the European Convention on Human Rights of 1949 (and of conventions applying to the Americas, to Africa and to the Arab States), the International Covenant on Civil and Political Rights (ICCPR) of 1966, and the 1981 United Nations Declaration on the Elimination of All Forms of Intolerance and of Discrimination Based on Religious Belief (again a declaration only, rather than a convention committing signatories to legally binding actions). In 1993, the UN Human Rights Committee published its General Comment No. 22 on Article 18 of the ICCPR, giving further definition to the scope of the right to freedom of religion, conscience and thought, and adding explicitly the critical point that the rights to freedom of religion and to freedom of expression cannot be derogated from[8] (although limits to this freedom in times of emergency are suggested in the UDHR and subsequent treaties).

The corpus of texts giving definition to international law in this area has included a wide range of thematic conventions as well, treating the rights of women, for instance, and the rights of the child. In war-time, too, the right to freedom of religious practice is anchored in the Geneva Conventions of 1949, irrespective of the less affirmative language about derogation in time of war of the UDHR. Though there has not been a binding convention devoted to either of the Article 18 or Article 19 rights, there is enough material in the preceding conventions for clashes to manifest themselves, over particular court cases and in the elucidation of areas in which states are accused of violations of the rights of large groups. A key arena in which international attention is drawn to these violations at the larger scale – the level of the rights of members of collectivities from which the drafters of the UDHR had shied away – was the expert Sub-Commission of the UN Commission on Human Rights, which before 1999 was known as the Sub-Commission on Prevention of Discrimination and the Protection of Minority Rights (dissolved in 2006). In 1986, the UN Commission on Human Rights instituted a Special Rapporteur on Religious Freedom, reporting initially to its expert Sub-Commission, and this has proven one of the most effective measures in the promotion of understanding about the application of this right . . . not without at-times-fierce resistance.

To characterise this resistance is one of the more interesting challenges presented as we seek to understand the rise of political divisions over religion and the freedom of expression at the United Nations in recent decades. Since the 1980s, inter-state discussions on these issues within the United Nations have been peppered with notions of a clash of ideologies: a conflict between West and non-West, or between North and South, between European, African and Asian states, between democracies and autocracies, or between Islamic and non-Islamic states. Yet these divisions all existed in the 1960s as well, when in stark contrast the Commission on Human Rights successfully forged the agreement between the Cold War blocs and the newly independent states, which led to a consensual acceptance of the Covenant on Civil and Political and the Covenant on Economic, Social and Cultural Rights. From the 1970s, the rise of the Islamic states has been seen by critics to be a force for division: between liberal and illiberal approaches, and applying to religious and to other political rights. From the time of the Rushdie Affair until 2010, representatives of an Islamic bloc sought repeatedly to define limits to the freedom of the individual to attack the divine, to attack or to defame established religion, limits which are not an accepted feature of the human rights mechanisms that have developed at the United Nations – since 2010, attention has shifted instead to efforts to combat offences to the feelings of the religious population in the context of countering intolerance. During this time, the proponents of protection for religion and for the followers of religious belief systems have won allies even amongst some secular, non-Islamic states that saw the issue not in religious terms, but as a matter of making common cause against the interventions of Western-style liberalism – evident, for example, in the Cuban government's support for the 'defamation of religion'.[9] For their critics, the politics of these defenders of Islamic perspectives on human rights were the product of a divisive, assertive or regressive approach to religious liberty. From the perspective of those states which sought to protect religious rights and sensibilities, many of which define themselves as partly secular, they were on the contrary seeking, as they saw it, a variety of balanced means by which to limit the impact of aggressive Western interference and internal political dissent. In this sensitive and politically charged context, distinguishing debate over principle from other more hard-nosed political interests is not straightforward.

Relating the clash over fundamental principles to political realities

The polarisation and the violence associated with clashes over religious liberty and the freedom of expression may provide evidence for the view that this is a battle over fundamentals, and yet this is a very incomplete picture.

The 'fundamentalist' views that present all rights as founded on a very few rights – potentially even solely on either the right to religious liberty or on the freedom of expression – such views may be said to be more associated with a campaigning voice than with the breadth of approaches taken in the academy, in courts, or even in quiet, backroom diplomatic negotiations. At the inception of the Universal Declaration, the moving spirits behind the Declaration held strongly to a religiously inflected rights foundationalism, albeit without construing the most fundamental rights to be in conflict with the other rights that they supported – for Roosevelt or Malik, this formulation would have appeared morally corrosive or nonsensical. Seventy years later, if this assumption of the inherent cohesion of different types of rights appears idealistic, it is chiefly because of the repeated conflicts in which antagonists have subsequently set rights against each other: religious liberty against the freedom of expression, or political against social rights.

Against this apparently titanic clash over foundational rights within the United Nations system, a more consensual approach has advanced from the time of the international covenants of the 1960s, and most particularly from the time of the Vienna Declaration on Human Rights of 1993, according to which all rights are indivisible. It follows that no one right or set of rights by dint of its nature takes automatic priority over other rights, and attempts to pursue a divisive approach are recognised as challenging the basis on which human rights are accepted. Whereas some contestants disputing the introduction of protection against the 'defamation of religion' may pit religious liberty and the freedom of expression against each other, it is more common to see the two rights described as intersecting, related or allied.[10]

At the conceptual level, too, a 'foundationalist' approach which accords exceptional status to one right over others has multiple problems.[11] Such an assertion locates the essence of a conflict over rights at an abstract conceptual level, rather than understanding conflicts to be a practical problem to be resolved in purely practical terms. It may be that additional practical arguments are made for enthroning religious liberty or the freedom of expression as the most basic right on which all others rest: arguments about the importance of that right for the functioning of society, for the flourishing of the individual, or for the defence of all rights in practice. In practice, however, the foundationalist approach isolates the abstract right from the context in which it is supposed to serve.[12] Where new, complex and socially challenging cases come to court, the intuition to set religion or the freedom of expression above other values can easily create harm as well as protect an individual's well-being. Where a case sets the religious right of a family against the religious right of their child, a simple assertion of the paramount value of religion cannot be free of other implied choices over values. Even where we may judge that historically there has been a special status accorded to religious freedom, as David Little memorably put it, in practical terms it would be unhelpful to seek to promote the supremacy of this over other rights.[13]

Against a paradigm setting the two rights against each other, legal theorist Peter Danchin sets a pluralism of rights and values, according to which judgements about rights in conflict with each other must be constructed not at an abstract level, but in the human and social context in which they occur.[14] Not because there are no potential clashes between expressions of a right at a conceptual level, but because such potential clashes are so intrinsic to the formulation of abstract rights that it would be irrational to seek to resolve them in the abstract. This more grounded approach proceeds from a description of rights conflicts as an inevitable feature of the development of international human rights law, one which is and can be dealt with through judicious compromise even in societies in which religious and secular perspectives are passionately held. Danchin takes his examples from the United States, South Africa, Russia, Denmark and France. Exemplary indications of such a rights-pluralism may equally be found in states with more contentious religious politics, in which the rights of established religious communities present regular challenges for public order, as Shimon Shetreet has shown in works comparing the institutional compromises made in India and Israel.[15] These compromises can be shown to represent an initial choice by the political leaders who shape the constitutional order, as Shetreet indicates. They also reflect, as he also indicates, a continuously renegotiated political settlement involving the divergent social components engaged in the making and remaking of national law. These different levels of analysis – constitutional, political and social – are distinguished in more recent research and religious liberty campaigning, separating trends within states with high levels of social discrimination but low levels of political or constitutional discrimination, from states which discriminate on religious grounds at all levels.[16] The UDHR did not provide for this type of distinction, focusing attention solely on the responsibility of states vis-à-vis individuals, regardless of the reasons for religious discrimination.

A pluralistic perspective drawing on these conceptual and practical dimensions is most easily evidenced in national contexts, marked by a degree of institutional cohesion and by the reinforcing political pressures in which conflicts are often resolved. What about at the United Nations? In the international realm, there is naturally less cohesion and less intensive pressure. This has allowed the continuation of fierce polemics across states, serving a range of political purposes, without the same expectation of timely practical or institutional results. Regional human rights systems present the nearest international equivalent to the nation state's intensive context for the resolution of conflicts over rights. Even in the most advanced European case, there are critics alleging systemic failures to advance a cohesive approach to the rights of religious minorities.[17] And yet, in his review of European and international legal developments, Malcolm Evans notes that the idea of a titanic battle does not describe the reality at either European or international levels, not least because the rights are so closely allied that either side in a European court case or a dispute in one of the UN treaty bodies could adduce arguments from each right.[18] The notion that the rights can be opposed therefore proceeds from a narrowing of perspective, either conceptually or in addressing a particular political context.

Where disagreements of principle meet political realities in the human rights mechanisms of the United Nations, it is most evident in the Charter-based political bodies rather than the specialist committees associated with specific treaties: the so-called treaty bodies. In the Commission on Human Rights, or in the committees at the General Assembly, the 'politicisation' or the 'politics' that complicates calculations about institutional reform or campaigning pressure is not simply characterised by the depth of the differences asserted by the actors most engaged in these conflicts, or most attached to one extreme position. UN politics is not so simple. On the contrary, it is also shaped by expectations about political relationships in UN bodies being more effective in being extensive than they are intensive: the politics is a politics of forging coalitions as large as possible, not simply forming blocking minorities. And so the politics undergirding clashes over the rights of religious majorities and religious minorities are also the politics of the formation of the largest possible coalitions and, in the long term, the strongest possible alliances. The Organisation of Islamic Cooperation must work with the League of Arab States, the African Union and the various formations that represent the non-aligned states; Danish or Dutch diplomats must secure the cooperation of the rest of the European Union; and the results will not be straightforward translations of a single ideological approach to institutionalising rights. This is the context in which coalitions of states ranged for and against a resolution on the defamation of religion jockeyed for over two decades, from 1999 to 2010, without result.

Prognosis: what can be said about the next 70 years?

The 70 years since the Universal Declaration have witnessed such unexpected changes that no prognosis for the next 70 years could be taken to be a firm prediction. Nevertheless, the conclusions reached in this essay may be extended into a prognosis for the next 70 years in two respects: descriptive and prescriptive.

The real-world conditions justifying assertive civil society campaigns on both of these issues have not abated over the past 50 years. Indeed, abuses of religious liberty are commonly said to be worsening globally. They have become, moreover, more widely associated with international conflict and instability – whether it be in Europe, in the Middle East, in Africa or in Central, South and South East Asia. Religiously inspired terrorism now threatens a widening range of countries, widening as internal conflicts become complicated by external state and non-state forces. These are the conditions in which conflicts between Article 18 and Article 19 rights are politicised. In light of this, religious expression becomes curtailed by dint of its association with sectarian ends. Legislators may see themselves now being presented with a variety of sectarian projects that appear harmful insofar as they are motivated – ideologically or merely in terms of alleged sympathy – by international political connections. The recognition that ostensibly sectarian conflicts are generally not religious in inspiration is a commonplace one. Still, over the course of a conflict, sectarian elements may strengthen to the point at which they dominate relationships at both the political and social levels. Given this state of affairs, it may seem overly optimistic to imagine pluralistic affirmations of religious freedom and freedom of expression becoming accepted where this is not yet the case. Even if we take the position that the perceived conflict between the two rights is conceptually unhelpful or conceptual nonsense, it is unlikely to disappear as long as the sharp real-world conflicts it feeds off persist.

Grounds for a similar pessimism about the development of more effective international mechanisms naturally exist as well. And yet the heightening connection between conflicts engaging religion and religious freedom issues may provide a basis for the kind of inter-state coalition that saw new treaty mechanisms designed to anathematise torture, to protect the rights of children and to counter terrorism. The terrorism parallel is worth bearing in mind: progress continues to be made in counter-terror activity at the United Nations, in spite of the challenge that states disagree about the conceptual nature of terrorism and its place in international society. The same may be said of Articles 18 and 19. States continue to disagree about the basis on which effective legal mechanisms could address the problems faced by religious minorities, the concerns of secular and religious majorities, and the freedom of others to exercise the right to dissent on the grounds of belief or conscience. And yet the need for common understanding and action is recognised, not least in the support granted to forthright interventions of the Special Rapporteur on Freedom of Religion or Belief.

If hopes for more effective legal mechanisms remain elusive, based on the as-yet-unachieved expectation of a global coalition in support of a new treaty, another ground for optimism may lie in greater inclusion or mainstreaming of divergent secular and religious sensibilities, and particularly of religious liberty concerns, in a comprehensive approach to conflict within UN institutions. This may be imagined not on the basis of a new unified doctrinal approach to religion within the UN institutions, but rather more gradually, as the challenges associated with religion gain recognition on a policy-by-policy basis. The Secretary-General's Special Adviser on Genocide Prevention, for instance, has supported a programme of action highlighting the role of religion in genocide prevention and in advancing the Responsibility to Protect. The importance of taking religion into account in designing and implementing humanitarian activity received renewed attention at the World Humanitarian Summit in Istanbul in 2016, not least because donor states have increasingly recognised the potential of religious leaders acting to promote a combined humanitarian, conflict prevention and human rights agenda. The notion of a comprehensive approach embracing the range of UN institutions to counter the risks associated with religiously inflected conflict would be an extension of the remit of the Special Rapporteur to advance coherent approaches in the field of religious freedom consistent with the latest legal developments, in the absence of new universally accepted treaty obligations.

While the conditions for the recurrence of conflict over religious freedom versus freedom of expression issues seem likely to pertain for the foreseeable future, the conditions for institutional change are less easy to predict with the same degree of confidence. In seeking to understand how this change might take place, we may move easily from judgements about what is likely to more prescriptive judgements about what would be necessary. Irrespective of the institutional path for change chosen, the advance will require a greater level of compromise, understanding, or dialogue than have been evident in the political disputes at the Commission of Human Rights over the defamation of religion. If the path of greater dialogue on these most political of political rights is to advance in the next 70 years, it may be couched in terms that suggest less the idealism of Articles 18 and 19 of the Universal Declaration and more the realism inspired by trends in international security politics. It may be the case that for the next 70 years this area remains without new treaties to give agreed enforcement institutions a new source of widespread support. If that is so, then we may safely hazard that Articles 18 and 19 of the UDHR will continue to be relied upon in legal and diplomatic advance as the most widely accepted expression of rights law in this area. In this area, the UDHR will continue to be conceived as a constraint on attempts to derogate from human rights approaches in times of continuing crisis. Reflecting the strength of its idealistic formulation, it will also continue to be used to signal the value of the aspiration to hold the flourishing of the human personality to be central to our understanding of international politics in a world divided by beliefs, group loyalties and sovereign powers.

Notes

1 E.g., Evans, 1997, 191–192, and Lindkvist, 2013.
2 The APPG for International Freedom of Religion or Belief, 2017
3 A useful review of the drafting process, with commentary on key features of the secondary literature, will be found in Lindkvist, 2013. The description of key features of the preparatory features in the following two paragraphs may be found in this article.
4 Lindkvist, 2013.
5 Lindkvist, 2013.
6 Lindkvist, 2013.
7 Lindkvist, 2013.
8 Evans, 2009, at 199–200.
9 See Report of the High Commissioner for Human Rights on the Implementation of Human Rights Council Resolution 7/19 Entitled "Combating Defamation of Religions", A/HRC/9/7, September 2008, 7–8.
10 Evans, 2009, passim; Mondal, 2016. For discussion of recent steps taken to clarify this relationship at the Commission on Human Rights, see Ohchr.org, 2017 and Article19.org, 2017
11 For more, see Danchin, 2008.
12 A related critique of the opposition drawn between the two rights in the United Kingdom in debate over the Racial and Religious Hatred Act 2006 is made in Mondal, 2016.
13 Little, 2001. Evans gives more detail on the limitations to the scope for states to judge according to a hierarchy of rights in Evans, 2009, esp. 214f.
14 Danchin, 2008.
15 See, e.g., Shetreet and Chodosh, 2015.
16 Henne, 2015.
17 E.g., Stinnett, 2005.
18 Evans, 2009, at 209.

References

The APPG for International Freedom of Religion or Belief. (2017). *Article 18 – The APPG for International Freedom of Religion or Belief.* [online] Available at: https://appgfreedomofreligionorbelief.org/article-18/ [Accessed 28 Nov. 2017].

Article19.org. (2017). ARTICLE 19 at the UN #HRC31: What Is at Stake for Free Expression? Article 19. [online] Available at: www.article19.org/resources.php/resource/38273/en/article-19-at-the-un- [Accessed 28 Nov. 2017].

Danchin, P. (2008). Of Prophets and Proselytes: Freedom of Religion and the Conflict of Rights in International Law. *Harvard International Law Journal*, 49(2), pp. 249–321.

Evans, M. (1997). *Religious Liberty and International Law in Europe.* Cambridge: Cambridge University Press.

Evans, M. (2009). The Freedom of Religion or Belief and the Freedom of Expression. *Religion & Human Rights*, 4(2), pp. 197–235.

Henne, P. (2015ii). *Latest Trends in Religious Restrictions and Hostilities.* [online] Pew Research Center's Religion & Public Life Project. Available at: www.pewforum.org/2015/02/26/religious-hostilities [Accessed 28 Nov. 2017].

Lindkvist, L. (2013). The Politics of Article 18: Religious Liberty in the Universal Declaration of Human Rights. *Humanity: An International Journal of Human*

Rights, Humanitarianism, and Development. [online], 4(3), pp. 429–447. Available at: http://humanityjournal.org/issue4-3/the-politics-of-article-18-religious-liberty-in-the-universal-declaration-of-human-rights/.

Little, D. (2001). Does the Human Right to Freedom of Conscience, Religion, and Belief Have Special Status? *BYU Law Review*, 2001(2), pp. 603–610.

Mondal, A. (2016). Articles of Faith: Freedom of Expression and Religious Freedom in Contemporary Multiculture. *Islam and Christian – Muslim Relations*, 27(1), pp. 3–24.

Ohchr.org. (2017). Cite a Website – Cite This for Me. [online] Available at: www.ohchr.org/Documents/Issues/Religion/RapporteursDigestFreedomReligionBelief.pdf [Accessed 28 Nov. 2017].

Shetreet, S. and Chodosh, H. (2015). *Uniform Civil Code for India: Proposed Blueprint for Scholarly Discourse.* Oxford: Oxford University Press.

Stinnett, N. (2005). Defining Away Religious Freedom in Europe: How Four Democracies Get Away with Discriminating Against Minority Religion. *Boston College International and Comparitive Law Review*, 28(2), pp. 429–451.

13 Rights for a democratic age? The development of freedom of assembly and association

Alexander Goldberg

This chapter focuses on the development of the rights to freedom of assembly and association at international and regional levels. It considers the limitations placed on these rights by the International Covenant on Civil and Political Rights and different regional instruments. It analyses how these rights relate to freedom of expression as well as other rights within the third column of the UDHR concerned with spiritual, public and political freedoms; how they have been viewed in terms of group and individual rights; and how the limitations and restrictions of these rights have been navigated, especially when they appear to clash with threats to life and liberty. Finally, the chapter considers how these rights have become increasingly relevant in the twenty-first century, particularly in respect of conflicts between different groups, between groups and individuals and between different rights. The Behzti case in the UK and growth of new religious and secular movements in France are used as examples to explore these issues. It is argued that the test of democracies in the twenty-first century is in how they maintain the default position of presuming the rights of freedom of assembly and association and minimise restrictions to these freedoms.

Definition of freedom of assembly and association (UDHR and ICCPR)

Freedom of assembly and freedom of association enable individuals to come together with others and collectively to promote, express or defend their views and ideas or to demonstrate against the views or ideas of others. Freedom of assembly is the freedom to gather in a public place and is considered to be a right of the individual to join a collective movement to protest in support for or against a particular cause, policy or movement. Freedom of association is the freedom to join an association and have membership of a collective body, such as a trade union. This approach is spelt out in the International Covenant on Civil and Political Rights that separates the two rights into separate articles: Article 21, "the right to peaceful assembly," and Article 22, "freedom of association with others, including the right to form and join trade unions for the protection of his interests."[1] The Covenant restricts and limits these rights "in the interests of national security or public safety, public order (*ordre public*), the protection of public health or morals or the protection of the rights and freedoms of others."[2]

Historical roots

The two rights have different historical roots. The inclusion of the right to peaceful assembly stems from the US Constitution and the 1791 US Bill of Rights that had been the model used by Sir Hersch Lauterpacht and others who had proposed an International Bill of Rights towards the end of World War II.[3] Freedom of assembly is a First Amendment right that is directly transposed both into the UDHR and the ICCPR. Freedom of association comes from a different tradition – the growth of the trade union movement and democratic socialism at the end of the nineteenth and beginning of the twentieth centuries.[4]

Workers' Rights have a separate history within international law and in the main are dealt with by the International Labour Organization (ILO) that was first founded as an agency of the League of Nations in 1919.

The ILO approach

Towards the end of World War II, the Allies convened a session of the ILO and adopted the Philadelphia Declaration.[5] The Declaration linked freedom of expression and of association, affirming them as fundamental rights that "are essential to sustained progress."[6] The Declaration contains a non-discrimination clause that arguably influenced equality legislation that emerged in the mid-to-late twentieth century, affirming that "all human beings, irrespective of race, creed or sex, have the right to pursue both their material well-being and their spiritual development in conditions of freedom and dignity, of economic security and equal opportunity."[7] This was followed in July 1948 with the adoption of the ILO Convention concerning Freedom of Association and Protection of the Right to Organise Labour.[8] To date, 154 countries have ratified the Convention. Both the Philadelphia Declaration and the Convention emphasise collective or group rights.

There was a conscious effort to cross-reference human rights with labour rights in the aftermath of World War II, and there is clear evidence of interplay between the UDHR and ILO processes. The UDHR is an important recognition by the drafters of the Declaration of a need for cross-referencing between human rights, workers' rights and non-discrimination.

Extension of UDHR principles to regional conventions and charters

Freedom of association and assembly have been incorporated into regional human rights instruments such as the European Convention on Human Rights,[9] the American Convention on Human Rights,[10] the African Charter on Human and Peoples' Rights[11] and the ASEAN Human Rights Declaration.[12] The limits and restrictions of these rights vary from region to region.

More recently, the European Union Charter of Fundamental Rights (2000) incorporated these rights, widening the interpretation of freedom of association in its Article 12:

> Everyone has the right to freedom of peaceful assembly and to freedom of association at all levels, in particular in political, trade union and civic matters, which implies the right of everyone to form and to join trade unions for the protection of his or her interests.[13]

The EU Charter approach differs in three respects. Firstly, through the explicit extension of freedom of association beyond the trade union movement. Whilst implied both in earlier instruments and in case law, the Charter spells this out more clearly. Secondly, the Charter specifies that "political parties at Union level contribute to expressing the political will of the citizens of the Union."[14] Thirdly, the Charter includes in Article 28 a separate right of collective bargaining and action.

The Organisation for Security and Co-operation in Europe (OSCE) issued advice by its Office for Democratic Institutions and Human Rights panel of experts on freedom of peaceful assembly that qualifies the right of assembly, noting that:

> Only peaceful assemblies are protected. An assembly should be deemed peaceful if its organizers have professed peaceful intentions and the conduct of the assembly is non-violent. The term "peaceful" should be interpreted to include conduct that may annoy or give offence, and even conduct that temporarily hinders, impedes or obstructs the activities of third parties.[15]

Collective versus individuals rights: international law

Whilst the language used in the third column of the UDHR is in the singular, implicit within freedom of assembly and association is a right given to a group to gather and form associations in the public space. There has been little formal recognition of collective or group rights within the UN human rights system. Where they are recognised, they seem at best totemic and rarely, if at all, used by the international community collectively. Nevertheless, the UN special procedures and treaty bodies have shown an increasing concern for group rights and routinely hold states to account for the treatment of an array of groups, including minorities, women, indigenous groups, children and those with disabilities.

The UN Human Rights Council appointed a Special Rapporteur[16] for Freedom of Assembly and Association in 2010, renewed in 2013 and 2016.[17] The early reports of the Special Rapporteur quickly point to the interplay of different actors, including the state, civil society, businesses, workers' and employers' groups, and multi-lateral forums. Contained within these reports is a tension between the rights of different groups – the limits placed on freedom of association and freedom of assembly as a result of businesses that have larger incomes than some of the states that they are dealing with, as well as the more traditional issues of limits on these rights for reasons of national security and public order. Increasingly, the street is not seen as the only place where these rights are targeted – the online world has come increasingly under the spotlight as internet rights have escalated up the international agenda. Seemingly the issues of freedom of expression and freedom of association and assembly are blurred, as some governments and businesses seek to limit access to the internet for reasons concerning public order or to quash dissent.

The former Special Rapporteur Maina Kiai has realised that group rights or the restriction of them will become increasingly problematic where one set of rights are privileged over another, where business interests trump workers' rights, or where governments use limitations or restrictions to suppress democratic rights. His concern is a fundamentalism in its broadest sense:

> Fundamentalism . . . can and should be defined more expansively, to include any movements – not simply religious ones – that advocate strict and literal adherence to a set of basic beliefs or principles. Adherence to the principles of free market capitalism, for example, has spawned what has been called "market fundamentalism." And the unbending belief in the superiority of one ethnic group, race, tribe or nationality can lead to what might be called "nationalist fundamentalism." Numerous other examples are detailed in this report. These non-religious forms of fundamentalism may not always be labelled as such, but the Special Rapporteur believes that they all share key similarities. Namely, they are based upon a set of strict, inflexible beliefs impervious to criticism or deviation.[18]

The challenge is how best to balance the rights to freedom of assembly and association with other individual rights. In the age of terror and with concerns about violent protests, there needs to be a balance between allowing freedom of assembly whilst ensuring that lives are not endangered and that property is not damaged. Every government has a duty to defend the lives of its citizens. The problem is when public authorities use blanket bans under the veil of upholding the right to life and property, where it is clear that the risk to either is minimal. Any restriction must be proportionate. Just as serious is the curtailment by states of freedom of association, both in terms of restricting trade union rights and impeding the operation of civil society.

Art and religion: Behzti *– freedom of expression and assembly*

The staging of the play *Behzti* at the Birmingham Repertory Theatre in December 2004 brought to the fore concerns relating to an apparent clash between freedom of expression[19] (to stage the play) and the grievances of a religious community who claimed to have been publicly misrepresented.[20] *Behzti* ('Dishonour') is a play written by Gurpreet Kaur Bhatti, a British Sikh playwright. The play includes a scene set in a Gurdwara (a Sikh temple) that depicts a rape, physical abuse and murder. Some members of the Sikh community found this offensive. The play opened on 9 December amidst protests. The protests turned violent on 18 December, and the play was cancelled on 20 December 2004.[21] The playwright faced death threats and went into hiding; the Sikh community in Birmingham found itself under public attack from the arts and media world; and proscribed extremist organisations managed to become involved (and are suspected of being responsible for the violence).

Freedom of expression issues surrounding Behzti

The Birmingham Repertory Theatre had tried to head off concerns about the play by showing some or all of it to a select Sikh audience. Some of those at the private staging/reading found it offensive. Some community leaders believed that as the theatre company had come to the community there was room to negotiate with the theatre over content. The artists felt this was censorship. The community elders argued that there was little positive representation of the Sikh religion or community in the media and that the play would show the community in a negative light.

Whilst the theatre company placed some information about the Sikh faith in the programme notes, elements of the Sikh community decided to protest. Their argument was that freedom of expression worked both ways – the community members had a right to express their opinion about the play and Sikh representation. The protests were peaceful at first, before turning violent.

Freedom of assembly issues surrounding Behzti*: Regina (Pritpal Singh) versus Chief Constable of West Midlands Police*

The protestors wanted to protest directly outside of the theatre. The police decided to use Anti-Social Behaviour Orders (ASBOs) under the Anti-Social Behaviour Act in the first few days of the protest to disperse the protests. This caused some resentment from the community, who felt their legitimate right to protest was being unnecessarily curtailed. The authorities would later point to the violent protests on 18 December 2004 as a justification for their initial concerns. One of the protestors, Pritpal Singh of Coventry, who was arrested on 16 December (two days before the protests turned violent) for failing to disperse, claimed that the Anti-Social Behaviour Act was being misused by police to restrict 'lawful protest'. His claim went to the Court of Appeal but was dismissed.[22]

According to a BBC news report,

> Lady Justice Hallett, giving the lead ruling on Friday, said Mr Singh's argument paid "scant regard" to the rights of those who wrote and staged the play and those who wanted to see it [stating] "They too had the right to freedom of expression, just as the adults and children who were at or near

> the theatre that day had the right to go about their business without being subjected to scenes which were unnecessarily frightening, intimidating and distressing" . . . and the use of the Act in the earlier demonstration "involved no deprivation of liberty or other sanction unless the direction order was disobeyed." She said she had watched the video recording of the event, which showed that police use of the powers to disperse had the desired effect. "They worked well. The protesters gradually, if reluctantly, left the scene and more trouble was averted."[23]

It appears from reports that a bin was kicked, which might have justified the dispersal on that night. Whether this persuaded the judges to rule in favour of the police, it is clear from Justice Hallett's ruling that the Court of Appeal thought the protest went too far in infringing upon the rights of theatre-goers, which included children visiting another play at the Birmingham Repertory at the time. The protection of children seems to be an important factor in Justice Hallett's ruling.

This ruling greatly extended the use of Anti-Social Behaviour Orders (ASBOs) as an instrument to control and disperse protests. The case was cited in police manuals as a justification for dispersal measures.

Growth of religious identity movements: France

Expression of religious identity in the public sphere is becoming more common throughout Europe and North America. Religious identity street movements have grown in places that have been traditionally strictly secular, such as France. The Catholic-backed and conservative Manif Pour Tous movement, which started as a movement against same-sex marriages but has extended its campaigning remit significantly, has claimed to have held demonstrations with up to one million protesters. Some of those demonstrations have ended in violence[24] and others have ended in LGBT counter-protestors being arrested. The feminist group Femen has been attacked, kicked and pepper-sprayed at Manif Pour Tous demonstrations. Femen originated in the Ukraine, although the group is growing in France. They have an anti-religious ideology with the Catholic Church as one of their targets. Radical religious and secular groups appear to act as a foil for one another in France, the actions of one attracting a reaction from the other. The growth of religious movements is challenging the French state ideology of *laicité* (secularism) as politicians on the right embrace elements of Manif Pour Tous.

Whilst Catholic protest movements have been given some latitude, this is not the case for all communities. *Laïcité* is used to strictly regulate religious dress code in the public sector (e.g., in schools and government offices) and praying in a public space. In schools in France, Sikh children are forced to remove their turbans, Jews their skullcaps and Muslims their hijabs. The French authorities claim that this approach is consistent with human rights norms and backed by the European Court of Human Rights in a case concerning a ban on head scarves in Turkey.[25] The adoption of new measures to 'reinforce *laïcité*' followed

Jihadist attacks on 7, 8 and 9 January 2015 on the newspaper *Charlie Hebdo*, a hostage-taking at a Kosher supermarket and a shooting of a French police officer outside a Jewish school. The events led to 3,700,000 protesters taking to the streets of France in solidarity with the victims, freedom of expression and French values.

In contrast, the Muslim community's freedom of assembly, association and religious life is regularly curtailed. The 8 million strong community of French Muslims do not have enough private Mosque or prayer space to accommodate all worshippers, and in recent years this has led to Friday prayers being held in the street. French government intervention occurs from time-to-time, and the issue has become politically charged, often becoming a platform used by the Republican Party and the far-right Front National. In Clichy-La-Garenne the local Republican mayor led a march against the prayers. However, the rules of *laïcité* seem to be applied in a discriminatory fashion when it comes to other groups. The same Republican Party opposed to Friday street prayers also has within it a group called Sens Commun, which though not explicitly Catholic is aligned to the Manif Pour Tous movement.

France is navigating waters where there is a resurgent Catholic movement, a large Muslim community and renewed secular movements (with leftist, centrist and right-wing versions). Naturally, legitimate arguments will be used in the light of security concerns and threats to life and property, but the complexities of *laïcité* and its seemingly asymmetric application when it comes to freedoms of assembly, expression and association may serve to heighten tensions if the perception remains that there is a discriminatory application of these rights.

Summary

The rise of liberal identity movements and the claiming of rights by gender, sexual orientation, environmental, pacifist, anti-globalisation and religious identity movements means that freedom of association and assembly have taken centre stage – the causes are different but the rights to associate and assemble are the same. Technological advances in terrorism and remote detonation devices makes the policing of protests more complex, as it does for all major gatherings such as sporting events. However, the issues remain the same – freedom of assembly and association must be taken as the default position unless there is sufficient evidence that harm will be done to others, specifically a legitimate expectation of threat to their life, liberty and/or property.

Freedom of association is changing – traditional trade union movements are not as powerful or large as they once were but are being replaced by civil society movements in some instances, or are under threat in others. Linked to both association and assembly rights is freedom of expression. Social media and the internet determines increasingly the ability to organise, assemble and legitimately express an opinion through a mass gathering.

Liberal democracies face duel challenges today – those who want to oppose them from the outside, but more importantly those who dismantle liberty and freedoms in the name of excessive security and limitations. The battle ground today is the set of rights concerned with the third pillar of the UDHR – the spiritual, public and political freedoms. Navigating the conflicts and reducing the restrictions on these rights is the challenge for all democracies today.

Notes

1 United Nations, 1966.
2 United Nations, 1966.
3 Lauterpacht, 1945.
4 Boisson, 2018.
5 Lee, 1994; International Labour Organization, 1944.
6 International Labour Organization, 1944.
7 International Labour Organization, 1944.
8 International Labour Organization, 1950 –entered into force 4 July 1950.
9 Council of Europe, 1950, Article 11.
10 Organisation of American States, 1969, Arts. 15–16.
11 OAU, 1981, Articles 10–11 – entered into force 21 October 1986.
12 ASEAN, 2012, Article 17 and Article 24.
13 European Union, 2000, Article 12.
14 European Union, 2000, Article 12.
15 OSCE/ODHIR Panel of experts on the Freedom of Assembly, 2010, principle 1.3.
16 Maina Kiai (from Kenya) took up his functions on 1 May 2011, and whose mandate was renewed for a second and final term on 1 May 2014, ending on 30 April 2017. A new mandate was given to Special Rapporteur Annalisa Ciampi (from Italy).
17 United Nations Human Rights Council, 2010.
18 UN Human Rights Council, 2016.
19 Index on Censorship, 2011.
20 Singh Raii, 2005.
21 Branigan, 2004.
22 *Regina (Pritpal Singh) v Chief Constable of West Midlands Police* (2006).
23 News.bbc.co.uk, 2006.
24 U.K. Reuters, 2013.
25 *Leyla Şahin v. Turkey* (2005).

References

ASEAN. (2012). *ASEAN Human Rights Declaration and the Phnom Penh Statement on the Adoption of the ASEAN Human Rights Declaration.* Phnom Penh: ASEAN.

Boisson, L. (2018). Bismarck Tried to End Socialism's Grip – By Offering Government Healthcare: The 1883 law was the first of its kind to institute mandatory, government-monitored health insurance. *Smithsonian Magazine*, 14 July 2017.

Branigan, T. (2004). Tale of Rape at the Temple Sparks Riot at Theatre. *The Guardian.*

Council of Europe. (1950). *European Convention on Human Rights.* Rome: Council of Europe.

European Union. (2000). *European Union of Charter of Fundamental Rights.* Luxembourg: European Union.

Index on Censorship. (2011). *Beyond Belief: Theatre, Free Theatre, Freedom of Expression and Public Order – A Case Study.* [online] London: Index on Censorship. Available at: www.indexoncensorship.org/wp-content/uploads/2012/09/Beyond-Belief-Index-On-Censorship.pdf [Accessed 7 Mar. 2018].

International Labour Organization (ILO). (1944). *Declaration Concerning the Aims and Purposes of the International Labour Organization (Philadelphia Declaration).* Geneva: International Labour Organization.

International Labour Organization (ILO). (1950). *Convention Concerning Freedom of Association and Protection of the Right to Organise.* Geneva: International Labour Organization.

Lauterpacht, H. (1945). *An International Bill of the Rights of Man.* Oxford: Oxford University Press.

Lee, E. (1994). The Declaration of Philadelphia: Retrospect and Prospect. *International Labour Review*, 133(467).

Leyla Şahin v. Turkey [2005] Application No 44774/98 (European Court of Human Rights (Grand Chamber).

News.bbc.co.uk. (2006). Sikh play protester loses appeal. [online] Available at: http://news.bbc.co.uk/1/hi/england/west_midlands/5223638.stm [Accessed 7 Mar. 2018].

OAU. (1981). *African (Banjul) Charter on Human and Peoples' Rights.* OAU Doc. CAB/LEG/67/3 rev. 5, 21 I.L.M. 58 (1982). Banjul: OAU.

Organisation of American States. (1969). *American Convention on Human Rights, 'Pact of San José, Costa Rica'.* B-32. San José: Organisation of American States.

OSCE/ODHIR Panel of experts on the Freedom of Assembly. (2010). *Guidelines on Freedom of Peaceful Assembly.* Warsaw: OSCE Office for Democratic Institutions and Human Rights (ODIHR).

Regina (Pritpal Singh) v Chief Constable of West Midlands Police [2006] (CA).

Singh Raii, J. (2005). Behind Behzti. *The Guardian.*

U.K.Reuters. (2013). French Gay Marriage Opponents Stage Big Paris March. [online] Available at: https://uk.reuters.com/article/us-france-gaymarriage/french-gay-marriage-opponents-stage-big-paris-march-idUKBRE94P0A320130527 [Accessed 7 Mar. 2018].

UN Human Rights Council. (2016). *Report of the Special Rapporteur on the Rights to Freedom of Peaceful Assembly and of Association.* A/HRC/32/36. Geneva: United Nations.

United Nations. (1966). *International Covenant on Civil and Political Rights (Adopted 1966: Entered into Force 1976).* Arts 21–22. Geneva: United Nations General Assembly.

United Nations Human Rights Council. (2010). *Resolution Adopted by the Human Rights Council 15/21 – The Rights to Freedom of Peaceful Assembly and of Association.* Geneva: United Nations.

Section V

Economic, social and cultural rights

(Articles 22–27)

Introduction to Section V

Michael Newman

The collection of articles affirming economic, social and cultural rights (ESCRs) reflects the desire of the framers of the UDHR to enshrine rights that provide for the personal development of humans alongside their general, civil and political rights. While ESCRs were not initially considered to be on a par with earlier clauses in the Declaration, they are now determined to be as essential. As Chirwa notes in his chapter, "ESCRs are recognised in international law and increasingly in comparative constitutional law as fundamental rights".

Articles 22–28 focus on human rights relating to the workplace, social security and family life; to participation in cultural life; and to access to housing, food, water, health care and education. Relatedly and collectively, these entitlements call for the right to social protection, including of one's family (specifically children), freedom from hunger and access to health facilities, as well as the right to compulsory primary education. In his article, Uprimny argues that this set of rights links to two very important concepts: human dignity and individual autonomy.

As well as featuring an essay on ESCRs and how they relate to the UDHR as a whole, the three chapters in this section focus in turn on individual articles and subjects: social security (Article 22), education (Article 26) and culture (Article 27). What is immediately apparent in these chapters is the interconnectedness of the subjects and themes, perhaps attesting, as Chirwa notes, to "the UDHR's commitment to the indivisibility, interdependence and interrelatedness of all human rights". While the authors focus on their individual areas of expertise, it is striking that this set of rights overlap such that their development, implementation and application is reciprocal.

In their essay on culture and the role of UNESCO in the protection of this specific human right, Boccardi and Evers repeatedly relate the promotion of cultural rights to the advancement of personal well-being and, ultimately, towards achieving peace. While they also note the value of "educational programmes on the importance of the cultural heritage and cultural rights", they conversely observe that the abrogation of cultural rights can lead to the destruction of communities. Similarly, Sobotka's chapter refers to the social dimension of the right to education.

The role of states in the advancement of ESCRs, and guaranteeing their provision, is also a noticeable thread running through the essays, itself reflecting the commitments in the articles in this section of the Declaration. As Chirwa reminds us, "States have the obligation to take positive steps to guarantee the enjoyment of human rights". In order to respect a person's right to autonomy, included here also, however, is the obligation and need for states to recognise when not to play a role. The state, as Chirwa describes it, simply has to "refrain (from) infringing the rights of the individual".

Also implicit is the responsibility of the international community to safeguard these rights, as provided for in Article 22 on social security, which calls for both "national effort and international co-operation". As Uprimny notes, citing the United Nations Charter, "all states pledge themselves to take joint and separate actions to promote universal respect for human rights".

Alongside the examples cited in the essays on how ESCRs apply to the world today, which include case studies of the challenges to provide education to Romani children and of the failure to protect the Ogoni community in Nigeria, the fate of the Rohingya people is an alarming illustration of what can happen to an individual community when these rights are withdrawn or abused, and of the failure of the international community to respond effectively.

While the despairing reality of a people being systematically murdered, dehumanised and displaced speaks to the failure to provide safety, justice and freedom of religion, the denial of the Rohingya's ESCRs is self-evident; the absence of social security, freedom of development and human dignity. It is a human catastrophe that not only demonstrates what can happen when society rejects the tenets of the Declaration, including of ESCRs, but also highlights the very real challenges the international community faces in addressing a humanitarian crisis of this proportion.

The parallels to the destruction of cultural property and theft of antiquities, as outlined by Boccardi and Evers, are readily apparent. Not only are they attacks on physical structures and on world heritage but also on the life of a society, impinging on the ESCRs of the people in the affected communities. They refer to the destruction of world treasures in Syria alongside the genocide they warn about when society breaks down. As with the Rohingya in Myanmar, in Syria we have witnessed the removal of all ESCRs as well as civil and political rights.

While Article 28, which provides for a "social and international order", brings together all rights and freedoms in the Declaration, as Chirwa notes, it also "underscores the significance of the broader local and international socio-economic and political context in which ESCRs are implemented and realised". With their focus on other articles covering ESCRs, the essays do not include an examination of the employment rights provided for in Articles 23 and 24.

Nevertheless, the common theme of the nexus between all the ESCRs can still be understood with the references in Article 23 to "protection against unemployment" (clause 1) and "social protection" (clause 3). Clause 3 also invokes the aforementioned notion of human dignity by demanding "favourable remuneration ensuring for himself and his family an existence worthy of human dignity". Article 24, meanwhile, which elucidates additional terms of employment, is worth mentioning precisely because of its brevity, and also to question why the framers saw fit to make it distinct and not integrate it into the preceding article.

It can also be observed in the essays that although the Declaration makes the initial provision of ESCRs, this collection of rights has been advanced and strengthened with the adoption of a series of subsequent charters, protocols, covenants and conventions. These in turn are complemented by a series of resolutions from international organisations and the accumulation of international humanitarian law. Furthermore, the ESCRs are the subject of specific measures and targets, witness The Sustainable Development (educational) Goals and the

World Programme for Human Rights Education, both of which are outlined in Sobotka's essay.

Opportunities to further develop ESCRs have also been achieved through the creation of a number of international organisations, such as the International Holocaust Remembrance Alliance (Education) and the International Alliance for the Protection of Heritage in Conflict Areas (Culture). An analysis of both these agencies as well as several other inter-governmental bodies and non-governmental organisations also appear in the essays.

Taken altogether it is therefore even more apparent that there have never been more effective mechanisms for measuring the accountability of human rights as well as the monitoring of states to ensure their provision. As Chirwa observes, these include "non-judicial or quasi-judicial . . . together with judicial remedies". Nonetheless, despite the numerous advancements in the protection and delivery of ESCRs, the failure to prevent genocide and ensure the safety of oppressed minorities since the advent of the Declaration is glaringly apparent.

Stemming from a response to the atrocities of the Holocaust and World War II, the Declaration itself has not been enough to prevent further genocide in disparate areas of the world. The crimes perpetrated by the Khmer Rouge in Cambodia, against the Tutsis in Rwanda and against Muslims in Bosnia are three indelible stains on the post-war international community that has repeatedly called for 'never again'. Common to these tragedies is the identification of 'others' in the respective communities as well as the absence of human dignity and – most notably – opportunities for the self-development of the individual.

Although located towards the end of the Declaration and after all other rights, the ESCRs help balance and round off the document, identifying and providing for a strong personal dimension that aims to facilitate the development of people and, specifically, an individual's personality to their fullest potential. Situated alongside civil and political rights, the indispensable ESCRs complete the Declaration, as the essays demonstrate.

And yet, perhaps reflecting the Declaration as a whole, despite the great moves forward to provide ESCRs, strengthened by the adoption of subsequent documents, serious challenges lie ahead for their introduction, protection and development. As Professor Chirwa notes, "The UDHR expected that the realisation of human rights was not going to be achieved at once, but was a goal towards which states had to constantly steer".

14 Article 22 and the role of economic, social and cultural rights in the realisation of social justice

Rodrigo Uprimny

Article 22 is essentially an 'umbrella' norm (Andreassen, 1999: 453) that introduces the full range of economic, social and cultural rights (ESCRs) of the UDHR. This idea is the point of departure of this commentary, which aims to analyse the vast potential that Article 22 continues to hold for the promotion of social justice and a holistic approach for the realisation of ESCRs.

Before embracing this task, however, an earlier difficulty must be addressed because Article 22 has a strange and even puzzling structure, as it begins by recognising a particular ESCR – the right to 'social security' – but at the same time this right is the entrance to all ESCRs. This ambiguity is even more troubling if we take into account that the specific content of what is technically understood today as 'social security' is developed in another article of the UDHR: Article 25(1). This article recognises everyone's right to "security in the event of unemployment, sickness, disability, widowhood, old age or other lack of livelihood in circumstances beyond his control", which is precisely the current technical notion of what we understand by social security.

Such ambiguity is perplexing, but the mystery can be dispelled by returning to the time of the drafting of Article 22, an episode carefully reconstructed by several scholars (Adreassen, 1999; Diller, 2012).

Against this backdrop, this commentary will begin with a short reference to the *travaux préparatoires* ('preparatory works') of Article 22 with the following caveat: I do not wish to fix the possible original intent of the drafters of the UDHR, as I am in general in favour of an evolutionary rather than originalist interpretation of human rights texts, which I see as living instruments. My aim is to solve the textual mystery arising from the reference to the right to social security at the beginning of Article 22, which is "perhaps the most puzzling and easily misunderstood clause of Article 22" (Diller, 2012: 46). This historical analysis will show that the inclusion of social security in the umbrella article for all ESCRs did not have the aim to introduce a specific right to social security to the UDHR in the technical sense that we now conceive it, since this right is fully developed in Article 25. Rather, its inclusion serves a different, two-pronged purpose, which is to establish a link between ESCRs and the pursuit of social justice, on the one hand, and to establish a general entitlement to social justice, on the other.

I will proceed then to study the normative content of this article and link it, when possible, to the evolution of ESCRs in international law. This analysis will reveal the enormous legal and political potential that Article 22 continues to have for the struggles for social justice and the realisation of ESCRs.

Dispelling a mystery: the drafting of Article 22

The inclusion of ESCRs in the UDHR, which was a novelty at the time, was nevertheless an "uncontroversial decision, tacitly agreed beforehand" (Samnoy, 1999: 11). The historical record shows that, contrary to certain interpretations that argue that the West was against this inclusion, there was broad support at that moment at the UN for including ESCRs in the Declaration (Whelan and Donelly, 2007: 914–917). Even the US delegate, Eleanor Roosevelt, staunchly sponsored this inclusion (Andreassen, 1999: 465). Today, this fact might seem perplexing given the US's current resistance to recognising ESCRs as fundamental rights. Nonetheless, it appears natural if we recall the well-known speech made by President Roosevelt in 1941 about the so-called four freedoms, which included, alongside more classical liberal rights (freedom of expression, religion and from fear), a fourth freedom, strongly linked with ESCRs: freedom from want.

The drafters then made the decision to have an introductory or umbrella article for this new set of rights. The idea of this umbrella article was neither to devalue ESCRs nor to place them in a second category in relation to civil and political rights. It was simply to introduce them more distinctly as the drafters were aware that previous human rights declarations, such as that of the French Revolution, did not make such provision, and that these rights needed special implementation mechanisms. It was clear that it was not enough to enumerate them in order to realise them.

The first formulation of this umbrella article, written by the French delegate René Cassin, was very simple. It stated that everyone, as a member of society, has the ESCRs enumerated in the subsequent articles of the UDHR, "whose fulfilment should be made possible in every state or by international cooperation" (Andreassen, 1999: 470).

Concurrently, an article related to the technical content of the right to social security was amalgamated in a single article with the right to an adequate standard of living and the right to health. The first sentence of that proposed article set out that everyone has "a right to social security", which included the right to a "standard of living and social services adequate to health and wellbeing" of the person and his family. That article also incorporated the technical content of social security, such as the protection of income in cases of unemployment, disability, old age or other similar situations (Adreassen, 1999: 468). That proposed article became in essence the current Article 25 of the UDHR. Nevertheless, there was opposition to the reference to "social security" in the heading of the article, especially by the representative of the International Labor Organization, for whom this proposal implied a new definition of the notion of social security, which was contrary to the technical and customary understanding of this right. His criticism was accepted, and the expression "right to social security" was eliminated from that article, although its content was maintained and became the basis for Article 25. This includes the right to health, the right to an adequate standard of living and the right to social security in the technical sense, but without mentioning the latter.

In subsequent discussions, some delegates, principally René Cassin, insisted that it would be unacceptable for the UDHR to fail to even mention the right to social security as this right played a very important role at that moment. A decision was taken to include this expression but with a change. The expression "right to social security" was not incorporated into the article concerning the adequate standard living, but it was included as the first part of the umbrella article.

The transfer of the expression "right to social security" to the umbrella article was not a purely formal modification as it has deep conceptual implications, of which the drafters were aware (Andreassen, 1999: 475). At the time of the drafting, the term 'social security' appeared in different documents and discourses with two meanings (Diller, 2012: 48–51). Some used it in a restricted technical sense, synonymous to a kind of social insurance to protect the income of individuals who were unable to work. Others used it in a very broad sense, synonymous to social justice and the realisation of all ESCRs, because they understood the phrase in the sense of the security that people feel when they know they will have the "social protection from insecurity, or injustice, that is necessary for well-being" (Diller, 2012: 48). The incorporation of the right to social security in the umbrella article implied that this expression should not be understood in the restricted technical sense suggested by the ILO but in a broad and general manner, almost as a synonym for the right to social justice or for the realisation of all ESCRs (Andreassen, 1999: 475). Some delegates even proposed other expressions, such as the right to 'social justice' or the right to "protection against social insecurity" or the right to "social security in general" (Diller, 2012: 59–63) to avoid a possible restrictive interpretation. Eventually, the expression "right to social security" was retained, as some delegates insisted that this right needed to be incorporated into the UDHR, with the understanding that it should be interpreted in a very broad manner and not in a restricted technical sense.

The rich normative content of a short article

Once the mystery of the expression "right to social security" is dispelled, thanks to the previous analysis of the *travaux préparatoires*, the meaning of Article 22, as an umbrella article to introduce all ESCRs, appears not only clear but also very substantial.[1] This short article encompasses at least five fundamental components: (1) a general right to social justice, which leads to a general entitlement of all persons to all ESCRs. This holistic view of ECSRs is based on (2) robust philosophical grounds (human dignity and autonomy) that provide a strong foundation for the idea of the universality, indivisibility and interdependence of all human rights. This philosophical justification (3) also has implications for the interpretation of the scope of these rights and for the progressive recognition of new ESCRs. In addition, this article also stresses (4) that the realisation of ESCRs entails not only national efforts but also international cooperation. Finally, (5) the article deals with the complex issue of the implementation of these rights. I will proceed to succinctly explain these five aspects.

A general entitlement to social justice and to all ESCRs

As explained previously, the recognition to everyone of the right to social security, which heads the article, has to be interpreted in a broad way and not in the restrictive and technical sense of a right to social insurance. This article thus establishes a general right of every person to social justice. There is, of course, a difficulty in defining the specific content of this right because social justice is a controversial concept, open to multiple understandings, as shown by the very different theoretical approaches to social justice in political philosophy.[2] Nevertheless, this expression conveys at least a particularly powerful idea: that individuals are entitled not only to certain specific and discrete ESCRs but also to a general claim that society shall be ordered in a manner that can be considered socially just. In that sense, and as has been stressed by other scholars (Andreassen, 1999: 523), Article 22 is strongly linked to Article 28, which establishes that everyone is "entitled to a social and international order in which the rights and freedoms set forth in this Declaration can be fully realized". Both norms establish a general entitlement for human beings to a structural order of society that allows for the full enjoyment of rights and goes beyond individuals' specific entitlements to particular rights. The difference is that Article 28 refers more to the international order and to all human rights, whereas Article 22 is related more specifically to ESCRs and makes a broad claim to social justice.

This notion of social justice in Article 22 is strongly linked to the full enjoyment of all ESCRs. The implicit message of Article 22 is that individuals can feel secured from injustice, and thus have their right to social justice realised, only when all their ESCRs are guaranteed. Individuals have a general entitlement to the fulfilment of all those ESCRs that are necessary for their dignity and the free development of their personality. The "logical consequence of the universal right to social security as social justice is an entitlement for everyone to realisation of the ESC rights indispensable to dignity and self-development" (Diller, 2012: 126). This leads to a holistic view of ESCRs. It is not enough that some ESCRs are protected for individuals to enjoy social security and have their dignity protected. It is necessary that all ESCRs are equally realised.

Philosophical foundations of ESCRs and their implications

Article 22 also provides the robust ethical and philosophical foundations for ESCRs, by linking this set of rights to two critical concepts: human dignity and individual autonomy.

Article 22 provides that these rights are indispensable for protecting individuals' dignity and their autonomy or free development of their personality. This statement implies a wide understanding of human dignity and freedom, which transcends the liberal notion developed by philosophers such as Kant. Human dignity is affected not only when a person becomes an instrument of others, as in the classical liberal approach, but also when the person has to live in poverty, deprived of basic material conditions that are necessary for his or her well-being, such as housing, food or access to health services. Besides, this situation of poverty and material deprivation violates not only human dignity but also infringes on autonomy as it becomes impossible for persons living in such circumstances to truly exercise their freedom, as they lack the minimum material elements to develop an autonomous action. Thus, they are unable to develop their personality in a free manner. "This indicates that the most minimal respect for person´s dignity requires protecting their access to basic necessities, in which case such protection must be among the rock-bottom moral claims each person has in virtue of their universal moral status" (Ashford, 2007: 213).

This philosophical justification of ESCRs provides a solid background for defending the universality, indivisibility and interdependence of all human rights and for avoiding any rigid separation between ESCRs and civil and political rights.[3] Certain philosophical approaches have denied the legitimacy of ESCRs because they do not consider them necessary for the protection of human dignity or freedom. All the more, they see these rights as undermining the rule of law and the protection of 'real' human rights, which are, according to such views, civil and political (Hayek, 1973: 103).

Contrary to these approaches, the UDHR, especially its preamble and Article 22, supports the idea that both sets of rights are necessary for the real and equal protection of human dignity and the autonomy of all individuals. Consequently, if both sets of rights are grounded on the same values, both should be guaranteed to all human beings and equally protected. This powerful idea was strongly reaffirmed by the common preamble of the two 1966 Covenants: The International Covenant on Civil and Political Rights (ICCPR) and the International Covenant on Economic, Social and Cultural Rights (ICESCR), when they stated that:

> the ideal of free human beings enjoying civil and political freedom and freedom from fear and want can only be achieved if conditions are created whereby everyone may enjoy his civil and political rights, as well as his economic, social and cultural rights.

Unfortunately, this strong affirmation of the principles of universality, indivisibility and interdependence of all human rights, made by both covenants, and reaffirmed by the Teheran Conference on Human Rights in 1968, occurred exactly at the moment in which the separation between ESCRs and civil and political rights was more acute than ever in international law (Whelan, 2010: 144–153). The best proof of this division was precisely the fact that it was impossible to agree on just one covenant to implement the UDHR, and thus two separate covenants, with different monitoring mechanisms, were established.

List and scope of ESCRs

The link between ESCRs, human dignity and free development of the personality also has consequences for two normative issues, which have important practical consequences: the enumeration and scope of these rights.

A first version of this umbrella article spoke of the ESCRs "set forth" in the UDHR. This expression could be interpreted as though Article 22 established a fixed list. However, the current wording reversed that interpretation: an individual is entitled to the realisation of the ESCRs "indispensable for his dignity and the free development of his personality". Thus, neither Article 22 nor the UDHR establish a closed list of ESCRs, as human beings are entitled to all ESCRs indispensable for their dignity and autonomy. Therefore, new ESCRs can be recognised. One example was the recognition of the right to water, whose legal basis and content was explained and developed by the UN Committee on ESCR (CESCR), although neither the UDHR nor the ICESCR refer explicitly to this right (CESCR 2002).

Furthermore, the interpretation of the scope or content of existing ESCRs should take into account their connection with human dignity and autonomy, especially to avoid restrictive interpretations. ESCRs should be interpreted in a broad and dynamic manner, taking into account the evolution of society and other legal standards, and focusing on their purpose: the protection of human dignity and the free development of individuals. Different treaty bodies, especially the CESCR, have developed this broad interpretation. For instance, the UDHR and the ICESCR recognise the right to housing as an element of a more general right to an adequate standard of living (UDHR Article 25, ICESCR Article 11), but neither of these texts develop the content of this right. The CESCR, taking into account the need to protect the dignity of all persons, said that:

> the right to housing should not be interpreted in a narrow or restrictive sense which equates it with, for example, the shelter provided by merely having a roof over one's head or views shelter exclusively as a commodity. Rather it should be seen as the right to live somewhere in security, peace and dignity.
> (CESCR, 1991: par 7)

The international dimension

One important aspect of Article 22 is that it clearly establishes that the realisation of ESCRs is not only a matter of national responsibility as it depends on a combination of "national efforts and international cooperation". Thus, states have a duty to cooperate in the realisation of ESCRs in other states. This principle stems from Articles 55 and 56 of the United Nations Charter, according to which all states pledge themselves to take joint and separate actions to promote universal respect for human rights. This was reiterated in Article 2 of the ICESCR. It is a principle with important implications: it means that states' responsibilities vis-a-vis ESCRs go beyond the territories under their jurisdiction. These are the "extraterritorial obligations of States," recently systematised in the so-called Maastricht Principles elaborated by a group of international experts (De Schutter et al, 2012). While it is still a controversial doctrine, as some states refuse to recognise extraterritorial obligations, it has been largely accepted by the CESCR in several Concluding Observations to some states and in several General Comments (CESCR, 2017: pars 25–37). Article 22 is in any case an important additional justification for the existence of these extraterritorial obligations, which are essential to enable the realisation of ESCRs in an increasingly globalised economy, in which corporations operate across borders. For instance, the CESCR has stated that among these extraterritorial obligations is the duty of states to,

> encourage business actors whose conduct they are in a position to influence to ensure that they do not undermine the efforts of the States in which they operate to fully realise the Covenant rights – for instance by resorting to tax evasion or tax avoidance strategies in the countries concerned.
>
> (CESCR, 2017: 37)

The implementation challenge

Article 22 also deals with the complex issue of implementation of ESCRs. Implementation was one of the justifications for the incorporation of this umbrella article, as most of the UDHR's drafters thought this set of rights needed special mechanisms for their realisation because they require positive actions by states and thus high costs. Three aspects are worth discussing regarding this relationship.

First, contemporary legal theory and sociological analysis contest the argument that civil and political rights are without costs as they only require negative duties by the state, whereas ESCRs are very expensive as they entail positive state actions. According to the now-accepted classification, states have three kinds of obligations or duties vis-a-vis any human right:[4] (1) the duty to respect, that is, to refrain from interfering with the enjoyment of the right; (2) the duty to protect, which requires states to protect individuals and groups against infringement of the right by third parties; and (3) the obligation to fulfil, which imposes on states' positive obligations to facilitate the enjoyment of the right. These triple categories of obligations apply to all rights, which means that states also have positive obligations in relation to civil and political rights. For instance, the right to privacy, a classic civil and political right, requires states not only to abstain from invading privacy but also to take positive action to protect individuals from threats or infringement of their privacy by third parties. Thus, the implementation of any right implies expenses for states, with no clear difference between ESCRs and civil and political rights (Holmes and Sunstein, 1999: 15–19).

Second, Article 22 accepts that the effective implementation of ESCRs depends on states' resources, a principle reiterated and even reinforced by Article 2 of the

ICESCR, which establishes that the full realisation of ESCRs is progressive and depends on the available resources of states. This reasonable qualification of the obligations of states requires nevertheless a clear understanding of its meaning in order to avoid a devaluation of ESCRs from 'real' rights to simple aspirations or desires. The CESCR has developed, at least since 1990, a robust doctrine to avoid this peril by stressing that not all obligations are progressive. Some are immediate, such as the ones concerning the prohibition of discrimination or the duty to realise the core content of ESCRs: states have to "ensure the satisfaction of, at the very least, minimum essential levels of each of the rights" (CESCR, 1990: para 10). Besides, the CESCR has also signalled that, beyond this core content, states cannot indefinitely postpone taking action to secure the full realisation of ESCRs. States must take deliberate, concrete and targeted steps in that direction and, in principle, they must avoid retrogressive measures (CESCR, 1990: paras 2 and 9). Article 22 provides clear support for this robust legal doctrine of the CESCR because, while it recognises that the varying resources of different states should be taken into account, the core idea of this article is, nevertheless, that all persons remain entitled to the full realisation of all ESCRs. That is the real meaning of the right to social security.

Finally, Article 22 is to a certain extent agnostic on how states will implement ESCRs because it indicates that the realisation of these rights is "in accordance with the organization" of each state. Thus, states can adopt different political and economic systems without infringing on the UDHR. This position has also been assumed by the CESCR, which stated that the ICESCR is "neutral" in this respect because ESCRs "are susceptible of realization within the context of a wide variety of economic and political systems" (CESCR, 1990: para 8).

This thesis is correct but requires nuance. In principle states can adopt a variety of economic and political systems and develop very different policies to implement ESCRs. Nevertheless, if there was evidence that a political arrangement makes it impossible to advance the realisation of ESCRs, then the right to social security, understood in its broad sense as a right to social justice, would imply that all persons would be entitled to contest the existence of such a political arrangement.

Conclusion

Article 22 has a paradoxical status in international law. On the one hand, it is a very powerful article, in the sense that it recognises that individuals have a broad right to social justice, which allows for a better understanding of the entitlements of individuals to all ESCRs and of the scope of the different national and international state obligations in this field. On the other hand, Article 22 remains largely "ignored or misunderstood" (Diller, 2012: 198), especially because of the tendency to apply a restrictive interpretation of the right to social security. Hopefully, a better understanding of the normative content of Article 22 and of the right to social justice will make evident the enormous potential of this norm to support the efforts and struggles for a better world based on the effective realisation of all

ESCRs. The awakening of Article 22 would be much welcomed because "if the vision of Article 22 is heeded, the security of social justice will become equally available some day for everyone in society" (Diller, 2012: 224).

Notes

1 This broad understanding of the meaning and potential of article 22 has been strongly influenced by the very rich and suggestive study of this same article by Janelle Diller in Diller 2012.
2 For a strong reference that shows the diversity of approaches to social justice, see Sen 2009, who distinguishes between the "transcendent institutionalism" (theories, such as Rawl's, that intend to establish the set of just principles that allow for the establishment of just institutions) and the "realization-focused comparative approach" (theories, such as Condorcet's, that renounce the notion of perfectly just institutions, but intend, with a comparative approach, to build a widespread consensus on the injustice of certain practices or situations).
3 See Chirwa, in this volume.
4 The CESCR has used this tripartite classification in all its General Comments concerning specific rights, at least since its General Comment No 11 in 1999 on the right to food (CESCR, 1999: para 15).

References

Andreassen, B. (1999). Article 22. In: G. Alfredsson and A. Eide, eds., *The Universal Declaration of Human Rights: A Common Standard of Achievement*. Leiden: Martinus Nijhoff.

Ashford, E. (2007). The Duties Imposed by the Human Right to Basic Necessities. In: T. Pogge, ed., *Freedom from Poverty as Human Right: Who Owes What to the Very Poor*. Oxford: Oxford University Press.

CESCR. (1990). *General Comment No. 3: The Nature of States Parties' Obligations*. Art. 2, Para. 1, of the Covenant. Geneva: United Nations.

CESCR. (1991). *General Comment No. 4: The Right to Adequate Housing*. Art. 11 (1) of the Covenant, E/1992/23. Geneva: United Nations.

CESCR. (1999). *General Comment No. 4: The Right to Adequate Food*. Art. 11. E/C.12/1999/5. Geneva: United Nations.

CESCR. (2003). *General Comment No 15: The Right to Water (Arts. 11 and 12 of the Covenant)*. E/C.12/2002/11. Geneva: United Nations.

CESCR. (2017). *General Comment No. 24 (2017) on State Obligations Under the International Covenant on Economic, Social and Cultural Rights in the Context of Business Activities*. E/C.12/GC/24. Geneva: United Nations.

De Schutter, O., Eide, A., Khalfan, A., Orellana, M., Salomon, M. and Seiderman, I. (2012). Commentary to the Maastricht Principles on Extraterritorial Obligations of States in the Area of Economic, Social and Cultural Rights. *Human Rights Quarterly*. [online], 34, pp. 1084–1169. Available at: www.jura.uni-bonn.de/fileadmin/Fachbereich_Rechtswissenschaft/Einrichtungen/Lehrstuehle/Herdegen/de_Wet/SoSe_2016_IWR_und_MR/35_Commentary.Maastricht.pdf [Accessed 30 Nov. 2017].

Diller, J. (2012). *Securing Dignity and Freedom Through Human Rights: Article 22 of the Universal Declaration of Human Rights*. Leiden: Martinus Nijhoff.

Eide, A. and Eide, W. (1999). Article 25. In: G. Alfredsson and A. Eide, eds., *The Universal Declaration of Human Rights: A Common Standard of Achievement*. Leiden: Martinus Nijhoff.

Hayek, F. (1973). *Law, Legislation and Liberty: A New Statement of the Liberal Principles of Justice and Political Economy. Volume II*. London: Routledge.

Holmes, S. and Sunstein, C. (1999). *The Cost of Rights: Why Liberty Depends on Taxes*. New York: W.W. Norton.

Samnoy, A. (1999). The Origins of the Universal Declaration of Human Rights. In: G. Alfredsson and A. Eide, eds., *The Universal Declaration of Human Rights: A Common Standard of Achievement*. Leiden: Martinus Nijhoff.

Sen, A. (2009). *A Theory of Justice*. Cambridge, MA: Harvard University Press.

Whelan, D. (2010). *Indivisible Human Rights*. Philadelphia: University of Pennsylvania Press.

Whelan, D. and Donnelly, J. (2007). The West, Economic and Social Rights, and the Global Human Rights Regime: Setting the Record Straight. *Human Rights Quarterly*. [online], 29(4), pp. 908–949. Available at: https://muse.jhu.edu/article/223909 [Accessed 30 Nov. 2017].

15 The Universal Declaration of Human Rights, economic, social and cultural rights and human rights discourse

Danwood M. Chirwa

Introduction

In defining the human rights referred to in general terms in the Charter of the United Nations[1] as including economic, social and cultural rights (ESCRs), the UDHR took an unprecedented step in international and comparative constitutional law. By 1948, ESCRs had not yet been universally accepted as legal rights worthy of recognition on par with civil and political rights. Although it was adopted as a non-binding international instrument, by declaring ESCRs, together with civil and political rights, as a 'common standard of achievement for all peoples and all nations', the UDHR set in motion a chain of international processes that would eventually result in the full recognition of these rights as legal rights in international law and, increasingly, in comparative constitutional law.

Major challenges to realising this broad vision of the UDHR were to be encountered in the years following its adoption. These included a period of regress, precipitated by the bifurcation of the UDHR into the International Covenant on Civil and Political Rights[2] (ICCPR) and the International Covenant on Economic, Social and Cultural Rights[3] (ICESCR) in 1966, which saw ESCRs being relegated to second-rate rights, junior to civil and political rights. As will be shown, in the long run, however, this retrogressive response to the UDHR proved crucial to the evolution and our understanding of ESCRs and other human rights.

This chapter seeks to demonstrate how, by recognising ESCRs, the UDHR laid the groundwork for transforming our understanding of human rights. After providing a brief overview of the manner in which the UDHR protects ESCRs, the chapter addresses its central concern by focusing on two broad themes: how the jurisprudence on ESCRs has over the last 70 years helped change the debate about the nature of human rights obligations and duty bearers and brought us back on a path the UDHR had marked; and how the practice of international human rights bodies has over the same period changed the conception of the implementation and enforcement of human rights to underline the UDHR's commitment to the indivisibility, interdependence and interrelatedness of all human rights.

Uniqueness of the UDHR with regard to the protection of ESCRs

The UDHR is remarkable not just for recognising ESCRs side by side with civil and political rights but also for the unique manner by which it recognises these rights. Unlike the International Covenant on Economic, Social and Cultural Rights (ICESCR) and other later treaties,[4] the UDHR underlines the similarities between civil and political rights and ESCRs by using the same language. The UDHR typically uses the universal term 'everyone' as the subject of the rights it protects. Thus, for example, the rights to education, social security, work and an adequate standard of living are inalienable to 'everyone'. By contrast, the ICESCR protects ESCRs through the intermediary of 'States Parties'. It repeatedly uses the formulation 'The States Parties to the Present Covenant recognise . . . ' or 'undertake to . . . ' before naming the right sought to be protected. The ICESCR does this to distinguish itself from the International Covenant on Civil and Political Rights (ICCPR), which predicates civil and political rights to the universal terms 'every human being', 'everyone', 'all persons', 'no one' and 'every child',[5] in an apparent effort to emphasise the programmatic nature of ESCRs and their dependence on the state's positive action and resources.

Secondly, the UDHR defined ESCRs in a manner that suggests that the realisation of these rights is as immediate or urgent as civil and political rights. Absent in its provisions on ESCRs are the notions of 'progressive realisation', 'available resources', and the states' duty to 'take appropriate measures'. At most, the UDHR mentions 'progressive measures' just after its preamble but before the individual articles it elaborates. By defining ESCRs without these qualifications, the UDHR underlined the immediacy and urgency of ESCRs and that states cannot postpone their implementation but continually work towards their full realisation.

All in all, the UDHR recognised at least six separate ESCRs: (1) the right to social security;[6] (2) the right to work and related rights;[7] (3) the right to rest and leisure;[8] (4) the right to a standard of living adequate for the health and well-being of oneself and one's family;[9] (5) the right to education;[10] and (6) the right to participate in the cultural life of the community, to enjoy the arts and share in scientific advancement and its benefits.[11] In addition, Article 28 of the UDHR recognises the much-neglected right to 'a social and international order' in which all rights and freedoms are fully realised. This right underscores the significance of the broader local and international socio-economic and political context in which ESCRs are implemented and realised. It serves as an anchor to the duty of states to cooperate to implement ESCRs and to the evolving idea of extraterritorial obligations of states.[12]

Being a general declaration, the UDHR focused on proclaiming the rights of every individual, not of specific groups. It is therefore not surprising that it did not say much about women and children beyond mentioning, in Article 25, that 'motherhood and childhood are entitled to special care and assistance. All children, whether born in or out of wedlock, shall enjoy the same social protection'. For a long time this article was the bugbear of the UDHR, especially as it problematically juxtaposed women with children, creating the presumption that women and children have similar needs or, worse still, that women need special care and assistance for the reasons that children do. The adoption of the Convention on the Elimination of All Forms of Discrimination Against Women (CEDAW)[13] and the Convention on the Rights of the Child (CRC)[14] has since corrected these shortfalls of the UDHR.

The evolution of human rights obligations and duty bearers

The retreat from the UDHR symbolised by the splitting of the UDHR into the ICESCR and the ICCPR created a false dichotomy between civil and political rights and ESCRs, which the UDHR had avoided. The period following the split saw the beginning of concerted efforts to interpret ESCRs simultaneously as unique rights and as rights that are similar to civil and political rights. Efforts to develop ESCRs as unique rights consisted in analysing and developing the concepts of 'progressive realisation', 'availability of resources' and 'appropriate measures'. Groups of academics produced documents, such as the Limburg Principles[15] and the Maastricht Guidelines,[16] which influenced the development of the ICESCR's general comments.

Some interpretations of these terms adopted by these documents sought to highlight the similarities between ESCRs and civil and political rights. For example, the Limburg Principles emphasised that '[a]lthough the full realization of the rights recognized in the [ICESCR] is to be attained progressively, the application of some rights can be made justiciable immediately while other rights can become justiciable over time'.[17] Again, the concept of 'unjustified retrogressive measures', introduced by ICESCR General Comment No. 3,[18] sought to prevent states from interfering with the enjoyment of existing access to ESCRs without justification. According to this concept, for a state to justify taking retrogressive measures, it has to show that the measures are reasonable, that it considered alternatives and that such alternatives have been made available, that the existing measures were independently reviewed, that it consulted all those affected by the measures, and that the impact of such measures on the realisation of the right in question is not too severe.[19] If the retrogressive measures are being justified on the ground of lack of resources, their justification will depend on the level of development of the state concerned, the extent of the breach (especially if it relates to the minimum core of a right), competing claims on the state's resources, and the state's efforts to find alternative options and seek international co-operation and assistance.[20] The concept of retrogressive measures resembles the concept of the duty of states to respect civil and political rights, which is based on the assumption of existing enjoyment of freedom and autonomy with which the state is obliged not to interfere.

Drawing attention to the significance of the duty to respect ESCRs was not the only strategy used to illuminate the similarities between ESCRs and civil and political rights. Over time, the ICESCR adopted and significantly expanded the typology of 'respect', 'protect' and 'fulfil' in the context of state party reporting and its general comments. The ICESCR's typology was preceded by Henry Shue's seminal work on 'subsistence rights' published in 1980, in which he argued that every basic right entails three duties: 'to avoid depriving', 'to protect from deprivation' and 'to aid the deprived'.[21] This classification of duties was adopted and refined by Asbjørn Eide in 1987, who termed these duties the duty to 'respect', 'protect' and 'fulfil'.[22] It has now become standard to associate these duties to all rights, not just ESCRs,[23] which brings us back to the position the UDHR had started.

The UDHR cleared the path for the development of these duties by proclaiming that the UDHR was 'a common standard of achievement for all peoples and all nations' obligating every individual and every organ of society 'to promote respect for these rights and freedoms and by progressive measures, national and international, to secure their universal and effective recognition and observance'.[24] In concretising this obligation, Article 2 of the ICCPR enjoins states parties 'to respect and to ensure to all individuals within its territory and subject to its jurisdiction the rights recognized in the Covenant'. The duty to 'ensure' suggests that states have the obligation to take positive steps to guarantee the enjoyment of human rights.[25]

In *Velásquez Rodríguez v Honduras*,[26] the Inter-American Court of Human Rights significantly developed the positive dimension of civil and political rights when it held that a human rights violation which was initially not directly imputable to a state could lead to an international responsibility of the state 'not because of the act itself, but *because of the lack of due diligence to prevent the violation or to respond to it*'.[27] The court understood the notion of 'due diligence' as requiring the state to 'take *reasonable steps* to prevent human rights violations and to use the means at its disposal to carry out a *serious* investigation of violations committed within its jurisdiction, to identify those responsible, to impose the appropriate punishment and to ensure the victim adequate compensation'.[28]

In this case, Honduras was found responsible for the disappearances of several people, even though it was not proven that the disappearances were committed by state officials. This decision effectively overturned the traditional position that rights only engender the state's duty not to interfere in the enjoyment of rights and affirmed instead that the realisation of human rights also depends on state action to ensure that individuals do not suffer from violations at the instance of third parties. In making this point, the Inter-American Court of Human Rights expanded the basis upon which states can be held responsible for human rights and extended the reach of human rights to the private sphere, albeit through the medium of the state.[29]

Velásquez Rodríguez v Honduras has been enormously influential. In *Social and Economic Rights Action Centre and the Centre for Economic and Social Rights v Nigeria*[30] (*SERAC*), the African Commission on Human and Peoples' Rights (African Commission) adopted the notions of the duty to protect and due diligence in connection with claims by the Ogoni community that the government of Nigeria had not taken sufficient steps to prevent oil companies from polluting soil, air and water and thus causing health hazards to the communities living in

Ogoniland. The Commission linked this duty to a wide range of rights, including the rights to water, food, life and a healthy environment, thereby underlining the interdependence of all human rights. Unlike *Velásquez Rodríguez v Honduras*, where it was not clear who had caused the disappearances, in *SERAC* there was no doubt that the pollution was committed by oil companies. This communication affirmed the indirect application of human rights to non-state actors.

The application of human rights to the private sphere, alluded to in the UDHR as part of the individual's duties,[31] has received increased prominence in the jurisprudence about women's rights, especially violence against women, and about business and human rights. With respect to women's rights, the notion of due diligence has become the main touchstone for describing what is expected of states with respect to combating violence against women in the private sphere.[32] With respect to business and human rights, the Special Representative for the UN Secretary-General on the issue of human rights and transnational corporations developed as the main framework for addressing human rights concerns raised by business enterprises the so-called Protect, Respect and Remedy Framework,[33] which essentially is a convoluted version of the principles enunciated in *Velásquez Rodríguez v Honduras*. This demonstrates that the duty to protect and its correlate, the due diligence standard, are concepts that attach to all rights.

There is therefore no doubt that what the UDHR had set in 1948 as a common standard of achievement for all peoples and nations with respect to duties that human rights entail and the spheres in which human rights have relevance has largely been accomplished, if only at the level of developing and applying these duties in concrete cases. What is yet to be accomplished, perhaps, is the application of the duty to fulfil civil and political rights. In ESCRs jurisprudence, the notion of the minimum core, has been used to hold states accountable at least via the state reporting procedure.[34] With respect to judicial proceedings, the concept of reasonableness has been used in South Africa[35] and codified in the Optional Protocol to the International Covenant on Economic, Social and Cultural Rights.[36] It is therefore now clear that in order for a state to be held responsible for failing to fulfil its obligations related to facilitating and providing access to ESCRs, a court will ask whether the state has taken reasonable measures. A similar question could be posed with respect to civil and political rights: has the state taken reasonable measures to ensure access to justice or fair trial, the exercise of the right to vote, or that vulnerable groups participate in public decision making? So far, no cases have been brought before international, regional and domestic human rights monitoring bodies or courts to pose this question in relation to civil and political rights.

The evolution of accountability for human rights

By the time the UDHR was adopted, Western domestic legal systems had long-established constitutional practices that defined human rights through the justiciability lens.[37] Accountability for human rights thus meant the deployment of judicial remedies to ensure that the state did not interfere with the enjoyment of human rights.[38] Given also that human rights were largely recognised in their negative form, talk of human rights implementation was meaningless, if not non-existent, since what was required of the state was simply to refrain from infringing on the rights of the individual. Where applicable, government accountability for positive obligations implicit in human rights was left to the vagaries of democratic processes.[39]

The acceptance by states of the idea that human rights were inherently justiciable or needed to be subjected to judicial remedies for their full recognition and protection affected the manner in which the struggle for the recognition of ESCRs at the international level was framed, namely, as an argument for recognising ESCRs as judicially enforceable rights.[40] As noted earlier, this was successfully done with respect to the UDHR, but not the ICCPR and the ICESCR. However, the division of human rights into civil and political rights and ESCRs, as symbolised by the two treaties, led to the evolution of a wide range of non-judicial mechanisms of accountability – peer review,[41] state reporting, inquiries, on-site investigations and special procedures.[42] Over the years, these non-judicial or quasi-judicial mechanisms have played an important role, together with judicial remedies, in holding states fully accountable for human rights.[43] These mechanisms evolved in recognition of the fact that human rights entailed both negative and positive obligations and that human rights implementation requires more than adherence to policing by the state to its duty to abstain from interfering with the enjoyment of human rights.

As noted earlier, the UDHR specifically requires every individual and every organ of society to strive through teaching and education to promote respect for human rights and, by progressive measures, to secure their universal and effective recognition and observance. In short, the UDHR introduced a new way of thinking about human rights that marked a shift from an emphasis on reactive and corrective remedies to proactive implementation. According to the UDHR, the process of implementing human rights is and must be continuous and requires a whole range of activities aimed at translating the international human rights obligations of states into domestic policies, laws, procedures and practices, and rendering human rights justiciable or enforceable by the courts and other monitoring bodies.[44] Understood in this way, human rights implementation goes beyond domestication to require the review of existing legislation, the adoption of new and additional legislation, the creation of new policies and programmes, and the review and introduction of (new) mechanisms, institutions, procedures and practices to ensure the full realisation of human rights. The way in which we think about accountability for human rights has thus fundamentally changed, for states are not just held accountable for interfering with existing access to human rights but also for the measures they have taken to anticipate violations, revise and reform law and policy, and establish suitable institutions, procedures and practices to implement and monitor the implementation of human rights.

Conclusion

The 70th anniversary of the UDHR must serve as a reminder of the ideals this important document set. One of those goals was for ESCRs to be treated as full rights just like civil and political rights. The full realisation of both sets of rights no doubt remains a challenge. However, the UDHR expected that the realisation of human rights was not going to be achieved at once, but was a goal towards which states had to constantly aim. After years of regress from the UDHR's broad vision, we have now reached a stage where ESCRs are recognised in international law and increasingly in comparative constitutional law as fundamental rights. It is also due in large measure to the UDHR that all human rights are now generally seen as engendering both negative and positive obligations and to have application to both public and private actors, and that quasi- and non-judicial means of monitoring the implementation of all human rights have evolved. More concerted efforts at domestic, regional and international levels – among state institutions, international agencies, civil society, individuals and other stakeholders – have to be made in order to ensure that the broad vision set by the UDHR is fully realised.

Notes

1 26 June 1945, 59 Stat 1031, TS 993, 3 Bevans 1153, entered into force 24 October 1945.
2 United Nations General Assembly (UNGA), 1966i, entered into force 23 March 1976.
3 United Nations General Assembly (UNGA), 1966ii, entered into force 3 January 1976.
4 Among the later treaties that brought ESCRs and civil and political rights together are the Convention on the Elimination of All Forms of Racial Discrimination (CERD), 660 UNTS 195, entered into force 4 January 1969; the Convention on the Elimination of All Forms of Discrimination against Women (CEDAW), GA Res 34/180, 34 UN GAOR Supp (No 46) at 193, UN Doc A/34/46, entered into force 3 September 1981; the Convention on the Rights of the Child (CRC), GA Res 44/25, annex, 44 UN GAOR Supp (No 49) at 167, UN Doc A/44/49 (1989), entered into force 2 September 1990; the Convention on the Protection of the Rights of All Migrant Workers and Members of their Families, GA Res Res 45/158, 18 December 1990, entered into force 1 July 2003; and the Convention on the Rights of Persons with Disabilities (CRPD), GA Resolution 61/106, Annex I, UN Doc. A/61/49 (2006), entered into force 3 May 2008. However, except the Convention on Migrant Workers, these treaties follow the ICESCR, not the UDHR, in defining rights by reference to what states parties 'undertake' or 'commit to'.
5 Exceptions are articles 1(3), 2, and 3 of the ICCPR.
6 Article 22.
7 Article 23.
8 Article 24.
9 Article 25.
10 Article 26.
11 Article 27.
12 See, e.g., Maastricht Principles on Extraterritorial Obligations of States in the Area of Economic, Social and Cultural Rights, adopted in 2011; De Schutter et al., 2012; Gibney and Skogly, 2010.
13 Supra note 5.
14 Supra note 5.
15 The Limburg Principles on the Implementation of the International Covenant on Economic, Social and Cultural Rights, 1987.

16 Maastricht Guidelines on Violations of Economic, Social and Cultural Rights, adopted in 1997, UN Doc E/C.12/2000/13 (2000).
17 Paras 8 and 22. This point was reaffirmed in (CESCR, 1990): para 1.
18 CESCR, 1990: para 9. See also CESCR, 2003: para 19; CESCR, 1999: para 45; and CESCR, 2006: para 21.
19 See CESCR, 2008: para 42.
20 CESCR, An evaluation of the obligation to take steps to the 'maximum of available resources' under an Optional Protocol to the Covenant, UN Doc E/C.12/2007/1, 10 May 2007, para 10.
21 See Shue, 1996: 52.
22 See A. Eide, Final report on the right to adequate food as a human right, UN Doc E/CN.4/Sub.2/1987/23.
23 For CESCR, see, e.g., General Comment No 13, supra note 19, para 46; CESCR, 2000: para 33.
24 See opening para.
25 Similar provisions can be found in regional instruments. See, e.g., article 1(1) of the European Convention for the Protection of Human Rights and Fundamental Freedoms, adopted 4 November 1960, entered into force 3 September 1953, ETS No 5, 213 UNTS 222; article 1(1) of the American Convention on Human Rights, adopted 29 April 1982, entered into force 18 July 1978, OAS Treaty Series No 36, 1144 UNTS 123; and, in relation to the African Charter on Human and Peoples' Rights, adopted 27 June 1981, entered into force 21 October 1986, OAU Doc CAB/LEG/67/3 Rev 5, 21 ILM 58 (1982).
26 *Velásquez Rodríguez v Honduras* (1988).
27 Ibid, para 172.
28 Ibid, para 174.
29 See Chirwa, 2010.
30 African Commission on Human and Peoples' Rights, 2001.
31 Article 29 of the UDHR provides that everyone has duties to his or her community and to have respect for the rights and freedoms of others.
32 See Rashida Manjoo's chapter.
33 OHCHR, 2011.
34 See United Nations, 1999, para 9; CESCR, 1990, para 10.
35 See, e.g., Liebenberg, 2016; Liebenbrg, 2002; Bilchitz, 2002; Scott and Alston, 2000.
36 UNGA, 2008, adopted 10 December 2008, entered into force 5 May 2013. See article 8(4).
37 As evidence of this, the European Convention for the Protection of Human Rights and Fundamental Freedoms, ETS 5, 213 UNTS 222, entered into force 3 September 1953, adopted as the founding treaty for the European regional system of human rights, initially protected predominantly civil and political rights in their negative form. See also *United States v Cruikshank* 92 US 514, 554–555, 318 (1875), *Retail, Wholesale and Department Store Union v Dolphin Delivery Ltd* [1986] 2 SCR 573, 595.
38 See, e.g., J. Akandji-Kombe, 2001. Positive obligations under the *European Convention on Human Rights: A guide to the implementation of the European Convention on Human Rights*, Human Rights Book No. 7, arguing that the concept of positive obligations did not appear until the late 1960s after the Belgian Linguistic Case (1968).
39 For a recent discussion of the consequences of judicial enforcement of positive rights for democracy, see Bellamy, 2014.
40 See, e.g., Dennis and Stewart, 2004; Alston, 1984. See also Centre on Housing Rights and Evictions (COHRE), 2005; CESCR, 2005, paras 37–38. Steiner, Alston and Goodman, 2008: 271–273.

41 For the Human Rights Council's peer review mechanism, see, e.g., United Nations General Assembly (UNGA), 2006i; United Nations General Assembly (UNGA), 2006ii.
42 See, generally, Alfredsson et al., 2009.
43 See, e.g., Saunders, 2012: 117–124.
44 See, e.g., OHCHR, 2003: paras 1, 13–65.

References

African Commission on Human and Peoples' Rights. (2001). *Communication No 155/96*. AHRLR 60. [online] Banjul: ACHPR. Available at: www.achpr.org/communications/decision/155.96/ [Accessed 11 Jan. 2018].

Akandji-Kombe, J. (2001). *Positive Obligations Under the European Convention on Human Rights: A Guide to the Implementation of the European Convention on Human Right*. Strasbourg: Council of Europe Human Rights Book.

Alfredsson, G., Grimheden, J., Ramcharan, B. and Zayas, A. (2009). *International Human Rights Monitoring Mechanisms: Essays in Honour of Jakob Th. Moller*. 2nd ed. The Hague: Martinus Nijhoff.

Alston, P. (1984). Conjuring up New Human Rights: A Proposal for Quality Control. *The American Journal of International Law*, 78(3), pp. 607–721.

Belgian Linguistic Case [1968] EHRR 252 (European Court of Human Rights).

Bellamy, R. (2014). The Democratic Legitimacy of International Human Rights Conventions: Political Constitutionalism and the European Convention on Human Rights. *European Journal of International Law*, 25(4), pp. 1019–1042.

Bilchitz, D. (2002). Giving Socio-Economic Rights Teeth: The Minimum Core and its Importance. *South African Law Journal*. [online], 118, pp. 484–501. Available at: http://heinonline.org/HOL/LandingPage?handle=hein.journals/soafl119&div=48&id=&page= [Accessed 28 Nov. 2017].

Centre on Housing Rights and Evictions (COHRE). (2005). *Information Provided by Non-Governmental Organisations: Written Submission Presented by the Centre on Housing Rights and Evictions (COHRE)*. UN Doc E/CN.4/2005/WG.23/CRP.3. Geneva: United Nations.

CESCR. (1990). *General Comment No 3: The Nature of States Parties' Obligations*. UN Doc E/1991/23 (1990). Geneva: United Nations.

CESCR. (1999). *General Comment No 13: The Right to Education (Twenty-First Session, 1999)*. UN Doc E/C.12/1999/10. Geneva: United Nations.

CESCR. (2000). *General Comment No 14: The Right to the Highest Attainable Standard of Health (Article 12 of the Covenant)*. E/C.12/2000/4. Geneva: United Nations.

CESCR. (2003). *General Comment No. 15: The Right to Water. (Arts. 11 and 12 of the ICESCR) (Twenty-Ninth Session)*. UN Doc E/C.12/2002/11. Geneva: United Nations.

CESCR. (2005). *Elements for an Optional Protocol to the International Covenant on Economic, Social and Cultural Rights, Analytical Paper by the Chairperson*. UN Doc E/CN.4/WG.23/2. Geneva: United Nations.

CESCR. (2006). *General Comment No 18, Article 6: The Equal Right of Men and Women to the Enjoyment of All Economic, Social and Cultural Rights (Thirty-Fifth Session)*. UN Doc E/C.12/GC/18. Geneva: United Nations.

CESCR. (2007). *An Evaluation of the Obligation to Take Steps to the 'Maximum of Available Resources' Under an Optional Protocol to the Covenant*. UN Doc E/C.12/2007/1. Geneva: United Nations.

CESCR. (2008). *General Comment No 19: The Right to Social Security. (Art. 9 of the ICESCR) (Thirty-Ninth Session, 2007)*. UN Doc E/C.12/GC/19. Geneva: United Nations.

Chirwa, D. (2010). State Responsibility for Human Rights. In: M. Baderin and M. Ssenyonjo, eds., *International Human Rights Law: Six Decades After the UDHR and Beyond*. Farnham: Ashgate, pp. 397–410.

De Schutter, O., Eide, A., Khalfan, A., Orellana, M., Salomon, M. and Seiderman, I. (2012). Commentary to the Maastricht Principles on Extraterritorial Obligations of States in the Area of Economic, Social and Cultural Rights. *Human Rights Quarterly*, 34(4), pp. 1084–1169.

Dennis, M. and Stewart, D. (2004). Justiciability of Economic, Social, and Cultural Rights: Should There Be an International Complaints Mechanism to Adjudicate the Rights to Food, Water, Housing, and Health? *The American Journal of International Law*, 98(3), pp. 462–515.

Gibney, M. and Skogly, S. (2010). *Universal Human Rights and Extraterritorial Obligations*. Philadelphia: University of Pennsylvania Press.

Liebenberg, S. (2002). South Africa's Evolving Jurisprudence on Socio-Economic Rights: An Effective Tool in Challenging Poverty? *Law, Democracy and Development*. [online], 6(2), pp. 159–191. Available at: www.ajol.info/index.php/ldd/article/view/138099 [Accessed 28 Nov. 2017].

Liebenberg, S. (2016). Direct Constitutional Protection of Economic, Social and Cultural Rights in South Africa. In: D. Chirwa and L. Chenwi, eds., *The Protection of Economic, Social Cultural Rights in Africa: Regional and International Perspectives*. Cambridge: Cambridge University Press, pp. 305–337.

The Limburg Principles on the Implementation of the International Covenant on Economic, Social and Cultural Rights. (1987). *Human Rights Quarterly*, 9(2), pp. 122–135.

OHCHR. (2003). *CRC General Comment No 5 (3003), General Measures of Implementation of the Convention on the Rights of the Child (Arts 4, 42 and 44, para 6)*. CRC/GC/2003/5. Geneva: United Nations.

OHCHR. (2011). *Human Rights and Transnational Corporations and Other Business Enterprises*. A/HRC/Res/17/4. Geneva: United Nations.

Retail, Wholesale and Department Store Union v Dolphin Delivery Ltd [1986] 2 SCR 573, 595 (Canadian Supreme Court).

Saunders, P. (2012). The Integrated Enforcement of Human Rights. *International Law and Politics*, 45, pp. 97–174.

Scott, C. and Alston, P. (2000). Adjudicating Constitutional Priorities in a Transnational Context: A Comment on Soobramoney's Legacy and Grootboom's Promise. *South African Journal on Human Rights*, 16, pp. 206–268.

Shue, H. (1996). *Basic Rights: Subsistence, Affluence, and US Foreign Policy*. Princeton: Princeton University Press.

Steiner, H., Alston, P. and Goodman, R. (2008). *International Human Rights in Context: Law, Politics and Morals*. 3rd ed. Oxford: Oxford University Press.

UNGA. (2008). *GA Resolution 63/117*. UN Doc A/63/435. Geneva: United Nations.

United Nations. (1987). *Final Report on the Right to Adequate Food as a Human Right*. UN Doc E/CN.4/Sub.2/1987/23. Geneva: United Nations.

United Nations. (1999). *Maastricht Guidelines on Violations of Economic, Social and Cultural Rights*. UN Doc E/C.12/2000/13 (2000). Geneva: United Nations.

United Nations General Assembly (UNGA). (1948). *GA Res 217A (III)*. UN Doc A/810. Geneva: United Nations, p. 71.

United Nations General Assembly (UNGA). (1966i). *GA Res 2200A (XXI), 21*. UN GAOR Supp (No 16) at 52, UN Doc A/6316 (1966), 999 UNTS 171. Geneva: United Nations.

United Nations General Assembly (UNGA). (1966ii). *GA Res 2200A (XXI), 21*. UN GAOR Supp (No 16) at 49, UN Doc A/6316 (1966), 993 UNTS 3. Geneva: United Nations.

United Nations General Assembly (UNGA). (2006i). *Human Rights Council*. GA Res 60/251. Geneva: United Nations.

United Nations General Assembly (UNGA). (2006ii). *Review of the Human Rights Council*. GA Res 65/281. Geneva: United Nations.

United States v Cruikshank [1875] 92 US 514, 554–555, 318 (US Supreme Court).

Velásquez Rodríguez v Honduras [1988] C No. 4 (Inter-American Court of Human Rights).

16 A promise of Sustainable Development Goal 4

Right to education and right to human rights education as a path to inclusion

Eva Sobotka[1]

Introduction

Education is a fundamental human right and essential for the exercise of all other human rights. It promotes individual freedom and empowerment and yields important development benefits. Education is a powerful tool by which economically and socially marginalised adults and children can lift themselves out of poverty and participate fully as citizens. Yet 70 years on from the adoption of the UDHR in which the right to education is underscored, millions of children and adults remain deprived of educational opportunities, many as a result of poverty and discrimination. Never before in human history has there been so many children and adolescents, and so many individuals under the age of 25.[2] The millennials are the 'Sustainable Development Goal generation', yet education still remains humankind's most effective tool for personal empowerment, fostering respect and a recognition of a common humanity beyond all the differences.

The potential of human rights education in fostering education in all its facets as social, cultural and economic human rights remains to be fully realised. In positing a human right to education, the framers of the UDHR relied axiomatically on the notion that education is not value-neutral. In this spirit, Article 26 lays out specific educational goals, which go straight to the objectives set under human rights education: (1) the full development of the human personality and the strengthening of respect for human rights and fundamental freedoms; (2) the promotion of understanding, tolerance and friendship among all nations, racial or religious groups; and (3) the furthering of the activities of the United Nations for the maintenance of peace.[3] Likewise, Article 29 of the Convention on the Rights of the Child provides directly for the education of the child towards development of respect for human rights and fundamental freedoms, and for the principles enshrined in the Charter of the United Nations. A number of UN-led and regional initiatives aimed to establish human rights education as a long-term strategy set on the needs of coming generations. To this end, the latest vision and impetus is offered within the scope of the Sustainable Development Goals, in particular target 4.7, while a number of policy and practice initiatives in different regions of the world make small steps towards creating a universal culture of human rights.[4]

While underscoring the potential to fully realise human rights education, this chapter looks at the protection of the right to education under international and European human rights law, highlighting two case studies: (1) the inclusion of Roma through education in the European Union and (2) human rights education and learning from the Holocaust and other genocides. Taking six priority human rights principles (individual rights, aims of education, dignity, equity, non-discrimination and participation), the first case study takes a particular focus on the European region, on inclusion of Roma in education in the European Union, in particular. The second case study takes a wider geographical scope, selectively looking at human rights education and learning from the Holocaust and other genocides. Both cases serve the purpose of illustration that the specific educational goals under Article 26 remain to be realised and, to this end, further changes to approaches, policy and practice may be needed in order to strive to fully realise the right to education, as intended by the drafters of the UDHR 70 years ago.

The right to education: closing the equality and accessibility gap

Looking at the first paragraph of Article 26, a belief in equality of all human beings and the fundamental unity of all human rights is embedded in the proclamation of the right to education. The international and regional legal frameworks reinforced these axioms and goals, focusing in particular on the principles of non-discrimination, accessibility and equality. UNESCO's Convention against Discrimination in Education was the first international instrument in this field, delivering the fundamental principles of non-discrimination and equality of educational opportunities into international norms. It stipulates that states have to ensure "all types and levels of education, access to education, the standard and quality of education, and the conditions under which it is given". Article 13 of the International Covenant on Economic, Social and Cultural Rights, which has been considered the most comprehensive article on the right to education, underlines the need for equal access to education at different levels and the positive obligation to make education accessible for all, without discrimination. This is called the social dimension of the right to education. In order to measure the enforcement of this obligation, the UN Committee on Economic, Social and Cultural Rights defined the right to education as encompassing the acceptability, accessibility, adaptability and availability of education. Also the Convention of the Rights of the Child, the International Covenant on Civil and Political Rights and the International Convention on the Elimination of all Forms of Racial Discrimination include provisions that have been interpreted as strengthening the right to education for minorities. Among the Council of Europe's documents, the European Social Charter supports the right to participate in education by vulnerable groups. The Charter of Fundamental Rights of the European Union proclaims the right to education and provides that "everyone has the right to education and to have access to vocational and continuing training. This right includes the possibility to receive free compulsory education". It also prohibits discrimination on the basis of, *inter alia*, race, colour, ethnic or social origin, language and membership of a national minority. After the entry into force of the Lisbon Treaty in December 2009, these provisions have the same legal value as the Treaties. However, the most relevant binding legislation which can be used to tackle discrimination in the field of education is the Race Equality Directive.[5] Thus far, the Directive has not led to case law of the European Court of Justice.

The UN designated two 'Decade' projects focusing on advancing education: (1) in 2005–2014 the United Nations Decade of Education of Sustainable Development and (2) in 2003–2012 the United Nations Literacy Decade: Education for All. The result of the two projects is both uplifting and sobering. While progress in literacy – particularly among youth – is positive and encouraging, the wider adult population has not benefited to the same extent in some regions. Though substantial progress was made towards the Millennium Development Goals, on education alone a lot more needs to be done to overcome the challenges. It is a troubling fact that there are now more illiterate adults compared with 50 years ago, meaning that efforts to realise the right to education for all have not kept pace with population growth. There are still 58 million children out of school globally. Of these, 25 million are in the rural, low-income regions and most are in Africa and Asia.[6] Today's generation of young people numbers slightly less than 1.8 billion in a world population of 7.3 billion, up from 721 million people aged 10 to 24 in 1950, when the world's population was 2.5 billion (United Nations Department of Economic and Social Affairs, 2014). The highest proportion of young people today is in poor countries, where barriers to their development and fulfilment of their potential are the highest. Poverty is the most prevalent, access to critical health care and schooling is the lowest, conflict and violence are the most frequent, and life is the hardest. Eighty-nine per cent of the world's 10- to 24-year-olds live in less developed countries, with half in Asia and the Pacific, including China and India.[7]

Thus, on the first goal to achieve access and ensure equality in the right to education, further progress is called for within the sustainable development agenda – which includes lifelong learning for all and will be increasingly mediated by people's interaction with technology. Providing access to education to the increasing population will not be met with measures that only try to fix the existing educational systems. Progress towards developing a culture of lifelong learning and a learning society will need to be made, and it will not become a reality without the recognition of non-formal and informal learning achievements, as we continue the search for the most equitable and relevant strategies to move forward, provide greater financial input not only by states but also from business and entrepreneurs.

The case of inclusion of Roma in education in the European Union

Education is a key instrument for promoting social cohesion within the European Union, because, apart from providing knowledge and developing skills, it also shapes attitudes and empowers young people to adapt to today's fast-changing social, economic and technological environment. Whereas Europe is one of the most economically and developmentally affluent regions, studies carried out at both the European and national level draw a discouraging picture of the educational situation concerning Romani children in most EU countries.[8] The case of the Roma, a diverse group with a population of 10 to 12 million, who experience substantial social exclusion, remains a challenge at a number of domains of the right to education under all human rights principles – individual rights, aims of education, dignity, equity, non-discrimination and participation.

While primary school attendance is compulsory in all EU member states, primary attainment rates for the Roma are very low. A 2011 survey administered to over 20,000 Roma in 11 EU member states found that on average 56% left school before the age of 16, while only 27% on average finished school after the age of 16. The out-of-school proportion average has been 17%, highest in Greece, where 44% of Roma children were not attending school (European Union Agency for Fundamental Rights, 2011). EU-MIDIS II survey results released in 2016 shows that Roma children lag behind their non-Roma peers on all educational indicators. Only about half (53%) of Roma children between the age of 4 and the starting age of compulsory primary education participate in early childhood education. On average, 18% of Roma aged between 6 and 24 years attend an educational level lower than that corresponding to their age. The proportion of Roma early school-leavers is disproportionately high compared with the general population (European Union Agency for Fundamental Rights, 2016).

The results also show a substantial gender gap. On average, in the nine countries surveyed, 72% of Romani women aged 16 to 24 years are neither in work nor in education, compared with 55% of young Roma men (European Union Agency for Fundamental Rights, 2011). School segregation remains a problem in Bulgaria, Greece, Hungary and Slovakia despite the legal prohibition of this practice and recent case law of the European Court of Human Rights (ECHR). In its first landmark judgement, the ECHR found in 2007, in the breakthrough case *D.H. and others v The Czech Republic*, a breach of Article 14 read in conjunction with Article 2 of Protocol No. 1. It held that, "the Court is not satisfied that the difference in treatment between Roma children and non-Roma children was objectively and reasonably justified and that there existed a reasonable relationship of proportionality between the means used and the aim pursued".[9]

Human rights education as a full development goal

I shall now turn my attention to the second paragraph of Article 26. The first sentence mentions two goals: "full development of the human personality" and "strengthening of respect for human rights and fundamental freedoms". The first goal speaks to the role of education in enabling a person to develop their potential to the full, thus enhancing their dignity as a person. The second goal encompasses the total menu of human rights: personal rights, such as privacy; political rights, including participation and the right to seek and disseminate information; civil rights like equality and non-discrimination; economic rights, for example, a decent standard of living; and the cultural right to participate in the life of the community. It is important to note that these two goals are asserted without being separated by so much as a comma. This implies that they are inextricably linked. So, the logic of the first sentence of the second paragraph of Article 26 is this: human rights education is an essential component of an education that promotes the full development of the human personality and the enhancement of dignity that this entails. Unless human rights education is incorporated into a programme of education, access to education – even if it is totally inclusive for a given population – will fail to capture in full the spirit of the right to education under Article 26 of the UDHR. In particular, it will fail to serve the ends specified in the second sentence of paragraph 2: promoting "understanding, tolerance and friendship among all nations, racial or religious groups" and furthering "the activities of the United Nations for the maintenance of peace".

The example of Janusz Korczak,[10] a Polish-Jewish educator, children's author, and paediatrician is worth citing when speaking of "full development of the human personality". His educational philosophy focused on these very principles, even during the Holocaust. In his words:

> Children are not the people of tomorrow, but people of today. They are entitled to be taken seriously. They have a right to be treated by adults with tenderness and respect, as equals. They should be allowed to grow into whoever they were meant to be – the unknown person inside each of them is the hope for the future.[11]

Moreover, his refusal to abandon the children even when he knew that they were being deported to their deaths is an educational legacy. He was a human rights practitioner even during the Holocaust when he could have easily despaired in light of the inhumanity around him.

With a view to encouraging human rights education initiatives, UN member states have adopted various international frameworks for action, such as the World Public Information Campaign on Human Rights (1988–ongoing), the United Nations Decade for Human Rights Education (1995–2004), the International Decade for a Culture of Peace and Non-Violence for the Children of the World (2001–2010), the United Nations Decade of Education for Sustainable Development (2005–2014) and the International Year for Human Rights Learning (2008–2009). On 10 December 2004, the General Assembly proclaimed the World Programme for Human Rights Education (2005–ongoing) in order to advance the implementation of human rights education programmes in all sectors. The World Programme is structured in consecutive phases, in order to further focus national human rights education efforts on specific sectors and issues. Human rights education is also integrated in Target 4.7 of the 2030 Agenda for Sustainable Development.

The World Programme for Human Rights Education is currently in its third phase (2015–2019), which focuses on strengthening implementation of the first two phases and promoting human rights training of media professionals and journalists. Member states are requested to report on their human rights education activities in the context of resolutions adopted by the UN Human Rights Council on the World Programme for Human Rights Education. At the request of the Human Rights Council (resolution A/HRC/27/12), the OHCHR prepared a global evaluation of implementation of the second phase of the World Programme for Human Rights Education (A/HRC/30/24); the evaluation, which was based on national reports submitted by member states, was submitted to the Human Rights Council at its 30th session in September 2015.

Analyses of over 500 lower and upper secondary social science textbooks produced from 1970 to 2008 in around 70 countries show interrelated trends. Discussion of human rights increased: about 20% of the textbooks before 1995 devoted a section or more to human rights, rising to 44% between 1995 and 2008, suggesting the impact of the UN Decade for Human Rights Education.[12] In addition, textbooks became more student-centred by including child-friendly pictures, illustrative figures, open-ended discussion questions and role-playing exercises, a shift associated with the focus on children's empowerment in global human rights treaties and organisations.[13] Finally, under the influence of broad global, cultural and environmental changes, the proportion of textbooks discussing environmental topics rose from 24% between 1970 and 1984 to 52% between 1995 and 2008.[14]

Yet, as educational systems across the globe provide vastly unequal opportunities for individual academic achievement, so too, they provide vastly unequal opportunities for students to develop their capacities for civic engagement. A variety of disparities in civic behaviour and attitudes between ethno-racial majority and minority communities are apparent, including knowledge of political institutions and affairs; rates of voting, contacting public officials, and engaging in political protest; and expressions of political trust, identification and perceived efficacy. But, while the evidence of a civic empowerment gap is unmistakable, it has received nowhere near as much public attention as has the disparity in attainment measurements etc.[15] While in recent years many educators have called for a renewed commitment to civic education, only within the last decade have policy makers devoted more consistent attention to including human rights and civic education (with learning from the past) in schools, and developed respective competences – knowledge, skills and attitude of students and teachers alike.

Last but not least, education is generally considered to play a critical role in the reconstruction of post-conflict countries, especially in transforming people's mind-sets and rebuilding social relations. Teachers' ability to build up their roles as educators for sustainable development and peace in the spirit of paragraph 3 of Article 26 of the UDHR will be crucial. In this context, concerns across countries arise with respect to remuneration, professional development of teachers, changing working conditions due to educational reforms and their own ability to become active citizens who address the injustices of the past.[16]

Human rights education and learning from the Holocaust and other genocides

The Preamble to the UDHR proclaims the instrument as a common standard for all peoples and all nations to "strive by teaching and education to promote respect for these rights and freedoms". Human rights education and learning from the 'failure of humanity' has therefore been part of the design and motivation of the framers of the UDHR. As much as the UDHR was an effort to re-establish a standard for human rights for humanity after they collapsed, a systematic reference to lessons from the Holocaust as well as linkages between learning from this historical period for human rights today came much later. The lessons from the Holocaust and the educational value of the experience of victims and, in recent years, the perpetrators and bystanders, have evolved only decades later – at best during the 1990s, when the world departed from the Cold War division and embraced a new world order and with it also ambitions to strive for better realisation of human rights globally.

Looking at the European region, from the early 1990s onwards, the European Parliament has regularly honoured victims of the Holocaust and called for greater awareness of what happened during this painful chapter of European history.[17] Signatory countries to the 2000 Stockholm Declaration[18] then collectively deepened the insights into methodological approaches and strategies in the context of education, remembrance and research of the Holocaust. The International Holocaust Remembrance Alliance was established on 7 May 1998 in Stockholm through the initiative of former Swedish Prime Minister Göran Persson as a unique forum of diplomats, educational experts, historians and those working in places of memory to preserve and enhance educational lessons for future generations.[19] In conjunction with the Stockholm meeting and 'Tell Ye Your Children' of the Living History Project, Persson proposed to former British Prime Minister Tony Blair, as well as former US President Bill Clinton, that their countries join an effort to foster international cooperation on disseminating information about the Holocaust. Today there is already strong evidence that the links between history teaching and human rights education are strongly desired by inter-governmental organisations, such as UNESCO, the EU, the UN, the Council of Europe and the Organisation for Security and Cooperation in Europe, as there is a consensus that this combination has a potential to create a moral compass and engagement in young people.[20]

Teaching about other genocides for human rights today remains a difficult matter to handle for teachers, in part due to the scarcity of available educational materials and guidance. The Kigali Genocide Memorial and Aegis Trust, in partnership with other Rwandan organisations such as the Educators' Institute for Human Rights, has, therefore, developed education programmes and in-service training to help teachers build capacity and acquire historical knowledge to deal with genocides and mass atrocities. Such programmes emphasise "critical thinking, empathy and individual moral responsibility".[21] The South African Holocaust Foundation is dedicated to creating a more caring and just society in which human rights and diversity are respected and valued. With three centres in Durban, Johannesburg and Cape Town, they serve as a memorial to the 6 million Jews who were killed in the Holocaust and all victims of Nazism. The Foundation teaches about the consequences of prejudice, racism, antisemitism, xenophobia and homophobia, and promotes an understanding of the dangers of indifference, apathy and silence.[22]

It is without doubt that learning from the past has gained prominence in human rights education today. What remains to be further addressed are adjustments of educational systems, capacity building and availability of resources that would allow us to integrate fully the goals expressed under the second paragraph of the UDHR – educating young people about human rights in an historical perspective with a view to building hope and a peaceful future.

New opportunity under the Sustainable Development Goal 4

A young person aged 10 in 2016 will have become an adult of 26 in 2030, the target year for achieving the sustainable development goals. Those charged with forging the post-2015 agenda would do well to imagine what the life of that 10-year-old is like now and what it could be in 2030. A meaningful future agenda to realise the right to education is one that recognises the protection of a young person's human rights and empowerment to ensure her well-being and role as a citizen, expand her opportunities for social and political participation, promote her abilities and innovativeness to become an entrepreneur, and support safe and healthy transitions from adolescence to adulthood and beyond.

Having tracked the Article 26 human rights education goals of (1) achieving equality and accessibility, (2) full personal development, (3) the promotion of tolerance and (4) the advancement of UN peace goals, it is instructive to link the human rights education potential with the sustainable development goal 4, which aims for inclusive, equitable and quality primary and secondary education. Of particular relevance is its target 4.7, which reads:

> by 2030, ensure that all learners acquire the knowledge and skills needed to promote sustainable development, including, among others, through education for sustainable development and sustainable lifestyles, human rights, gender equality, promotion of a culture of peace and non-violence, global citizenship and appreciation of cultural diversity and of culture's contribution to sustainable development.

and its global measurement indicator: (1) global citizenship education and (2) education for sustainable development, including mainstreamed gender equality and human rights, in (a) national education policies, (b) curricula, (c) teacher education and (d) student assessment.

This target can be evaluated in at least two ways. On the one hand, its explicit link to sustainable development is strong. Many, if not all, of the notions listed as promoting sustainable development are deeply embedded in principles established in existing international frameworks and conventions. The target is outcome oriented and universally applicable. More than other targets, it touches on the social, humanistic and moral purposes of education. Indeed, this target is one of the few international objectives to acknowledge the role of culture and the cultural dimensions of education and goes back to the goals of Article 26, namely: (1) the full development of the human personality and the strengthening of respect for human rights and fundamental freedoms; (2) the promotion of understanding, tolerance and friendship among all nations, racial or religious groups; and (3) the furthering of the activities of the United Nations for the maintenance of peace.

On the other hand, the current formulation reflects the interests of many organisations and institutions. Concepts need to be clarified, as several of them overlap. Clarity is also necessary to construct a limited set of valid and measurable indicators. Considerable work would be needed to develop qualitative indicators, sensitive to diverse country contexts as well as *de facto* segregated schools in impoverished urban communities, which must prepare their students to engage in modes of collaborative citizenship that address the structural conditions.

The high-level panel discussion on the implementation of the United Nations Declaration on Human Rights Education and Training: Good Practices and Challenges, held on 14 September 2016, marked the fifth anniversary of the UN Declaration on Human Rights Education and Training and generated recommendations to giving further impetus to national implementation of human rights education and training. This was based on good practice and current opportunities, in line with the United Nations Declaration on Human Rights Education and Training and Target 4.7 of the 2030 Agenda for Sustainable Development. The panel called specifically on countries to include, on a systematic basis, the national human rights institutions mobilising relevant public and private actors for human rights education.[23] A few encouraging examples connecting non-formal, wider lifelong human rights education learning within a formal educational setting can be mentioned in this regard. The Australian national human rights institution, the Australian Human Rights Commission, has promoted and provided education and training that sought to strengthen a human rights culture. The Global Alliance of National Human Rights Institutions has encouraged states to invite national human rights institutions to support the advancement of the implementation of human rights education in the formal education sector, and have them act as independent advisers to parliaments. In this context, it could be mentioned that the Danish Institute for Human Rights has acted as a key advisor to the Ministry of Education on education reform, curricula development and human rights education. The International Organisation for the Right to Education and Freedom of Education (OIDEL), on behalf of civil society organisations, noted that human rights education was part of international law and stressed that states should include human rights education in all of their reports to the United Nations human rights treaty bodies and agencies.

Conclusion

To reinforce our responsibilities to support human rights education, consider this poignant comment by Eleanor Roosevelt. As if talking to us today, she said in 1948:

> It will be a long time before history will make its judgment on the value of the Universal Declaration of Human Rights, and the judgment will depend, I think, on what the people of different nations do to make this document familiar to everyone. If they know it well enough, they will strive to attain some of the rights and freedoms set forth in it, and that effort on their part is what will make it of value in clarifying what was meant in the Charter in the references to human rights and fundamental freedoms.

However, better educational outcome rates do not necessarily mean increased tolerance. Looking back on lessons from history, Nazi Germany, in the geographic centre of well-developed Europe, with cultured, highly educated people, carried out genocide. In this sense, education is not a guarantee for humane behaviour and must be firmly anchored within established human rights commitments and educational systems based on human rights and values. The commitment to access to education must be equalled by a focus on learning and relevance. Focusing on quality will also ensure that public education can become a vehicle for social mobility for disadvantaged populations and where appropriate formal and informal settings of educational achievements reinforce each other.

National and international commitments to primary education have led to considerable progress. Gains achieved through both demand and supply-side initiatives are impressive, especially considering the challenges faced by many countries in this period, from economic crises and natural disasters to conflict and population growth. Governments and civil society must work together in a concerted way to promote universal primary education for the larger population, and to increase community ownership as well as understanding of the major benefits for everyone in society of improved education and development outcomes for marginalised groups. Multilateral institutions and civil society advocates that work on these issues globally, regionally and locally cannot compensate for a lack of involvement by national governments. Greater inclusion of human rights education in educational settings and increasing the role of national human rights institutions as advisors and partners to Ministries of Education would positively contribute to the realisation of the right to education and strengthen solid human rights cultures as well as the development of a global culture of tolerance, patience and cohesion.

Notes

1 The views expressed in this article are the author's own and do not reflect the view of the European Union Agency for Fundamental Rights (FRA). I would like to thank, for their very helpful comments and suggestions Friso Roscam Abbing, Head of Department Fundamental Rights Promotion of the EU Agency for Fundamental Rights; Richelle Budd Caplan, European Department

Director, International School for Holocaust Studies of Yad Vashem; and Dr. Brian Klug, Senior Research Fellow in Philosophy, St. Benet's Hall, University of Oxford.

2 Office of the Secretary-General's Envoy on Youth, 2017; UNFPA, 2017.
3 Claude, 2005.
4 http://www.undp.org/content/undp/en/home/sustainable-development-goals.html
5 See Racial Equality Directive, available at: http://eur-lex.europa.eu/legal-content/en/TXT/?uri=CELEX%3A32000L0043.
6 Global Monitoring Report, Education For All 2000–2015: Achievements and Challenges, 2015.
7 See United Nations Populations Fund, *The state of world population report 2016*, available at: www.unfpa.org/swop
8 See *Report on discrimination of Roma children in education* (2014), available at: http://ec.europa.eu/justice/discrimination/files/roma_childdiscrimination_en.pdf
9 *DH and others v The Czech Republic* (2007).
10 After spending many years working as director of an orphanage in Warsaw, he refused sanctuary repeatedly and stayed with his orphans when the entire population of the institution was sent from the Ghetto to the Treblinka extermination camp, during the Grossaktion Warsaw of 1942 in Poland.
11 Korczak, 2009.
12 Meyer, Bromley and Ramirez, 2010.
13 Bromley, Meyer and Ramirez, 2011i.
14 Bromley, Meyer and Ramirez, 2011ii.
15 Levinson, 2010.
16 Rubagiza, Umutoni and Kaleeba, 2016
17 Discover the past for the future: The role of historical sites and museums in Holocaust education and human rights education in the EU: Summary report, 2011: 9.
18 Declaration of the Stockholm International Forum on the Holocaust (Holocaustremembrance.com, n.d.i).
19 International Holocaust Remembrance Alliance (Holocaustremembrance.com, n.d.ii).
20 Discover the past for the future: The role of historical sites and museums in Holocaust education and human rights education in the EU: Summary report, 2011: 9; Education about the Holocaust and preventing genocide, 2017.
21 Gasanabo, Mutanguha and Mpayimana, 2016.
22 South African Holocaust and Genocide Foundation (Ctholocaust.co.za, 2017).
23 Ohchr.org, 2016.

References

Bromley, P., Meyer, J. and Ramirez, F. (2011i). Student-Centeredness in Social Science Textbooks, 1970–2008: A Cross-National Study. *Social Forces*, 90(2), pp. 547–570.

Bromley, P., Meyer, J. and Ramirez, F. (2011ii). The Worldwide Spread of Environmental Discourse in Social Studies, History, and Civics Textbooks, 1970–2008. *Comparative Education Review*. [online], 55(4), pp. 517–545. Available at: www.journals.uchicago.edu/doi/10.1086/660797.

Claude, R. (2005). The Right to Education and Human Rights Education. *International Journal on Human Rights*, 2, pp. 36–59.

Ctholocaust.co.za. (2017). South African Holocaust & Genocide Foundation – Cape Town Holocaust Centre – Durban Holocaust Centre – Johannesburg Holocaust Centre. [online] Available at: www.ctholocaust.co.za/ [Accessed 25 Aug. 2017].

DH and others v The Czech Republic [2007] App. No. 57325/00 (European Court of Human Rights).

Discover the Past for the Future: The Role of Historical Sites and Museums in Holocaust Education and Human Rights Education in the EU: Summary Report. (2011). Luxembourg: Publications Office of the European Union.

Education About the Holocaust and Preventing Genocide. (2017). Paris: UNESCO.

Gasanabo, J., Mutanguha, F. and Mpayimana, A. (2016). Teaching About the Holocaust and Genocide in Rwanda. *Contemporary Review of the Middle East.* [online], 3(3), pp. 329–345. Available at: http://cme.sagepub. com/content/3/3/329. full.pdf [Accessed 7 Nov. 2016].

Global Monitoring Report, Education for All 2000–2015: Achievements and Challenges. (2015). Paris: UNESCO.

Holocaustremembrance.com. (n.di.). Declaration of the Stockholm International Forum on the Holocaust | IHRA. [online] Available at: www.holocaustremembrance.com/about-us/stockholm-declaration [Accessed 25 Aug. 2017].

Holocaustremembrance.com. (n.dii.). History of IHRA | IHRA. [online] Available at: www.holocaustremembrance.com/about-us/history-ihra [Accessed 25 Aug. 2017].

Korczak, J. (2009). *The Child's Right to Respect: Korczak Lectures.* [online] Council of Europe. Available at: www.coe.int/t/commissioner/source/prems/PublicationKorczak_en.pdf [Accessed 25 Aug. 2017].

Levinson, M. (2010). The Civic Empowerment Gap: Defining the Problem and Locating Solutions. In: L. Sherrod, J. Torney-Purta and C. Flanagan, eds., *Handbook of Research on Civic Engagement.* [online] Hoboken: John Wiley & Sons. Available at: http://nrs.harvard.edu/urn-3:HUL.InstRepos:8454069 [Accessed 25 Apr. 2017].

Meyer, J., Bromley, P. and Ramirez, F. (2010). Human Rights in Social Science Textbooks: Cross-National Analyses, 1970–2008. *Sociology of Education.* [online], 83(2). Available at: http://worldpolity.files.wordpress.com/2010/07/meyer-bromley-ramirez-human-rights-intextbooks- soe-may-4–11–10.pdf [Accessed 24 Aug. 2017].

Office of the Secretary-General's Envoy on Youth. (2017). *10 Things You Didn't Know About the World's Population – Office of the Secretary-General's Envoy on Youth.* [online] Available at: www.un.org/youthenvoy/2015/04/10-things-didnt-know-worlds-population/ [Accessed 30 Apr. 2017].

Ohchr.org. (2016). OHCHR | High-Level Panel Discussion on the Implementation of the UN Declaration. [online] Available at: www.ohchr.org/EN/Issues/Education/Training/Pages/HighLevelDiscussionImplementationDeclationHREducation.aspx [Accessed 25 Aug. 2017].

Rubagiza, J., Umutoni, J. and Kaleeba, A. (2016). Teachers as Agents of Change: Promoting Peacebuilding and Social Cohesion in Schools in Rwanda. *Education as Change.* [online], 20(3), pp. 202–224. Available at: www.scielo.org.za/pdf/eac/v20n3/11.pdf.

UNFPA. (2017). The Power of 18 Billion: Adolescents, Youth and the Transformation of the Future. [online] Available at: www.unfpa.org/sites/default/files/pub-pdf/EN-SWOP14-Report_FINAL-web.pdf [Accessed 30 Apr. 2017].

17 Safeguarding heritage in armed conflict – how UNESCO protects the human right to culture

Giovanni Boccardi and Léonie Evers[1]

Introduction

Seventy years ago, the world was still recovering from what remained of one of the deadliest conflicts it had ever seen. Beyond the barbarity that cost the lives of millions of people, World War II was also the theatre of one of the largest and most systematised attempts at looting of cultural objects, iconoclasm and destruction of cultural heritage to date.

Based on the premise that "since wars begin in the minds of men, it is in the minds of men that the defences of peace must be constructed" (UNESCO Constitution, 1945), the United Nations Educational, Scientific, and Cultural Organization (UNESCO) was established on 16 November 1945 by 37 countries (UNESCO, n.d.), with the fundamental objective to:

> contribute to peace and security by promoting collaboration among nations through education, science and culture in order to further universal respect for justice, for the rule of law and for the human rights and fundamental freedoms which are affirmed for the peoples of the world.
>
> (UNESCO Constitution, 1945: Article I(1))

Just three years after the founding of UNESCO, the adoption of the UDHR anchored culture as a fundamental right indispensable for the dignity of humankind (Article 22) and guaranteed to "everyone . . . the right freely to participate in the cultural life of the community [and] to enjoy the arts" (Article 27(1)).

Today, despite the institutional and legal frameworks put in place in the wake of World War II, we yet again witness widespread destruction of cultural heritage, looting and illicit trafficking of cultural objects, as well as the persecution of ethnic and religious minorities. Attacks against culture have occurred especially in the context of the on-going conflicts in the Middle East and Africa, notably in Iraq, Syria and Mali.

On the 70th anniversary of the adoption of the UDHR,[2] this paper recalls the reasons why culture was originally integrated within the framework of human rights law and argues for an enhanced consideration of culture as a foundation for peace and sustainable development. It does so by outlining, first, the legal references to culture in human rights law and in international humanitarian law (IHL). Secondly, the paper explains why the protection of culture is fundamental, particularly during armed conflict. Thirdly, it introduces the role of UNESCO in protecting the human right to culture, before giving an overview of recent normative developments in the field at the international level. Finally, the paper concludes by pointing to possible future perspectives, with a view to expanding the scope of the application of existing normative frameworks as well as leveraging culture as a tool for peace-building and reconciliation.

Legal references to culture in human rights law

Culture is an integral part of the rich body of international human rights law (IHRL), referenced throughout the various treaties. These Conventions and Declarations attribute a central space to culture in the fundamental rights any human should be able to freely enjoy, and testify to the international community's recognition of the importance of culture for sustainable development and peace.

As the foundation of IHRL, the UDHR (1948) stipulates everyone's entitlement to realise their cultural rights (Article 22) and guarantees everyone "the right freely to participate in the cultural life of the community" (Article 27(1)).

Two subsequent main Covenants make it legally binding for ratifying states "to respect, to protect and to fulfill" the respective human rights set out within them (United Nations, n.d.). The International Covenant on Civil and Political Rights (1966) prohibits that "ethnic, religious or linguistic minorities . . . be denied the right . . . to enjoy their own culture, to profess and practice their own religion, or to use their own language" (Article 27). Moreover, Article 1 specifies the scope of all peoples' right to self-determination to include "their cultural development". The same article is repeated in the International Covenant on Economic, Social and Cultural Rights (1966). In addition, this Covenant ensures the recognition by its States Parties of the right "to take part in cultural life" (Article 15.1.a.) and makes explicit that, to ensure this, the necessary steps for "the conservation, the development and the diffusion of . . . culture" must be taken (Article 15.2.). In further recognition of the relationship between culture and the enjoyment of fundamental human rights, the two Covenants, as well as the UDHR, are referred to in the preamble of the 2003 UNESCO Convention for the Safeguarding of the Intangible Cultural Heritage.

Beyond these core human rights treaties applicable to all people, additional instruments of IHRL protect the cultural rights of distinctive groups of people, such as the United Nations (UN) Declaration on the Rights of Indigenous Peoples, notably in its Articles 3, 5, 8 and 11.

While IHRL is "inalienable and equally applicable to everyone" (United Nations, n.d.), in both war and peace (ICRC, 29 October 2010), the specific conditions of armed conflict have been warranted by the international community to require complementary legal instruments. As such, IHL "regulates the way war is conducted" (*idem*), notably concerning the protection of civilians and other non-combatants and the effects of the war upon them. Contrary to IHRL that contains provisions allowing the suspension, under certain conditions, of some human rights, the rights protected under IHL are always applicable and cannot be waived (*idem*). Henceforth, the inclusion in multiple legal instruments of IHL of the protection of cultural property, considered by IHRL as an integral element in the enjoyment of cultural rights, hints at the importance given to culture in contributing substantively to the well-being and dignity of individuals, *including* in situations of armed conflict.

Following previous codifications of Cultural Property Protection (CPP), such as in the Lieber Code of 1863 (Article 35) as well as the Hague Conventions on the Laws and Customs of War on Land of 1899 and 1907 (Article 27), the new world order following World War II enshrined CPP in Article 16 of the Protocol Additional to the Geneva Conventions of 12 August 1949, and Relating to the Protection of Victims of Non-International Armed Conflicts (Protocol II) of 1977, which prohibits anyone "to commit any acts of hostility directed against historic monuments, works of art or places of worship which constitute the cultural or spiritual heritage of peoples, and to use them in support of the military effort". The 1998 Rome Statute of the International Criminal Court (ICC) goes further in that it qualifies as a war crime in both international and non-international armed conflicts the act of "intentionally directing attacks against buildings dedicated to religion, . . . art, . . . historic monuments . . . provided they are not military objectives" (Article 8.2.(b)(ix) and Article 8.2.(e)(iv)). Finally, the 1954 Hague Convention concerns exclusively the protection of cultural property in the event of armed conflict and is considered customary IHL, applicable beyond its current 128 States Parties (as of June 2017). However, it is noteworthy here that IHL protects the physical embodiments of culture but does not specifically protect its practitioners, that is, the people linked to a given culture. In this context, the increased attention attributed to the destruction of cultural heritage, be it intentional or collateral, and particularly to its implications for international security, humanitarian response and, underlying all, human rights, has resulted in reflections regarding the need to better protect cultural rights in general, and not only cultural property.

Why safeguard culture and cultural heritage in armed conflict?

As has been outlined already, the practices around a given culture, as well as the physical expressions of these practices, are the subject of explicit protection and entitlement in various foundational legal bodies both in times of peace and war. Why, then, is culture so important that it must be safeguarded at all times?

Tylor defines culture as "that complex whole which includes knowledge, beliefs, arts, morals, laws, customs, and any other capabilities and habits acquired by [a human] as a member of society" (Seymour-Smith, 1986: 65). It touches and defines people and communities on a daily basis, guides their actions and shapes their understanding of the world around them. In its tangible and intangible forms, it is an expression and integral part of their identity, defining their position and role in the society they live in. Developed over centuries by individual communities or larger groups such as nations and states, culture is an expression of accumulated knowledge, tradition and positioning in the surrounding world.

Because of their high symbolism as expressions of cultural identity, cultural assets, be they objects or monuments, are attributed a special value by communities and must be protected in order to strengthen the resilience of people in the face of traumatic events such as armed conflict. Indeed, the populations themselves are often at the origin of protective measures for their cultural heritage, such as the human chain formed around the National Museum in Cairo, Egypt, during the political unrests of 2011, when it was at risk of being plundered (ICOM, 2011: 1).

The current era of globalisation, with its unprecedented acceleration and intensification in the global flows of capital, labour and information, is having a homogenising influence on local culture. While this phenomenon promotes the integration of societies and has provided millions of people with new opportunities, it may also bring with it a loss of uniqueness of local culture, which in turn can lead to loss of identity, exclusion and even conflict. This is especially true for traditional societies and communities, which are exposed to rapid 'modernisation' based on models imported from outside and not adapted to their context. In this sense, while contributing to the rapprochement of different cultures and communities, globalisation can also exacerbate tensions between them.

As a source of identity, meaning and belonging, culture can be used both to bring people together or to polarise and divide communities, forcing people to take sides in conflicts based on their heritage, a strategy that is fuelled through a propaganda of hatred and, in extreme cases, by deliberate attempts at erasing diversity, which the Director-General of UNESCO, Irina Bokova, has termed "cultural cleansing" (24 August 2015). It is precisely because of its role in shaping people's identities and as a source of resilience and strength for its claiming community that cultural heritage can also become the *target* of violence. In these circumstances, attacks are waged as a means to subjugate populations, control them and undermine social cohesion and resilience. Expressions of culture, in their tangible form, as heritage sites, monuments, or museums, or intangible form as embodied by the populations as bearers of culture, are hence particularly at risk during conflicts and necessitate therefore specific safeguarding measures integrated in security, humanitarian and peace-building strategies.

It is based on such considerations that in 1944 the Polish lawyer Raphael Lemkin sought to include a cultural component in the initial draft of the Convention on the Prevention and Punishment of the Crime of Genocide. While this suggestion was not retained in the final text, acts of cultural cleansing have been recognised as potential early warning signs of the intention to commit atrocities or even genocide (Nersessian, 2005). Indeed, the Trial Chamber of the International Criminal Tribunal for the Former Yugoslavia (ICTY) in the *Krstic* case stated that, "where there is physical or biological destruction there are often simultaneous attacks on the cultural and religious property and symbols of the targeted group as well, attacks which may legitimately be considered as evidence of an intent to physically destroy the group" (2001). In the same vein, the "destruction or plundering . . . of property related to cultural and religious identity" is considered by the UN (2014) as an indicator of "an environment conducive to the commission of atrocity crimes" (p. 16), while "attacks against or destruction of . . . cultural or religious symbols and property [of a protected group]" is considered one of the "signs of an intent to destroy in whole or in part a protected group" (p. 19), that is, to commit genocide. Moreover, "signs of patterns of violence against civilian populations, or against members of an identifiable group, . . . and [their] cultural or religious symbols" presents a risk factor for the commission of crimes against humanity (p. 20).

Most recently, in a report presented by the Independent International Commission of Inquiry (15 June 2016) on the Syrian Arab Republic to the Human Rights Council, the Yazidi community, thousands of whom have been or continue to be held captive in the country, has been recognised to be the victim of the crime of genocide as well as of multiple crimes against humanity and war crimes committed by the Islamic State in the Levant (ISIL/Daesh), that have resulted in "cutting them off from beliefs and practices of their own religious community, and erasing their identity as Yazidis" (p. 36).

It is hence because of the intrinsic symbolic value and importance for peoples' identities that heritage and cultural rights must be protected both in peacetime and situations of armed conflict, as the basis for peaceful and tolerant societies

UNESCO's action to protect cultural rights

UNESCO has worked for many decades to safeguard heritage through its normative instruments and programmes, notably the World Heritage Convention. In implementing these initiatives, heritage has in effect been protected and promoted for its own intrinsic value and as an objective in its own right. The shocking images of destruction of monuments, museums, libraries and religious buildings by ISIL/Daesh in Iraq and Syria, however, have led to a renewed awareness, on the part of UNESCO, of the original reasons why culture must be protected, as enshrined in its Constitution. In this context, UNESCO has reoriented many of its initiatives by explicitly focusing on culture as a vector of tolerance and dialogue, as well as on its role for social cohesion.

In Mali, the shrines and mausoleums destroyed in Timbuktu during the conflict in 2012 were reconstructed by the local population with the support of UNESCO, based on the understanding that they were essential to the practice of local cultural traditions and the population's resilience in the face of violent extremism and conflict (UNESCO, n.d.: 9). Similarly, a comprehensive project for the Emergency Safeguarding of the Syrian Cultural Heritage, currently being implemented, aims at contributing to "restoring social cohesion, stability and sustainable development" (UNESCO Observatory of Syrian Cultural Heritage, n.d.).

In order to allow an integrated and comprehensive response more efficiently federating the various UNESCO Cultural Conventions in emergency contexts, the General Conference of UNESCO adopted a comprehensive Strategy for the Reinforcement of the Organization's Action for the Protection of Culture and the Promotion of Cultural Pluralism in the Event of Armed Conflict (November 2015, 38C/49).

In this context, a number of measures have been initiated with the intention to protect culture and cultural heritage for their broader human rights value and their related contribution to security and humanitarian action. Initiatives aimed at building a larger understanding of cultural diversity and at promoting cultural pluralism, thereby contributing to sustainable peace and the prevention of violent extremism, have also been launched. As such, the Action Plan for the *Strategy*'s implementation (UNESCO, 2017) foresees "cooperation and exchange of information with the Human Rights Council and the UN Special Rapporteur on Cultural Right" aimed at "mainstream[ing] culture into Human Rights policies", the "integration of the protection of cultural heritage into UN peace-keeping operations", the "integration of culture into humanitarian relief efforts related to displacement", as well as the "integration of culture into peacebuilding efforts".

In addition, "Community-based recovery projects" and activities focused on creative cultural expressions aimed at "reconcil[ing] communities, foster[ing] dialogue, promot[ing] sustainable development", as well as social inclusion and peaceful societies, are also planned. Moreover, educational activities, both formal and informal, aimed at "promoting cultural pluralism and enhancing youth engagement around culture" are foreseen, their expressed objective being to facilitate "access to and enjoyment of heritage among the younger generation as related to the development of their self-identities" and thereby "build more tolerant and inclusive societies and to contribute to the Prevention of Violent Extremism".

In this context, new and innovative technology has been increasingly used to support awareness-raising and sensitisation initiatives, particularly aimed at youth. Indeed, beyond the physical protective measures that can be implemented before or in the aftermath of an emergency such as an armed conflict, the individual members of each society are at the basis of cultural heritage protection through their respect for cultural diversity and tolerance. It is in this vein that UNESCO has launched, in March of 2015, the global social media campaign '#Unite4Heritage', that seeks to engage youth in the protection of cultural heritage by promoting an alternative narrative to extremist propaganda, based on tolerance for diversity and intercultural dialogue. Another example of the use of IT for raising awareness of the importance of cultural heritage and the need to protect it is the use of three-dimensional reconstructions of monuments and artefacts, allowing the greater public to experience the richness of the world's cultural diversity remotely in a museum context. Most recently, the Grand Palais in Paris, France, made accessible such three-dimensional renderings of Iraqi and Syrian World Heritage sites in an exhibition, recognised in the press as a necessary visit for everyone (Chassagnon, 2016).

Increased recognition in security, humanitarian and human rights policies

Initial reactions to UNESCO's forceful intervention at the international level for an enhanced consideration of culture in security and humanitarian policies were questioning the immediate necessity to 'save stones', when human lives were at risk (Bokova, 1 July 2015i: 8). However, UNESCO's position has incrementally gained recognition at the highest levels of the international community, as well as among the public.

On the occasion of a high-level international Conference on Heritage and Cultural Diversity at Risk in Iraq and Syria, hosted by UNESCO in December 2014, the Special Representative of the UN Secretary-General (UNSG) for Iraq, Mr Nickolay Mladenov, and the UNSG's Special Envoy to Syria, Mr Staffan de Mistura, underlined the role of culture in the future of both countries in the foundation of peace and stability (UNESCO, n.d.: 6–7). Against the background of their mandates that do not explicitly include culture, but "aimed at bringing an end to all violence and human rights violations, and promoting a peaceful solution" (UN News Centre, 2014), their contributions marked an important recognition of the role of culture in political processes, including humanitarian and security issues.

Most recently, the UN Security Council adopted Resolution 2347 (2017), which for the first time focuses exclusively on the protection of cultural heritage in conflict situations. In an historic development, the Resolution affirms that UN Peacekeeping operations' mandate may include assisting in the protection of cultural heritage, whenever considered appropriate (Article 19). In his briefing to the Council following the vote, Jeffrey Feltman, UN Under-Secretary-General for Political Affairs, borrowed the often-used quote by Ms Bokova, according to which, "protecting heritage was . . . not only a cultural issue, but also a security and humanitarian imperative" (United Nations, 2017).

In the context of the fight against impunity, the International Criminal Court (ICC) decided, in a succession of historic steps, to prosecute and condemn for the first time for the war crime of intentionally directing attacks against historic monuments and buildings dedicated to religion, namely of the shrines and mausoleums in Timbuktu, Mali, during the occupation by extremist groups in 2012 of the city listed as a World Heritage property (2016). In the judgement, the prosecutor made explicit the human impact of the destructions by underlining the moral harm suffered by the victims (*idem*, p. 47). This human dimension is also reflected in the reparations order which requests the moral harm to be addressed "by giving compensation to the applicants as individual and collective reparations" (ICC, 2016: 36).

Beyond the security realm, a consideration for culture was also increasingly given in humanitarian and human rights policies. As such, the 56 states and 11 international and regional organisations that participated in the International Conference on the Victims of Ethnic and Religious Violence in the Middle East

(8 September 2015), convened by the governments of France and Jordan, underlined in the resulting Paris Action Plan the "pressing necessity to protect and preserve those communities and cultures whose very existence is threatened in Iraq and Syria". The Action Plan included the relevance of culture in different fields of action, namely the support to refugees and internally displaced persons (IDPs), through improved access to education for young people belonging to ethnic or religious communities; preventing and fighting radicalisation, violent extremism and terrorism, through strengthened intercultural and interreligious dialogue, education sensitive to cultural diversity as well as awareness-raising on the latter; and finally "protecting and promoting the cultural heritage of the communities concerned".

Underlining the recognition, as enshrined in the preambles of the aforementioned bodies of IHRL that "the ideal of free human beings enjoying civil and political freedom and freedom from fear and want can only be achieved if conditions are created whereby everyone may enjoy his civil and political rights, as well as his economic, social and cultural rights", Farida Shaheed, former Special Rapporteur in the field of cultural rights at the UN Office of the High Commissioner for Human Rights (OHCHR), focused on the right of access to, and enjoyment of, cultural heritage in her second thematic report. She stressed that cultural heritage is important not only in itself, but also in relation to its human dimension, in particular its significance for individuals and communities in terms of both their identity and development processes (Human Rights Council, 21 March 2011).

In continuity with her predecessor, Ms Karima Bennoune, the current Special Rapporteur in the field of cultural rights, has pleaded for a human-rights-based approach to cultural heritage, focussing specifically on its intentional destruction and the related human rights implications (UN General Assembly, 9 August 2016). In doing so, she supported UNESCO's advocacy for the impact of cultural heritage destruction on individuals and their human rights. She also addressed, in a subsequent report, the impact of violent extremism on the enjoyment of cultural rights, as well as the contribution of cultural rights to preventing violent extremism (Human Rights Council, 16 January 2017). Based on the Special Rapporteur's reports and upon the impulse of the Republic of Cyprus, the Human Rights Council itself adopted landmark Resolution 33/20 on the destruction of cultural heritage in the framework of armed conflicts and in particular by terrorist groups (6 October 2016).

Finally, further evidence of the increased recognition of the importance of the protection of cultural heritage is provided by initiatives taken by two members of the UN Security Council, the United Kingdom and France. In addition to their creation of two financial mechanisms – the Cultural Protection Fund (British Council, 2017) and the International Alliance for the Protection of Heritage in Conflict Areas (ALIPH) (France Diplomatie, 3 May 2017), respectively – both states are in the process of ratifying the Second Protocol of the 1954 Hague Convention (Woodhouse, Lang, & Mills, 2016, and Assemblée nationale, n.d.).

Conclusion

As has been outlined here, the recent escalation of violence directed towards individuals and sites associated with cultural heritage, notably in Iraq and Syria, has led to a renewed awareness, within the international community, of the need to protect culture in situations of armed conflict as a security, humanitarian and human rights issue. Despite this, damage and destruction have continued, leading to growing feelings of powerlessness and frustration, particularly among experts and scholars (e.g., Bin Talal, 2 September 2015), some of whom suggested that the existing legal tools for the protection of cultural property in armed conflict needed to be strengthened.

In this context, the authors believe that the main shortcoming is not related to gaps in the existing normative instruments, but rather to their insufficient level of ratification and national implementation. While recognising that in an armed conflict situation it is often not possible to prevent acts of violence, including against cultural assets, existing legal frameworks, if applied to their fullest, can provide the necessary means for appropriate protection of cultural property, which is key to ensuring access to culture and the enjoyment of cultural rights.

As far as international cooperation mechanisms are concerned, similarly, it is not so much a lack of policies, but the inadequate means for their actual implementation that is at stake. The UNESCO Strategy, close to two years after its adoption by member states, remains only partially funded (UNESCO, 2017).

Nevertheless, it is undeniable that stronger attention should be paid to the human rights dimension of attacks against culture and heritage in situations of armed conflict, which are too often considered only for their effects on monuments and sites. This would mean, in addition to protecting cultural heritage as an end in itself, to ensure the affected populations' access to culture and participation in cultural life, including free artistic expression. Thereby, culture would be more strongly anchored in the wider humanitarian and security framework and policies, so that its potential as a source of resilience and social stability could be fully harnessed.

In the context of on-going armed conflicts, special consideration should therefore be given to the unprecedented number of refugees and IDPs, with the aim of ensuring, insofar as possible, their continued access to culture and enjoyment of cultural rights. The 2003 UNESCO Convention for the Safeguarding of Intangible Cultural Heritage and the 2005 UNESCO Convention on the Diversity of Cultural Expressions may provide a useful framework in this regard. Article 11(a) of the 2003 Convention, for example, calls on State Parties to "take the necessary measures to ensure the safeguarding of the intangible cultural heritage present in its territory". While it may not have been in the minds of the Convention's authors that this could apply to the intangible cultural heritage of refugees or migrants present in a State Party's territory, its relevance in the context of globalisation and in relation to cultural rights is undeniable. This is also one of the recommendations made by Special Rapporteur Karima Bennoune (UN General Assembly, 2016, §78(i)), in addition to others, such as the value of "educational programmes on the importance of the cultural heritage and cultural rights" (§78(c)(iv)).

Indeed, perhaps the most effective way of protecting the cultural rights of groups and individuals is through sensitisation and educational initiatives in peacetime. In this regard, two complementary objectives should be pursued: on the one hand, strengthening the awareness of one's own culture and its transmission to the youth, including through intergenerational dialogue. On the other hand, promoting a pluralistic and inclusive approach to the culture of others, through intercultural dialogue and learning to facilitate tolerance and understanding. Such dialogue and exchange can be supported by leveraging the positive aspects of globalisation, including greater mobility across communities and the spread of new digital technologies, such as virtual reality, social media and others.

Notes

1 The ideas and opinions expressed in this article are those of the authors and do not necessarily represent the views of UNESCO and do not commit the Organisation.

2 A collection of essays specifically dedicated to cultural rights was published by UNESCO and the Institute of War and Law on the occasion of the 50th Anniversary of the adoption of the UDHR, in 1998 (See Niec, H. (Ed.). (1998). *Cultural rights and wrongs: a collection of essays in commemoration of the 50th anniversary of the Universal Declaration of Human Right*. UNESCO Publishing and Institute of Art and Law, London, UK).

References

Ap.ohchr.org. (2016). Human Rights Documents. [online] Available at: http://ap.ohchr.org/documents/dpage_e.aspx?si=A/HRC/RES/33/20 [Accessed 3 May 2017].

Ap.ohchr.org. (2017). Human Rights Documents. [online] Available at: http://ap.ohchr.org/documents/dpage_e.aspx?si=A/HRC/34/56 [Accessed 5 May 2017].

Assemblée Nationale. (n.d.). *Traités et conventions: protection des biens culturels en cas de conflit armé*. [online] Paris: French National Assembly. Available at: www.assemblee-nationale.fr/14/dossiers/protection_biens_culturels_conflit_arme.asp [Accessed 12 Dec. 2017].

Bin Talal, H. (2015). The Right to Protect Our Common Heritage. *Jordan Times*. [online]. Available at: www.jordantimes.com/news/letters/right-protect-our-common-heritage [Accessed 3 May 2017].

Bokova, I. (2015i). *Cultural Heritage: Extremism's New Target*. [online] UNESCO. Available at: http://unesdoc.unesco.org/images/0023/002336/233661E.pdf [Accessed 3 May 2017].

Bokova, I. (2015ii). Fighting Cultural Cleansing: Harnessing the Law to Preserve Cultural Heritage. *Harvard International Review*. [online] August 2015. Available at: http://hir.harvard.edu/article/?a=11723 [Accessed 1 May 2017].

Bokova, I. (2017). *Cultural Heritage: Extremism's New Target*. London: Chatham House.

Britishcouncil.org. (2017). Cultural Protection Fund | British Council. [online] Available at: www.britishcouncil.org/arts/culture-development/cultural-protection-fund [Accessed 10 May 2017].

Chassagnon, M. (2016). "Sites éternels" au Grand Palais, l'expo que tous les Français (et les autres) devraient aller voir. *Huffington Post.* [online] Available at: www.huffingtonpost.fr/2016/12/13/sites-eternels-au-grand-palais-lexpo-que-tous-les-francais/ [Accessed 10 May 2017].

Daccess-ods.un.org. (2011). Cite a Website – Cite This for Me. [online] Available at: http://daccess-ods.un.org/access.nsf/Get?Open&DS=A/HRC/17/38&Lang=E [Accessed 5 May 2017].

En.unesco.org. (2005). The Convention | Diversity of Cultural Expressions. [online] Available at: http://en.unesco.org/creativity/convention [Accessed 12 May 2017].

En.unesco.org. (n.d.). The Emergency Safeguarding of the Syrian Cultural Heritage project | UNESCO. [online] Available at: http://en.unesco.org/syrian-observatory/emergency-safeguarding-syrian-cultural-heritage-project [Accessed 10 May 2017].

France Diplomatie: Ministry for Europe and Foreign Affairs. (2015). *The Paris Action Plan (08.09.15).* [online] Available at: www.diplomatie.gouv.fr/en/country-files/north-africa-and-middle-east/events/article/the-paris-action-plan-09-08–2015 [Accessed 5 May 2017].

Human Rights Council. (2011). *Report of the Independent Expert in the Field of Cultural Rights, Farida Shaheed.* A/HRC/17/38. Geneva: United Nations.

Human Rights Council. (2016). *Cultural Rights and the Protection of Cultural Heritage.* A/HRC/RES/33/20. Geneva: United Nations.

Human Rights Council. (2017). *Report of the Special Rapporteur in the Field of Cultural Rights.* A/HRC/34/56. Geneva: United Nations.

Icom.museum. (2011). ICOM Preliminary Report on Museums in Egypt. [online] Available at: http://icom.museum/fileadmin/user_upload/pdf/working_groups/110207_ICOM_preliminary_report_Egypt.pdf [Accessed 10 May 2017].

Ihl-databases.icrc.org. (2017i). Treaties, States Parties, and Commentaries – Hague Convention (II) on the Laws and Customs of War on Land, 1899. [online] Available at: https://ihl-databases.icrc.org/applic/ihl/ihl.nsf/Treaty.xsp?action=openDocument&documentId=CD0F6C83F96FB459C12563CD002D66A1 [Accessed 12 May 2017].

Ihl-databases.icrc.org. (2017ii). Treaties, States Parties, and Commentaries – Hague Convention (IV) on War on Land and its Annexed Regulations, 1907. [online] Available at: https://ihl-databases.icrc.org/applic/ihl/ihl.nsf/Treaty.xsp?documentId=4D47F92DF3966A7EC12563CD002D6788&action=openDocument [Accessed 12 May 2017].

International Committee of the Red Cross. (2010). *IHL and Other Legal Regimes.* [online] Available at: www.icrc.org/en/document/ihl-and-other-legal-regimes [Accessed 30 Apr. 2017].

Judgment and Sentence Situation in the Republic of Mali: The Prosecutor v Ahmad Al Faqi Al Mahdi [2016] ICC-01/12–01/15 (International Criminal Court).

Kim, A. (2014). The Monuments Men. *The Harvard Crimson.* [online] February. Available at: www.thecrimson.com/article/2014/2/4/the-monuments-men-cover/ [Accessed 27 Apr. 2017].

Krstic´ [2001] IT-98–33-T (International Criminal Tribunal for the former Yugoslavia), Para 580.

Lieber, F. (1863). *Instructions for the Government of Armies of the United States in the Field.* Washington: GPO.

Lostal, M. (2016). Opinio Juris " Blog Archive Prosecutor v Al Mahdi: A Positive New Direction for the ICC? – Opinio Juris. *Opiniojuris.org.* [online] Available at: http://opiniojuris.org/2016/10/26/prosecutor-v-al-mahdi-a-positive-new-direction-for-the-icc/?utm_source=feedburner&utm_medium=email&utm_campaign=Feed%3A+opiniojurisfeed+%28Opinio+Juris%29 [Accessed 12 May 2017].

Nations, U. (2017). *Protection of Heritage – UNESCO's Participation in the Founding Board of ALIPH (03.05.17).* [online] France Diplomatie: Ministry for Europe and Foreign Affairs. Available at: www.diplomatie.gouv.fr/en/french-foreign-policy/united-nations/events/events-2017/article/protection-of-heritage-unesco-s-participation-in-the-founding-board-of-aliph-03 [Accessed 10 May 2017].

Nersessian, D. (2005). Rethinking Cultural Genocide Under International Law | Carnegie Council for Ethics in International Affairs. *Carnegiecouncil.org.* [online] Available at: www.carnegiecouncil.org/publications/archive/dialogue/2_12/section_1/5139.html/:pf_printable [Accessed 16 Apr. 2017].

Nieć, H. (1998). *Cultural Rights and Wrongs: A Collection of Essays in Commemoration of the 50th Anniversary of the Universal Declaration of Human Right.* London: UNESCO and Institute of Art and Law.

Ohchr.org. (1966i). OHCHR | International Covenant on Civil and Political Rights. [online] Available at: www.ohchr.org/EN/ProfessionalInterest/Pages/CCPR.aspx [Accessed 30 Apr. 2017].

Ohchr.org. (1966ii). OHCHR | International Covenant on Economic, Social and Cultural Rights. [online] Available at: www.ohchr.org/EN/ProfessionalInterest/Pages/CESCR.aspx [Accessed 30 Apr. 2017].

Ohchr.org. (1977). OHCHR | Protocol II Additional to the Geneva Conventions of 12 August 1949. [online] Available at: www.ohchr.org/EN/ProfessionalInterest/Pages/ProtocolII.aspx [Accessed 30 Apr. 2017].

Ohchr.org. (1998) OHCHR | Rome Statute of the International Criminal Court. [online] Available at: www.ohchr.org/EN/ProfessionalInterest/Pages/InternationalCriminalCourt.aspx [Accessed 30 Apr. 2017].

Ohchr.org/Documents. (2016). "They came to destroy": ISIS Crimes Against the Yazidis. [online] Available at: www.ohchr.org/Documents/HRBodies/HRCouncil/CoISyria/A_HRC_32_CRP.2_en.pdf [Accessed 3 May 2017].

Petropoulos, J. (1998). *Art Looting During the Third Reich: An Overview with Recommendations for Further Research, in Proceedings of the Washington Conference on Holocaust-Era Assets.* [online] Available at: https://fcit.usf.edu/holocaust/resource/assets/heaca.pdf [Accessed 27 Apr. 2017].

Portal.unesco.org. (1945). UNESCO Constitution. [online] Available at: http://portal.unesco.org/en/ev.php-URL_ID=15244&URL_DO=DO_TOPIC&URL_SECTION=201.html [Accessed 27 Apr. 2017].

Reparations Order. Situation in the Republic of Mali. The Prosecutor v Ahmad Al Faqi Al Mahdi [2017] ICC-01/12–01/15 (International Criminal Court).

Seymour-Smith, C. (1986). *Macmillan Dictionary of Anthropology.* Basingstoke: MacMillan Press.

UN News Service Section. (2014). *UN News – UN chief appoints Staffan de Mistura as special envoy for Syria crisis.* [online] Available at: www.un.org/apps/news/story.asp?NewsID=48244#.WQzWSlLwdok [Accessed 5 May 2017].

Un.org. (2008). United Nations Declaration on the Rights of Indigenous Peoples. [online] Available at: www.un.org/esa/socdev/unpfii/documents/DRIPS_en.pdf [Accessed 30 Apr. 2017].

Un.org. (2014). Framework of Analysis for Atrocity Crimes: A Tool for Prevention. [online] Available at: www.un.org/en/preventgenocide/adviser/pdf/framework%20of%20analysis%20for%20atrocity%20crimes_en.pdf [Accessed 2 May 2017].

Un.org. (2016). Report of the Special Rapporteur in the Field of Cultural Rights. A/71/317. [online] Available at: www.un.org/ga/search/view_doc.asp?symbol=A/71/317 [Accessed 5 May 2017].

Un.org. (2017). Security Council Condemns Destruction, Smuggling of Cultural Heritage by Terrorist Groups, Unanimously Adopting Resolution 2347 (2017) | Meetings Coverage and Press Releases. [online] Available at: www.un.org/press/en/2017/sc12764.doc.htm [Accessed 3 May 2017].

Un.org. (n.d.). The Foundation of International Human Rights Law. [online] Available at: www.un.org/en/sections/universal-declaration/foundation-international-human-rights-law/index.html [Accessed 30 Apr. 2017].

Undocs.org. (2017). S/RES/2347(2017) – E. [online] Available at: http://undocs.org/S/RES/2347(2017) [Accessed 5 May 2017].

Unesco.org. (2017). History | United Nations Educational, Scientific and Cultural Organization. [online] Available at: www.unesco.org/new/en/unesco/about-us/who-we-are/history/ [Accessed 6 Sep. 2017].

Unesco.org. (n.d.). *UNESCO Report. "Heritage and Cultural Diversity at Risk in Iraq and Syria" International Conference*. [online] Available at: www.unesco.org/fileadmin/multimedia/HQ/CLT/CLT/pdf/IraqSyriaReport-en.pdf [Accessed 5 May 2017].

Unesdoc.unesco.org. (2003). Convention for the Safeguarding of the Intangible Cultural Heritage. [online] Available at: http://unesdoc.unesco.org/images//0013/001325/132540e.pdf [Accessed 5 May 2017].

Unesdoc.unesco.org. (2015). Reinforcement of UNESCO's Action for the Protection of Culture and the Promotion of Cultural Pluralism in the Event of Armed Conflict. 39C/49. [online] Available at: http://unesdoc.unesco.org/images/0023/002351/235186e.pdf [Accessed 5 May 2017].

Unesdoc.unesco.org. (2017). Report on the Implementation of the Strategy for the Reinforcement of UNESCO's Action for the Protection of Culture and the Promotion of Cultural Pluralism in the Event of Armed Conflict. 201 EX/5 Part I (E). [online] Available at: http://unesdoc.unesco.org/images/0024/002477/247706e.pdf [Accessed 5 May 2017].

Unesdoc.unesco.org. (n.d.). UNESCO's Response to Protect Culture in Crises. [online] Available at: http://unesdoc.unesco.org/images/0024/002449/244984e.pdf [Accessed 10 May 2017].

Woodhouse, J., Lang, A. and Mills, C. (2016). *Cultural Property (Armed Conflicts) Bill [HL] (Bill 66 of 2016–2017): Briefing Paper 7745*. London: House of Commons Library.

Section VI

The challenge of hope

18 Challenges for the human rights movement

Jimmy Carter

In 1941 Franklin Delano Roosevelt outlined what he called the Four Freedoms upon which government policies should be based. One of them was the freedom of religion, and another was freedom of speech. Then he gave two warnings – that progress would be impossible unless people enjoy freedom from want, or poverty, and the freedom from fear of violence and warfare. Roosevelt understood that basic social and economic well-being are just as important to democratic life as civil and political rights. He also pointed to the danger posed by a fearful population and the importance of channelling our resources into constructive enterprises that would reduce fear and increase hopefulness. This comprehensive view of human rights, security and governance is just as relevant now as it was all those years ago, as free speech and religious freedom are under assault, the extremes of wealth and poverty are widening and warfare and violence are increasingly normalised.

***

I was on a battleship in the Atlantic Ocean in 1945 when the world's powers got together and formed the United Nations with a clear and express purpose of preventing war in the future. A few years later, the same global powers assembled and, under the leadership of Eleanor Roosevelt, adopted the UDHR. The United Nations became the only organisation that would include every nation in its deliberations on peace, security, as well as human rights and development. Now, those two great commitments have largely been abandoned by the world. The United Nations is no longer a repository and guarantor of peace, and even the greatest of nations have not met the expectations of the UDHR.

Recently, the leaders of the United States announced that no longer will we try to have as a key to one of our foreign policy commitments the upholding of the standards that have made our country and others admirable and trustworthy. This is very troubling to me. When I was a young man listening to my president on that battleship, I was proud of my country and the role we would play in advancing human freedom. I never dreamed that the United States of America would cease to be the most admired democratic country in the world, but the erosion of human rights is a reality we are facing, and it is even worse in some other countries.

When I was elected, and later when awarded the Nobel Peace Prize, I quoted my high school teacher, Miss Julia Coleman, who told us students that we must accommodate changing times but cling to principles that never change. That has been a guiding statement for me throughout my life; we must accommodate what is happening now, make the most of it, improve it if we can, but never default on our commitment to the principles expressed in our Constitution, The Lord's Prayer, and in our own ideals, which never change. Those things that never change include a commitment to peace and a commitment to the UDHR.

As President of the United States, I decided to emphasise human rights in our foreign policy because I believed that human freedom would be the best guarantor of stability and peace within and among nations. I still believe this to be true. During my administration, the United States signed the major global human rights treaties, invested in the United Nations' human rights agencies and supported democratic movements in many countries, sometimes securing the release of political prisoners who suffered abuse and torture for their activities on behalf of human rights. We even confronted our Cold War allies, especially the military dictators of Latin America, when they abused, tortured and disappeared non-violent human rights activists. I was criticised for this by those who believed geo-political allegiances should have been a singular priority. Over time, however, it has been shown that the hemisphere's nations that are committed to expanding freedom for more people become more successful and stable partners.

We did not believe that instigating violence and warfare would serve American interests or hasten the advent of democracy throughout the world, so we sought to resolve conflict with diplomacy and dialogue. We knew that democracy and human rights must be fought and won from inside, and that the most productive approach would be to offer various types of encouragement. As much as possible, we backed this up with a commitment to peace and reciprocity that would signal our belief that human rights, including the right to peace, are universal and should be constantly demanded, even of our own government when warranted.

A broad global embrace of human rights took hold in subsequent years, and we saw a dramatic increase in the demand for accountable governance and justice in more nations. The promise of equal rights for women and girls came into greater focus, and a global consensus began to emerge that women's rights must be protected to the same degree as the basic rights of freedom of speech and religion, or the right to a fair trial. The United Nations built upon the promise of the UDHR by establishing and strengthening institutions like the Office of the High Commissioner for Human Rights, the International Criminal Court and the Human Rights Council. The Carter Center and I participated in these efforts directly, working with other human rights organisations and like-minded governments to create these and other institutions that would monitor and intervene in cases of human rights abuse when conditions demanded.

However, after the attacks against the United States in 2001, these many gains in the field of human rights were eroded. The threat of terrorism led even established democracies to embrace an overly militaristic approach to national security. My own country launched a "pre-emptive war" in violation of the United Nations Charter, which limits the use of force to cases of self-defense. While military force obviously is sometimes justifiable or necessary, the distinction between justifiable self-defense and aggressive war has been undermined because of the global war on terror, which continues to be expanded into more and more nations.

The grave consequences can be seen throughout the Middle East and the entire world, as the reach of terror groups has only expanded. Young people are being recruited into terror groups under the banner of righteous warfare against what they see as Western invasion, and many nations face a growing threat of homegrown terrorism. Taking advantage of the understandable public anxiety about this threat, many governments are actively fomenting fear and xenophobia to justify the expansion of authoritarian policies and broaden their powers. Torture against people suspected of terrorist crimes has been carried out with impunity, including in my own country; the right to privacy has disappeared; and freedoms of religion, association and speech are under attack in many nations.

The deployment of excessive military force has been extended to the wars on drugs and crime as state-sanctioned violence has become normalised in the form of police brutality and mass incarceration. Governments also increasingly use force against citizens, especially indigenous communities, protesting economic and environmental exploitation, including by private corporations.

Meanwhile, the concentration of wealth at the very top has eroded public trust in political elites and parties. This disparity between the rich and the poor is growing both within nations and between nations. In the United States, average hard-working middle-class people believe that they are being cheated by the government and by society; they feel that their basic rights to healthcare, quality education and a political voice are being taken away. Unlimited amounts of money going into political campaigns means that an average person's vote is almost cancelled out because of the influence wielded by those who use their wealth to exert political influence, causing the average person to believe that her/his choice of a candidate is not equally valuable as a rich person's choice. Once that candidate gets into office, quite often the average person feels that the elected official must re-pay the contributions with their support of policies that favour the rich. This is a form of legal bribery that has undermined the confidence that citizens once had in our institutions.

America's criminal justice system has also become weaker. When I left office in 1981, only one out of a thousand Americans was in prison. Now, seven out of every thousand, seven times more people, are in prison. There can be no doubt that continuous racial discrimination in our country has resulted in African Americans bearing the brunt of this expansion of a massive private prison industry that profits from high occupancy of its facilities. A disturbing level of anger toward and even hatred for immigrants has risen in recent years, and now many immigrants seized in a growing number of government raids are also filling private prisons or simply being deported, sometimes to countries where they have never lived and have no family.

I have described here a loss of trust that we have had previously, in democracy and freedom, in our political leaders and institutions, in the sanctity of truth and basic fairness. This has come about due to the lack of adherence to the high ideals of peace and human rights in the broadest possible terms. That our nation's top leaders would actively undermine the trust of the people in our institutions and founding principles by fanning flames of hatred and fear is shocking.

Many of these trends came to a climax in 2016, including in my country's presidential election. The dissatisfaction of the average person with our political system resulted in many voters taking a chance on a leader who would obviously place less emphasis on human rights because they have lost trust in the major political parties. They were willing to abandon even basic principles of democracy and human rights just to try something new, no matter what it was. Similar political trends are present in nearly every region of the world, and it will take a concerted effort to turn the tide in favour of peace and human rights.

We have a great challenge before us if we are going to revitalise a global human rights movement. But, we have faced such challenges before, and we have seen incredible progress. During the darkest days of the two World Wars that engulfed Europe, we could barely imagine that one day the continent would become, even with all its challenges, an integrated community committed to resolving its differences peacefully. We must rededicate ourselves to an even higher aspiration than we have held in previous generations by promoting peace, an adequate standard of living, and the full inclusion and empowerment of women as basic human rights.

Where the threat of war exists, let us devote every possible effort to reduce fear and promote dialogue and understanding. When any brave human rights defender faces retaliation for shedding light on important information or government abuses, let us raise our voices to ensure their safety. When women and girls are excluded from decision making or are subjected to discrimination or violence, let us stand up and demand equality of representation and treatment. When religion is misused to promote violence or justify the oppression of anyone, let us remember that the essential teaching of every major religion is love and reciprocity. When a policy or law is debated in the parliaments and congresses of the world, let us consider whether the policy will give people opportunity and hope, alleviate suffering and dispel fear, or will it foment hatred or produce suffering among our fellow human beings?

If we are to revitalise a global human rights movement, we must work to strengthen our societies' commitments to peace and human rights so that future generations inherit a less violent and more just world.

Appendix

Universal Declaration of Human Rights

Preamble

Whereas recognition of the inherent dignity and of the equal and inalienable rights of all members of the human family is the foundation of freedom, justice and peace in the world,

Whereas disregard and contempt for human rights have resulted in barbarous acts which have outraged the conscience of mankind, and the advent of a world in which human beings shall enjoy freedom of speech and belief and freedom from fear and want has been proclaimed as the highest aspiration of the common people,

Whereas it is essential, if man is not to be compelled to have recourse, as a last resort, to rebellion against tyranny and oppression, that human rights should be protected by the rule of law,

Whereas it is essential to promote the development of friendly relations between nations,

Whereas the peoples of the United Nations have in the Charter reaffirmed their faith in fundamental human rights, in the dignity and worth of the human person and in the equal rights of men and women and have determined to promote social progress and better standards of life in larger freedom,

Whereas Member States have pledged themselves to achieve, in cooperation with the United Nations, the promotion of universal respect for and observance of human rights and fundamental freedoms,

Whereas a common understanding of these rights and freedoms is of the greatest importance for the full realization of this pledge,

Now, therefore,

THE GENERAL ASSEMBLY,

Proclaims THIS UNIVERSAL DECLARATION OF HUMAN RIGHTS as a common standard of achievement for all peoples and all nations, to the end that every individual and every organ of society, keeping this Declaration constantly in mind, shall strive by teaching and education to promote respect for these rights and freedoms and by progressive measures, national and international, to secure their universal and effective recognition and observance, both among the peoples of Member States themselves and among the peoples of territories under their jurisdiction.

Article 1

All human beings are born free and equal in dignity and rights. They are endowed with reason and conscience and should act towards one another in a spirit of brotherhood.

Article 2

Everyone is entitled to all the rights and freedoms set forth in this Declaration, without distinction of any kind, such as race, colour, sex, language, religion, political or other opinion, national or social origin, property, birth or other status.

Furthermore, no distinction shall be made on the basis of the political, jurisdictional or international status of the country or territory to which a person belongs, whether it be independent, trust, non-self-governing or under any other limitation of sovereignty.

Article 3

Everyone has the right to life, liberty and security of person.

Article 4

No one shall be held in slavery or servitude; slavery and the slave trade shall be prohibited in all their forms.

Article 5

No one shall be subjected to torture or to cruel, inhuman or degrading treatment or punishment.

Article 6

Everyone has the right to recognition everywhere as a person before the law.

Article 7

All are equal before the law and are entitled without any discrimination to equal protection of the law. All are entitled to equal protection against any discrimination in violation of this Declaration and against any incitement to such discrimination.

Article 8

Everyone has the right to an effective remedy by the competent national tribunals for acts violating the fundamental rights granted him by the constitution or by law.

Article 9

No one shall be subjected to arbitrary arrest, detention or exile.

Article 10

Everyone is entitled in full equality to a fair and public hearing by an independent and impartial tribunal, in the determination of his rights and obligations and of any criminal charge against him.

Article 11

1 Everyone charged with a penal offence has the right to be presumed innocent until proved guilty according to law in a public trial at which he has had all the guarantees necessary for his defence.
2 No one shall be held guilty of any penal offence on account of any act or omission which did not constitute a penal offence, under national or international law, at the time when it was committed. Nor shall a heavier penalty be imposed than the one that was applicable at the time the penal offence was committed.

Article 12

No one shall be subjected to arbitrary interference with his privacy, family, home or correspondence, nor to attacks upon his honour and reputation. Everyone has the right to the protection of the law against such interference or attacks.

Article 13

1 Everyone has the right to freedom of movement and residence within the borders of each State.
2 Everyone has the right to leave any country, including his own, and to return to his country.

Article 14

1 Everyone has the right to seek and to enjoy in other countries asylum from persecution.
2 This right may not be invoked in the case of prosecutions genuinely arising from non-political crimes or from acts contrary to the purposes and principles of the United Nations.

Article 15

1 Everyone has the right to a nationality.
2 No one shall be arbitrarily deprived of his nationality nor denied the right to change his nationality.

Article 16

1 Men and women of full age, without any limitation due to race, nationality or religion, have the right to marry and to found a family. They are entitled to equal rights as to marriage, during marriage and at its dissolution.
2 Marriage shall be entered into only with the free and full consent of the intending spouses.
3 The family is the natural and fundamental group unit of society and is entitled to protection by society and the State.

Article 17

1 Everyone has the right to own property alone as well as in association with others.
2 No one shall be arbitrarily deprived of his property.

Article 18

Everyone has the right to freedom of thought, conscience and religion; this right includes freedom to change his religion or belief, and freedom, either alone or in community with others and in public or private, to manifest his religion or belief in teaching, practice, worship and observance.

Article 19

Everyone has the right to freedom of opinion and expression; this right includes freedom to hold opinions without interference and to seek, receive and impart information and ideas through any media and regardless of frontiers.

Article 20

1 Everyone has the right to freedom of peaceful assembly and association.
2 No one may be compelled to belong to an association.

Article 21

1 Everyone has the right to take part in the government of his country, directly or through freely chosen representatives.
2 Everyone has the right to equal access to public service in his country.
3 The will of the people shall be the basis of the authority of government; this will shall be expressed in periodic and genuine elections which shall be by universal and equal suffrage and shall be held by secret vote or by equivalent free voting procedures.

Article 22

Everyone, as a member of society, has the right to social security and is entitled to realization, through national effort and international co-operation and in accordance with the organization and resources of each State, of the economic, social and cultural rights indispensable for his dignity and the free development of his personality.

Article 23

1 Everyone has the right to work, to free choice of employment, to just and favourable conditions of work and to protection against unemployment.
2 Everyone, without any discrimination, has the right to equal pay for equal work.
3 Everyone who works has the right to just and favourable remuneration ensuring for himself and his family an existence worthy of human dignity, and supplemented, if necessary, by other means of social protection.
4 Everyone has the right to form and to join trade unions for the protection of his interests.

Article 24

Everyone has the right to rest and leisure, including reasonable limitation of working hours and periodic holidays with pay.

Article 25

1 Everyone has the right to a standard of living adequate for the health and well-being of himself and of his family, including food, clothing, housing and medical care and necessary social services, and the right to security in the event of unemployment, sickness, disability, widowhood, old age or other lack of livelihood in circumstances beyond his control.
2 Motherhood and childhood are entitled to special care and assistance. All children, whether born in or out of wedlock, shall enjoy the same social protection.

Article 26

1 Everyone has the right to education. Education shall be free, at least in the elementary and fundamental stages. Elementary education shall be compulsory. Technical and professional education shall be made generally available and higher education shall be equally accessible to all on the basis of merit.
2 Education shall be directed to the full development of the human personality and to the strengthening of respect for human rights and fundamental freedoms. It shall promote understanding, tolerance and friendship among

all nations, racial or religious groups, and shall further the activities of the United Nations for the maintenance of peace.

3 Parents have a prior right to choose the kind of education that shall be given to their children.

Article 27

1 Everyone has the right freely to participate in the cultural life of the community, to enjoy the arts and to share in scientific advancement and its benefits.

2 Everyone has the right to the protection of the moral and material interests resulting from any scientific, literary or artistic production of which he is the author.

Article 28

Everyone is entitled to a social and international order in which the rights and freedoms set forth in this Declaration can be fully realized.

Article 29

1 Everyone has duties to the community in which alone the free and full development of his personality is possible.

2 In the exercise of his rights and freedoms, everyone shall be subject only to such limitations as are determined by law solely for the purpose of securing due recognition and respect for the rights and freedoms of others and of meeting the just requirements of morality, public order and the general welfare in a democratic society.

3 These rights and freedoms may in no case be exercised contrary to the purposes and principles of the United Nations.

Article 30

Nothing in this Declaration may be interpreted as implying for any State, group or person any right to engage in any activity or to perform any act aimed at the destruction of any of the rights and freedoms set forth herein.

Index

For Product Safety Concerns and Information please contact our EU representative GPSR@taylorandfrancis.com
Taylor & Francis Verlag GmbH, Kaufingerstraße 24, 80331 München, Germany

www.ingramcontent.com/pod-product-compliance
Ingram Content Group UK Ltd.
Pitfield, Milton Keynes, MK11 3LW, UK
UKHW010959180926
475701UK00004B/464
* 9 7 8 0 3 6 7 4 8 1 5 0 6 *